In 18[...]
erectio[...] [...] the
Dallas *Morning News*. At the age of
26 he was the business manager of the
new paper.

Mr. and Mrs. Dealey in Galveston in 1939 on the occasion
of his 65th anniversary with the *News*.

G. B. DEALEY OF THE DALLAS *NEWS*

G. B. DEALEY

of

The Dallas News

by ERNEST SHARPE

HENRY HOLT AND COMPANY   NEW YORK

87830-115

Printed in the United States of America

ACKNOWLEDGMENTS

SURELY IT MUST NOT BE UNCOMMON FOR A BIOGRAPHER TO FEEL he owes his first acknowledgment to the subject himself. Because of his interest in preserving the history of the *News,* Mr. G. B. Dealey left a vast collection of materials. Besides the many cabinets of personal files, his large brown envelopes with selected letters, clippings, pictures, souvenirs, and the like for each year from 1885 to the 1940's were veritable treasures. To read the contents of one was like having a talk with Mr. Dealey.

For help in many ways I am indebted to the members of the Dealey family and in particular to Mrs. G. B. Dealey, whose vivid memory could recall the details of 70 years ago, and to Mr. E. M. (Ted) Dealey, who made the writing of the book possible, read the manuscript at various stages, and contributed materially to it.

Mr. Sam Acheson, author of the history of the *News; 35,000 Days in Texas,* and Mr. Stuart McGregor, Editor of *The Texas Almanac,* assisted me in my research in the files at the *News* and kindly complied with my request that they read my manuscript and give me their criticisms.

Employees of the *News* who contributed assistance are too numerous to mention. In hundreds of conversations over the last three years many stories and much useful information were brought to light.

I am particularly indebted to Mr. George Waverley Briggs for his help in writing the chapter on the acquisition of ownership of the *News* by Mr. Dealey and his associates, and also for information relating to other parts of the book. Special appreciation goes to Dr. Herbert Gambrell, who helped in the writing of the chapter dealing with Mr. Dealey's interest in history and for information relating to the Critic Club.

Outside the *News* organization, many persons contributed information regarding certain incidents or interests in Mr. Dealey's life. Their names have usually been mentioned in the book.

Finally, thanks to Margarette.

PREFACE

Ernest sharpe's biography of george bannerman dealey is essentially the history of the *News* from 1874 to 1946, the period of his service.

During those 72 years the *News* rose to new heights of journalistic progress and achievement. For more than 60 of those years Mr. Dealey had an important role in guiding the enterprise through what came to be called its golden years.

Mr. Sharpe has cited the major events in the development of the *News* during that period and has revealed the growing influence of Mr. Dealey upon the decisions which shaped the course and character of the newspaper.

It was generally recognized at the time he became vice-president and general manager that he was the personification of the *News;* its mind and its conscience. Not only does the biography reveal this truth but with delicate strokes it sketches the soul of a truly great man.

To those who were privileged to work with him, Mr. Dealey was great because of virtues which no material yardstick can measure—courage, faith, understanding, and charity.

Evidence of those virtues may be found in Mr. Sharpe's recital of the steps by which the office boy rose to president of the corporation and owner of the property.

The author caught the impact of those virtues, not by delving into the written records, but by the testimony of those who work on the *News*.

He was impressed by the large number of them who regarded Mr. Dealey as an incomparable newspaper man but whose highest esteem for him was as a friend in need, a counselor in trouble, a leader with an understanding mind and a generous heart.

Mr. Dealey regarded all who worked for the *News* as members of his official family. His door was open to them, his hand helped them over the rough places, his counsel guided them in the solution of their personal problems. He welded them into a harmonious unit devoted to the service of the *News* and its high principles of responsible journalism.

Those who are familiar with the history of the institution recognize and acclaim him as one of the ruling triumvirate which conceived and guided its destiny through more than 100 years.

They were Willard Richardson, Alfred H. Belo, and George B. Dealey. Each of them, in his turn, directed the ship through rough waters and smooth so that neither chance nor death could divert it from its course.

Each of them established or strengthened foundations upon which his successor could move to new frontiers of progress without the impediment of a dead hand at the controls.

In no case did their passing serve to end the golden days of the *News,* to forfeit its place of leadership, or to sully its traditions. Capable hands were appointed and prepared to take up the torch and keep it shining more brightly than ever.

No man could be happier than G. B. Dealey to know that in the eight years since his passing the *News* has made more progress in growth and service than in any like period of its history.

Those whom Mr. Dealey taught that "except the Lord build the house they labor in vain that built it" recommend this biography of their late and beloved leader who strove to build the *News* on the rock of truth and righteousness.

HARRY C. WITHERS
Executive Editor
The Dallas *Morning News*

October 21, 1954

CONTENTS

G. B. DEALEY OF THE DALLAS *NEWS*

CHAPTER ONE

1874-1875

GALVESTON, 1874. YOUNG GEORGE DEALEY,
WITH AN ITCH TO WORK. THE BIG FAM-
ILY. COL. BELO HIRES AN OFFICE BOY.
THE *NEWS* GANG. WILLARD RICHARDSON
MAKES A PREDICTION.

*In the fading twilight of a summer's day in 1870, the old
English sea captain pointed out Galveston Island from the deck
of the sailing bark* Herbert, *and George Bannerman Dealey,
11 years old, caught his first glimpse of America.*

*Thirty-five years later he was in complete charge of the two
foremost newspapers of Texas, the Galveston* Daily News *and
the Dallas* Morning News.

*Forty years after that, at 86, he began his seventy-second
year with the same newspaper institution—a career that spanned
from Presidents Ulysses S. Grant to Harry S. Truman . . .
from a three-dollar-a-week copy boy to owner and publisher,
and, finally, to "Dean of American Journalism."*

How did it come about? What was he like?

This is the story.

FOUR YEARS AFTER THAT SUMMER'S DAY . . . 1874 . . . AUTUMN.

The first week of October found a cocky exhilaration spreading among the Galveston populace. The searing summer, hanging tenaciously on, snapped with the arrival of a norther. There was new life in brisk mornings, in cool Gulf breezes, and in the dew-laden nightfall.

The feeling of well-being among Galveston's 17,000 souls sprang of something deeper than mere good weather. They were beginning to feel free again. The Civil War had ended ten years ago, but a long, humiliating bondage had followed for cities like Galveston. Not until January of 1874 were true Texans able to drive the Radicals out of the state capitol in Austin, and even then it took time to shake out the depressed spirits.

October was the happy month. Plans laid in the spring began to materialize. Crops were coming in. Cargoes were arriving. Through Galveston funneled the state's commerce, in and out. It was the largest city and the port of Texas. Never were the bales of cotton stacked as high. Boats were crowded at the wharves and standing, impatient, off the bar. Scores of immigrant families, many in colorful European peasant dress, were camping on the strand. Up and down Market Street freshly posted handbills heralded a circus coming to town.

Somehow 15-year-old George Dealey was out of tune. With him things weren't right. His pockets were empty, no job, and his last employer, a harness maker, owed him four months' wages. Since arriving from England four years ago, he had felt a constant itch to work. He was small for his age, but eager and full of energy, and his bright blue eyes, shy smile, and North Country English appealed to employers when he asked for a job, and he was seldom turned down. But that no-good harness maker . . . four months without pay! To even the score he had decamped and taken a saddle. It wasn't worth what the man owed him, but even so his mother disapproved his taking it.

One evening early in October, with his troubles running through his mind, George walked along the strand, instinctively seeking out the calming effect of the rolling waves. Dusk was coming on, and newly arrived immigrant families could be counted by the fires they had kindled on the clean white sand to cook the evening meal. The smells of frying fish and boiling pots mingled in the breeze. The plop of waves and the low, rushing sound of the incoming tide were friendly noises . . . remindful of earlier years in Liverpool.

He had been thinking about the future, not just during the last few days, but for months. If a young man wanted to make money quick, he ought to join a trail-driving outfit. The newspaper said 100,000 cattle needed to be driven to Kansas before winter set in. But for real excitement a fellow ought to join the cavalry or the Texas Rangers and fight the Indians. Scarcely a day passed without news of Indian troubles somewhere in Texas. Or perhaps the surveying crew for the new railroad needed a boy. A surveying job would take a man places, and the Gulf, Colorado, and Santa Fe paid in gold coin. Of course, to get jobs like these, he might need to grow a few whiskers yet, but in a year or two . . .

For a moment George thought he heard a band playing, but the wind was blowing and the waves were slapping and he wasn't sure. There . . . now . . . it was a band! It seemed to be coming nearer. The *rat-ta-tat-tat* of the drums made his heart beat faster. This was something he had to see, and he hurried on in the direction of the town.

He could see them now coming toward him on Market Street. It was the Washington Guards and the Cadet Band. Near the corner of Seventeenth, they drew up smartly, arranged themselves in front of a large, two-story house, and the band began to play with unusual vigor. The front door of the big house opened and out on the porch stepped Captain Kelly. A shout went up from the troops. The captain swelled his chest and addressed the men. He was glad to be back from his stay in Virginia, he said, and this display of loyalty by his company made him a proud man.

George looked on in awe. This was what he would like to be— an officer in the Army and a commander of troops.

"Lieutenant," Captain Kelly shouted as he stiffened to attention, "about-face the company. I'll stand a drink at the Two Brothers down the street. By two's. File right! March!"

The band struck up the march, and the Washington Guards headed for the Two Brothers.

For a moment George stood watching the little puffs of white dust that each boot kicked up from the shelled street. Something pulled irresistibly, and he followed the parade.

For a 15-year-old the Galveston of 1874 held a new spectacle, a new adventure, every day.

On Saturday night at the Dealey residence there was always much commotion, the kind that eight children create at nightfall, especially when their father is not on hand to help get the young ones to bed. Father Dealey invariably arrived home late on Saturdays, as that was the busiest day of the week with his coffee and tea business. Then, too, preparations had to be made for Sunday. Dresses to be ironed for the girls and shirts for the boys, so the family would be presentable at church next day. If there was one thing George Dealey, Sr., insisted on, it was that the whole family attend church . . . both morning and evening services. For most of the members of the family there was not much choice as to what clothes to wear. The family exchequer was still "recovering," four years later, from their personal financial misfortune in England. George Dealey, Sr., had gone surety on a friend's note, who later defaulted, and it had cost the Dealeys their home and shoe shop.

The Saturday night of October 10, 1874, began as usual in the Dealey household, but it was to turn out to be a very special Saturday night. By 9:00 P.M. Mr. Dealey was home, and that made the family circle complete except for T.W., the eldest son, who had not come in from his job at the Galveston *News* office. It was customary for all hands at the newspaper office to work late on Saturday, getting out the Sunday paper, which was four pages more than the weekday issues, and ten columns wide.

"Well, I see by the paper," Father Dealey said, as he sat down to a late supper and picked up the newspaper on his plate, "that the great New York and New Orleans Zoological and Equestrian Exposition will be in Galveston next week."

"It just means more flies, if you ask me," Mrs. Dealey said.

"Do you know how many flies in a pound?" 13-year-old James asked.

"Don't be ridiculous, James," Mrs. Dealey admonished.

"There are forty-eight thousand," James said. "I read it."

"So," Mr. Dealey interjected, "then we've got a few pounds buzzing about!"

The conversation on flies ended abruptly as T.W. came in from work. He was 19 now, and raising his first mustache. He had been a breadwinner for the family ever since they came to America, and the younger boys were obliged to him for having good clothes to wear. With the money he earned at the Galveston *News,* he was able to buy good-quality suits, and as he outgrew them, they were handed down the line.

T.W. was excited. "Colonel Belo told me today that he is going to promote me to be mailing clerk," he announced. Turning to George, who was seated near a table polishing his shoes for Sunday, he said, "George, Colonel Belo asked if I had a brother who could come in and take my old job as office boy. Want to try it?"

"Do I?" George answered, glancing up. "Sure I do!"

What better job could a boy want? In Galveston people lived by the Galveston *News,* and everyone said it was the leading newspaper in the state. Colonel Belo, who ran the paper, was one of the most important men in Galveston.

"Tell Colonel Belo I'll take it," George said, and something inside made him feel excited.

On Monday morning a light breeze through the screenless windows made it pleasant for sleeping, but George waked up with a start at the shrill toot of the 6:10 train for Harrisburg. Ordinarily he never heard the whistle, but this was an extraordinary morning. He had gone to sleep thinking about the interview for the new job on the *News.* He was sure he would get the job, but thoughts of the interview with Colonel Belo made his hands sweat.

On the way to the *News* building George grew impatient with the mule car and told T.W. they could walk it faster. Never had he seen such a slow mule. *Clop-clop-clop*—the beat of the hoofs on the boardwalk dragged out painfully.

T.W. cautioned George that the men at the office would prob-

ably play some sort of joke on him as soon as they discovered he
was the new office boy, and he should take it good-naturedly. He
should know, too, that Colonel Belo sometimes had bad days with
his Civil War wounds. Never should he hand anything for the
colonel to take with his left hand. His left arm was shattered between the elbow and the shoulder by a bursting shell at the Battle
of Cold Harbor. It was patched up, but not too good. Colonel
Belo had been the colonel of the Fifty-fifth North Carolina Regi-
ment at 25, one of the youngest colonels in the Confederate Army.

As they approached the four-story building on Market Street,
in a silent prayer, George asked the Lord to help him, that he
might speak up well to the colonel when T.W. introduced him.
Today was not the first time he had entered the arched doorway
of this building, which stood two stories above any around it. But
today the building appeared more impressive to him than ever
before. He had been told that the iron front, with its elaborate
cast iron decorations over each window, had come from England,
probably Liverpool. The ships made ballast of heavy materials like
this iron facing when they came over to load cotton at Galveston.
This idea that he and the front of the building had come from the
same place intrigued him.

As a Western Union messenger boy he had delivered telegrams
to the *News* office, and when he was working for one of the cotton
factors in the city, he took orders for printing to the large job
shop on the second floor. There he had watched a wood engraver
carve a ship that was used to print a picture on a poster. The man
was an expert from the North, and said to be the best wood engraver south of St. Louis.

Before seeing Colonel Belo, T.W. took George first by a small
desk just behind the counter on the ground floor. For three years
this had been T.W.'s desk.

"This desk will be yours, if you get the job," T.W. told him.

The desk was not a beautiful piece of furniture, but George
immediately felt a possessive pride in it. The tall, round legs were
sturdy, and it had a slanted top for easier writing and contained
one wide, flat drawer. He thumped the top and liked the solid
ring to it.

He followed T.W. to the third floor, and when T.W. said, "Here on the right is the colonel's private office," George almost quailed.

The colonel greeted them warmly, and George felt more at ease. Of course he had seen the colonel before at a distance, but now he was just across the desk. The colonel sat very straight, and George thought he surely looked the military man. His mustache was thick and bushy.

The colonel could see that good material for an office boy stood before him. George wore a neat black suit, and the black string tie showed precisely just under his stiff white collar. He was small and would have passed more for 13 than 15, but the colonel knew that small lads usually made the best office boys.

"Sit down and tell me what experience you have for this job," the colonel said.

Confidence came to George with this question, because if there was anything he had to offer it was a variety of experience. He thought quickly of the job that would impress the colonel the most, and told him that he had worked as office boy for Ranger and Company, the largest cotton buyers in the world.

"My task," he said, "was to decode the cipher telegrams and cablegrams. They come from everywhere—Savannah, Mobile, New Orleans, New York, Bremen, Liverpool, and other places. I also acted as petty cashier."

While George was talking, a kindly-looking middle-aged man entered the office and told Colonel Belo he would be interested in the dispatch from Denison. Putting on his spectacles, the colonel read the telegram thoughtfully.

"So President Grant won't accept Galveston's hospitality," the colonel said. "For tomorrow's paper," the colonel instructed, "say that President Grant left Denison for the Indian Nation and now there is no probability that he will come to Galveston. No editorial comment."

The colonel introduced George to the kindly-looking man, Mr. Donaldson Jenkins, the chief editor. A good man to know, the colonel remarked. George wondered if Mr. Jenkins' eyes were puffy because he read so much. His Adam's apple protruded noticeably, and his hair appeared uncombed and thatchy.

Mr. Jenkins left, and the colonel asked George what else he had done. George said his first job, shortly after the family arrived in Galveston, was for the Trinity Episcopal Church. He pumped the organ and rang the bell. The pay wasn't much, because church services came only twice a week, but then, he admitted, he wasn't too good either. He had a string tied around his leg, and the choir leader would pull the string when the services called for music. But the sermons were long and it was hot back of the organ, and sometimes he went to sleep. The choir leader had to come around back of the organ and wake him up.

The colonel seemed amused at this experience.

The easiest job he ever had, George said, was pulling the strings that waved the paper streamers in the Fifth Avenue Hotel dining room. All he had to do was sit there and keep the flies moving . . . keep them off the tables and the diners.

When George was finished, Colonel Belo laughed.

"Well, George, you're versatile, and that's what we need in the newspaper business," the colonel said, ending the interview. He reached for the speaking tube and called T.W. to the office. Take George, he told T.W., to Frank Corbin and get him on the payroll at three dollars a week. Then turn him over to Mr. Brittingham.

On the way to Frank Corbin's desk, George and T.W. passed through the press and engine room. T.W. explained about the machinery, because an office boy was expected to know about everything. The big press was called a Hoe double-cylinder, and it printed 3500 papers per hour. The paper came in quires, and some time during the afternoon the quires for the night run would be dipped through a water trough. The paper would print better if it was slightly wet.

George saw a middle-aged man writing away at a long table in the mailing room. In a low voice he was singing:

"Shout! Shout! The Devil's about.
Shut the door and keep him out."

T.W. said the man singing was Will Cherry, Mr. Corbin's helper in the mailing room. He was preparing the addresses for the next day's mail circulation. Mr. Corbin was outside at the moment, lending some money to one of the printers. While waiting for Mr. Corbin to return, George was counseled on the improvidence of printers by both Cherry and T.W. The printers got paid on Saturday and by Monday they didn't have a cent. If they didn't spend it all on cheap whisky and women, they gambled it away playing cards or buying Mexican lottery tickets.

"Old Frank Corbin is the banker around here," Cherry said. "He gets ten per cent, and he can't lose, because he's the paymaster. Come Saturday he just takes out the money they owe him. And that's ten per cent for a week he collects, mind you. He has an eye to the main chance, that Corbin."

After finishing the formalities of getting on the payroll with the affluent Mr. Corbin, George and T.W. returned to the counting room to meet Mr. Brittingham. They approached the cashier's cage where two men were talking, one inside the cage and the other outside leaning on the rail.

"Look here, T.W., boy, look at this big apple," called the medium-sized, slightly corpulent man behind the railings. He held up a large red apple. "This apple was grown in Galveston, would you believe it? This man here brought it in . . . said he grew it on his place on Tremont Street . . . measures twelve inches in circumference . . . this just proves Galveston doesn't need to import any more apples, yes, sir."

The talkative man behind the cage was Mr. Brittingham. When Mr. Brittingham learned that T.W. had a new office boy for him, he got out his tobacco plug, bit off a big chew, turned around on his stool, made himself comfortable, and said, "Now, George, let's you and I get acquainted."

Mr. Brittingham proved to be George's good friend and practical teacher in the newspaper business. "Brit," as he was called by his contemporaries, was both cashier and business manager of the *News*. It was the office joke that "Brit" could be softened for a touch if one was willing to listen to him relate his exploits in the Confederate Navy. George soon learned that his own working hours were governed by the length of Mr. Brittingham's conversations. The longer his stories, the later he began his letters. Only after Mr. Brittingham had finished could George get on with his task, which was to copy the letters word for word into the office book . . . then to seal them and hurry to the post office. Nine P.M. became his usual hour of departure for home.

From the very first day on the new job, George became enthralled with the many-sided business of newspaper-making. This knowing the news before it was printed, the clatter and bang of the big press, the daily rush to get the paper printed before the trains departed—all this excited him.

In going from office to office he learned things that he had never imagined before. One morning during the first week, he overheard Colonel Belo and Mr. Jenkins discuss what seemed to him to be the whole truth about the Ku Klux. The next day when George read the editorial on the Ku Klux matter in the *News,* he experienced a new sensation; here was something he knew more about than the public did . . . he knew "the inside."

On the third floor, given over to the editorial department, George felt a little awed by these men who appeared so serious and thoughtful, but he promptly made friends with Captain J. W. Colvin, a good-natured, jovial man, who in size and manner somewhat resembled the occasional Falstaff at the Tremont Opera House. Captain Colvin was the paragrapher and exchange editor and was always ready with some wit. "Hey, boy, get me three trays and an ace," he would say when he wanted some stamps.

George thought the liveliest bunch were the printers up on the fourth floor. Their big joke during his first week concerned a certain paragraph which Captain Colvin had sent through for Wednesday's paper. He had written:

> **The news comes from Germany that some chemist with a name hard enough to resist all the acids in his laboratory, has discovered "the manner how" to make first-rate brandy "out of sawdust." Who will drink bad whisky now when he can take his saw, go to the**

> woodpile, and get staving drunk on an
> article that has not a headache in a
> whole cord?

The printers loved it.

"Listen, Bill," one would call across the room, "it's pretty good when a man can get drunk on his own clapboards, eh?"

Everybody would guffaw as the retort came back, "Yeah, and then have a bit of old shingle to get sober on."

There were 30 or more in the composing room, and George marveled at the speed with which the compositors picked each letter from the type cases. When setting a lengthy speech, they had a favorite expression: "Throw it away and tell 'em the man said three stickfuls of minion matter."

On the wall there was a yellowed clipping that read:

> Pick and click!
> Go the type in the stick,
> As the printer stands at his case!
> His eyes glance quick,
> And his fingers pick
> The type at a rapid pace!

George's acquaintance with the old "Chief Proprietor" of the *News,* Willard Richardson, was short-lived but impressionable. Later, as the years passed, George was to realize that this stately but quaint old gentleman in broadcloth suit, Prince Albert coat, and high hat, whom he saw occasionally around the office during his first few months on the job, was more than just a figurehead. He was the living symbol of the traditions that made the Galveston *News* superior to the other newspapers of the Southwest. In 30 years he had breathed a soul and spirit into the *News,* and now his work was all but over.

Willard Richardson had assumed command of the Galveston *News* in 1843, the second year of its life when it had not more than 200 circulation. By 1874 he had built it editorially to a rank of considerable eminence, and the circulation was, according to

the double-column boast carried daily in the masthead: CIRCULA-
TION MORE THAN DOUBLE THAT OF ANY PAPER IN TEXAS. Richardson had nursed the paper through financial panics, weathered
bitter political attacks that would have crushed an ordinary publisher, and survived a disastrous fire and a four-year war. During
the Civil War, prior to the capture of Galveston Island by the
Union troops in 1862, he evacuated press, paper, and files to
Houston and continued to publish daily. When newsprint ran out,
he printed on yellow straw wrapping paper.

Willard Richardson cast the canons of journalism for his paper
on such a high plane that they became the enduring creed of the
News. On the hundredth anniversary of the institution, his policy
of "political independence but not neutrality" was to be acclaimed
as the steadfast principle from which the paper never wavered. He
inscribed the policy indelibly in these lines:

> Independent of existing political organizations, we shall endeavor
> to do each evenhanded justice. The days of ultra-partisan journal-
> ism have passed; men of intelligence have discovered that an organ
> of party leaders or of political caucuses is not the most entitled to
> their confidence. . . . Yet we have never pretended to publish a
> neutral paper. We believe it our duty to have decided opinions
> upon all public questions and to declare them frankly, giving our
> reasons for them, regardless of whether they are considered as
> favoring one party or the other.

But to George Dealey, newly hired office boy, Willard Richardson was better known for his eccentricities than for his policies.
George was most impressed by Mr. Richardson's small dun pony
and the little low phaeton in which he drove around the city and
along the strand. For a rich man, he was uncommonly thrifty.
Each morning he had two copies of the *News* delivered at his
house. After he and his wife had read them, he brought them back
to the office to be sold.

One morning a few weeks after George had gone to work at the
News, Mr. Richardson came into the counting room. His stove-
pipe hat seemed higher than usual, and he was holding his cigar
between two fingers while he drew little short puffs. George

started to chuckle at the sight, but he quickly contained his mirth as the stern old gentleman caught his eye and headed straight for his desk. He shook hands. So, another one of the Dealey boys? Well, T.W. was a good one. How did he like his work? Had he met everybody? What did he think of the new folding machine? They didn't have contraptions like that when he started in the business . . . had to fold by hand.

"And how much money are you getting, young fellow?" Mr. Richardson asked.

"I get three dollars a week, sir."

"Well, son," he said, as he smiled and patted George on the shoulder, "keep working and maybe you'll get more some day."

CHAPTER TWO

1875-1882

THE HERITAGE FROM RICHARDSON. A VIOLENT STORM. KINDRED SOULS AND CAREFREE DAYS. "SHIP THE PAPER BY WIRE." A GIRL FROM MISSOURI.

MR. BRITTINGHAM SAT IDLE IN THE CASHIER'S CAGE SINGING HIS favorite ditty: "All a-r-o-u-n-d my h-a-t . . . I w-e-a-r a g-r-e-e-n ro-sette." The Christmas holiday had made everyone at the office lazy. George leaned on his desk practicing his signature with a new penstaff. He wished for a whole week of Christmases . . . a plum pudding at every meal. In his daydreaming he thought of the pleasant events of the day before. On Christmas morning he accompanied his father to the city jail, where his father visited with the prisoners and read the Bible, as he often did on Sundays. There they unexpectedly met Captain Hill of the sailing bark *Herbert,* the boat on which the Dealey family had come to America. Captain Hill was going bail for a crew member. The captain was full of news from England, and he told them how he had come up from first mate to captain of the *Herbert.* They recalled the voyage of four years earlier and how they had to build a shelter on deck to provide a cabin for all the Dealey family, and how the boat had been becalmed for five days off Jamaica Island. George could still picture in his mind the sight of that beautiful green island.

Thoughts of Christmas and of his old home in England [1] reminded George of the time when he worked in a grocery store in Liverpool and how he bottled ginger wine from the big, heavy barrels, especially at the yuletide season. He could almost taste it. Why not write for some? So he would: "26th December, 1874, Messrs. Jacob Stower & Sons, 46 Harrington St., Liverpool, England, Gentlemen: I beg to request that you be so kind as to furnish latest quotations on ginger wine . . ."

Of course an office boy whose wages had been raised to five dollars a week beginning the first of January could easily afford a luxury like ginger wine, even when the Liverpool price quotation came back: "One shilling eight pence the bottle."

The months flew by, and George thrived on his work. As each day passed, he had a stronger sense of belonging to the *News*. He was at that "formative period between boyhood and young manhood when impressions meant lessons, and associations meant ideals." He did not realize then but later he came to appreciate the rare good fortune he had in knowing and seeing and talking with the esteemed Mr. Willard Richardson. But the association was short-lived. Willard Richardson, the senior partner of the *News,* died July 26, 1875. The fiery pen, which for three decades had made many a lax politician dance lively, was now at peace.

Word of Mr. Richardson's death did not mean too much to George at first, but after noting Colonel Belo's preoccupation with funeral arrangements, seeing the messages from important men in faraway cities, and how Mr. Donaldson Jenkins and Mr. Hamilton Stuart worried over the editorial tribute, he sobered to the significance. Tuesday's paper was printed with the column rules turned, and all the employees were given mourning bands to wear on their coat sleeves. Funerals were something George had managed to evade most of his life, except when his three-year-old sister, Minnie, had died a few months after the family came to Galveston. The rites for Mr. Richardson, therefore, were all the more solemn to him. In the afternoon the *News* force gathered in the editorial department on the third floor. Also present were numerous members of the Odd Fellows lodge. Colonel R. G. Lowe, one of the compositors, called the meeting to order and asked Mr. Hamilton Stuart, the "State Press" of the *News,* to take charge.

"We are assembled for the purpose," intoned Mr. Stuart, "of testifying our regard for the memory of one who, in life, was ever our friend . . ."

As the 57 office employees lined up to march as a group from the building to the Richardson home, George took his appointed place with the "attachés of the counting room," immediately behind the editorial workers and in front of the composing room employees.

For a week and more sympathetic editorials were printed widely in other papers, and perhaps the best summation of Richardson's work was carried by the San Antonio *Herald:* ". . . the history of Willard Richardson's paper is really the history of Texas." For George the ideals and newspaper traditions of Willard Richardson took on a new meaning, in time to become part of his faith.

The equinoctial gale was a habitual visitor to Galveston Island. It was seldom alarming, but at 11 o'clock on the morning of September 15, 1875, a warning went out to expect the worst. The wind lashed with a fury. Oldsters said the blow might equal the storm of 1867 if it got worse. The high water began to crawl up into town covering street after street until by 2:30 in the afternoon it had reached Avenue L, only six blocks from the Dealey house, which was on Church Street between Twelfth and Thirteenth. George hoped James and Charles and Nora and Sam had gotten home from school safely. Under the shed at the back of the building he helped take care of the two horses being used by the reporters. One of the reporters, as he bundled on his raincoat, remarked, "That invention they call a telephone would be handy at a time like this!"

Darkness came on early, and all during the evening reports came in of destruction in the flooded areas. Numerous houses in the East End were gone. Several wharves on the bay side were breaking up. The G. H. & H. railroad yards were under water, and two miles of the newly laid Santa Fe tracks were washed out. George and T.W. remained at the office, waiting for a break in the storm and listening to the reports. About 9 o'clock they stepped outside with several of the staff to watch a rowboat tying up at the curb across the street. Three men got out and went into the saloon.

"To wet up," T.W. said. Water began to rise in the *News* building, and within an hour it was five inches deep on the ground floor. But the rain stopped sharply at 11 o'clock, and George and T.W. made a dash for home in the dark. They arrived safely and found all well. After midnight the fury of the winds increased. The whole family stayed awake. About 3 A.M. Father Dealey, T.W., George, and James made an inspection trip along Thirteenth Street. They found the water at least two feet deep only five blocks away from their house. A church bell was ringing frantically to the east, and they could hear distressful cries that seemed to sail in on the howl of the wind. It must be coming from the Negro Baptist Church, Mr. Dealey said. "Those poor souls! Have mercy, O God," he prayed with a bowed head. After getting back to the house, Mr. Dealey told the family that if the water got any higher, they would move as much of the furniture to the second story as they could.

About 4 o'clock in the morning the wind abated slightly, and some of the family went to bed. George and T.W. kept on their clothes, and as soon as it was daylight, they left for the office. Large numbers of men were headed for town. People were gathering at the corner of Tremont and Market Streets in front of the *News*. By 7:00 A.M. a large crowd stood around, talking and gazing at the sky. A change in the wind from any direction but east would help, they said. A turn to the north—the mainland—would be like a miracle. The weathervane over the Opera House made a few false jerks. "Look!" a man cried. All eyes fixed anxiously on the arrow. Slowly the point moved to the northwest and steadied there. A great shout went up. The "miracle" had happened.

Although the storm continued throughout Thursday and into the next day, it did less damage and gradually died down. When it was over, George had a new respect for the business he worked for. The *News* printed many pages of details, and the people had wanted more. They seemed to think the paper—somehow, by saying so, perhaps—could rescue the marooned and put a stop to the havoc. They looked to the *News* to tell them what to do to repair the wreckage.

For two and a half years George served the *News* as office boy, without a promotion in rank but with an increase in wages to ten dollars a week. By June of 1877 he was more than ready for his next opportunity. In one seven-league stride, he became chief mailing clerk and doubled his salary to 20 dollars a week, more than six times his starting wage. Willard Richardson's prophecy was coming true: "Keep working and you'll get more." For a young man still a few months shy of 18, it was an achievement. Veteran printers and reporters were getting no more than 25 dollars a week. Each week T.W. had been putting the payroll entry on the books as "George—$10." On June 11 it became "Geo. B. Dealey—$20." Out of the boys' ranks and up among the men.

The mailing clerk had a regular night stint, beginning at 2 A.M., the hour the paper went to press. For a time George enjoyed the feeling of responsibility in getting up shortly after midnight, dressing in the dark, and walking the 13 blocks to the office in the pleasant solitude of the island night. He liked this nocturnal world—the brilliant moon riding over the restless waves, the moist salt air, the palm fronds rustling in the wind, the light fragrance of the abundant oleanders and the heavy sweetness of the honeysuckle, the unseen insects chirping and shrilling, the mute but faithful lighthouse on the point throwing a beam into the endless Gulf. He relished the brief stop at the Market House, which remained open all night. Old Jack knew he wanted his coffee in the big mug, and hot. Two cups and a piece of pastry was his standing order. It made George feel more the man to sit down alongside the sailors and printers. They talked mostly of women and Civil War experiences and getting drunk.

After winter weather became inclement, George, together with a young pressroom employee, Jim Buckley, fixed up a room in the bindery, which adjoined the main building of the *News*. The bindery was a vast, unfriendly, second-story floor. It stretched a half-block long and 50 feet wide. By partitioning off one corner, they made a comfortable, livable room, complete with two cots, writing desk, wash stand, book shelves, gas jet lamp, gas burner for cooking, and an odd assortment of wall decorations, including clippings of several poems. One dark night in going to the "bindery room," George was feeling his way through the inky blackness. Nothing could be heard but the squeak of shifting boards and the scurrying of a rat across loose paper. Getting near the door of the little room, George paused a moment to listen. Jim must be out tonight, he thought. He could not hear the usual telltale snoring. He opened the door. A faint ray of light from across the street was shining through the back window. Stepping inside, he brushed a tall figure. It was a man! He lunged at the figure, instinctively grabbing his throat. They crashed to the floor.

Roars of laughter echoed in the bindery. Someone lit the gas jet. Jim Buckley and a friend stood slapping their thighs and laughing madly, pointing down at George. There he was lying side by side with a clothing store dummy, one hand still on the dummy's throat.

These were the good days when George was experiencing the feeling of boundless freedom that comes to maturing young men, when he was discovering kindred souls with harmonious ideas, when he was making the dances and learning an approving glance from a pretty girl was heady wine. Friendships were firm and fast, never to be forgotten . . . Frank Doremus . . . Dave Ryan . . . Otis Eaton . . . Reub Bowen . . . John Lubben . . . Henry Meyer . . . Dick Ennis . . . Frank Singer . . . George Dunlop and others.

Nearly a score of years after these carefree days were over, this echo came back down the corridor of time from one of the "bindery roommates":

> . . . Years ago the writer abided under the same roof with George B. Dealey and had ample opportunity to know him well . . . When we were at the aspiring-to-manhood age, George was the object of great solicitude on the part of his friends on account of a habit he had of working eighteen hours a day and dancing the balance of the time . . . Yes, George, we wonder how you could be engaged to three girls at the same time in the same neighborhood and not get caught.[2]

In late August of 1878 two office activities of the first magnitude preoccupied most of the *News* employees. The Annual Review of Business edition was scheduled for September 1. That task had the editorial and composing rooms working overtime. The pressroom was in a dither over the arrival of a Hoe web-perfecting press—newest thing of its kind in Texas. George, too, had problems : how to handle 50,000 copies of the Business Review edition, several times the regular daily circulation, and most of them to go by mail.

The press arrived late, and installation proceeded slowly, and there was trouble with a new piece of machinery called a "stereotyping apparatus." From the long mailing table in the back of the building, George could hear the clank of hammers and grunts of the pressmen. After each trial run of the press the factory man from New York would sing out as he slowed the rollers to a stop :

> "Whoa, Emma! Whoa, Emma!
> You put me in an awful dilemma,
> Whoa, Emma! Whoa, Emma!"

"Emma" wasn't ready when September 1 arrived, and George inserted the following notice on the front page of several consecutive issues of the *News:* ". . . it is necessary to postpone issuing the annual review of business . . . until such time as the new press and stereotyping apparatus are in working order."

"Emma's" stubbornness, however, suddenly became inconsequential compared to the problem which, on September 4, confronted the *News,* and in particular the mailing department. All Galveston had been apprehensively watching reports on the yellow fever epidemic in the Mississippi Valley. The headlines were frightening day after day : COURSE OF THE SCOURGE . . . NEW ORLEANS, SUNDAY'S DEATHS, 88 . . . MEMPHIS ONE VAST CHARNEL HOUSE. There was talk of a quarantine in Galveston, but no one on the *News* staff foresaw a crisis for the paper. Trouble, however, came from an unexpected quarter. On September 2 the health officer of Harris County declared a quarantine that isolated the City of Houston from all out-of-state commerce. Of course Houston's out-of-state commerce came mainly through Galveston only 50 miles away.

At 8 :00 P.M., September 4, the G. H. & H. freight train from

Galveston was turned back at the Harris County line. Wrote the *News* in a late-hour editorial: "This discriminating order . . . is suggestive of malice and rapacity, rampant and riotous over-pros-trate reason and conscience. . . . Sam Bass and his gang took the trouble to mask their faces when they stopped the trains." There was no yellow fever in Galveston, and the entire city was fuming mad at Houston. Commercially, Houston had throttled them. Of course no business was more choked off than the Galveston *News*, with its important state-wide circulation. The scene in Colonel Belo's office early Thursday morning resembled a small council of war. Oddly enough, the youngest member present—George Dea-ley—was the key man. He was the "chief mailing clerk." The big question was: How can we get the papers past Houston to the interior of the state?

George said possibly they could take the papers in a wagon and drive them beyond Houston. That would be about 60 miles . . . take two or three days. Would it work? Perhaps, Colonel Belo said, but here's what could be done. The Santa Fe has laid tracks almost as far as Houston. Get the Santa Fe to hook on a car to their work engine. Run the papers to the end of their track. That's 40-odd miles. Hire a hack at Arcola, and send the papers on. Catch the G. H. & H. at the first stop north of Houston.

The Santa Fe was willing. George was deputized as U. S. Mail Agent—complete with official documents—and went along with the papers. At Arcola he found a hack driver who was game for the 15-mile run to the north of Houston. The plan worked per-fectly. The arrangements continued for several days until Houston relaxed its quarantine against the trains from Galveston.

With the emergency past, attention centered again on the new press, and near the end of the month it was ready to roll. Satur-day was the big day. They started early. In the late afternoon Mr. Hand, the backshop foreman, brought over a barrel of "strong punch" from the saloon next door. By 5:00 A.M. the edition was printed, folded, wrapped, and on its way. Before turning in for some sleep, just as dawn was breaking, George stopped long enough to take the woodpile ax away from Frank Singer, who was about to chop the sleeping form of Dick Ennis in half right on the top of the mailing table. Both Singer and Ennis had imbibed too much of the "strong punch."

On an autumn evening very close to his twentieth birthday, George sat in on one of those rare conversations in which shop talk takes an unusual turn and a man discloses a vision and each listener catches the spirit of the something big and vague he describes, something remotely in the future but so definitely in the trend of events that no one doubts its reality and its certainty. On this autumn evening the man with the vision was Colonel R. G. Lowe, a compositor who had gradually switched to the editorial staff of the *News*. Each summer for the last three years Colonel Lowe had been compiling and helping edit the Annual Business Review editions of the *News*. This September—1879— he had prepared the biggest of them all, called the "Empire State Edition." He had spent many weeks traveling over Texas gathering information and statistics and piecing together the story that told of the remarkable progress and hinted at the vast opportunities in the immense state. On this autumn evening Colonel Lowe enraptured his office audience with the spell that a prophet casts. North Texas is the promised land, he told them. Cotton grows a bale to the acre. In 12 months the towns double their populations. They say 100,000 settlers passed through Jefferson alone last year, spreading from Texarkana to Fort Worth. Villages are becoming cities: Denison . . . Sherman . . . Gainesville . . . Denton . . . Dallas . . . Bonham . . . Paris . . . Greenville . . . Marshall. It's a great migration. And what brought all this about? The railroads. Ten years ago it was nothing. Then the H. & T. C., and the Texas & Pacific and the Trans-Continental and the Missouri-Pacific came along. Why, they say Dallas on the Trinity doubled in six months when the H. & T. C. reached there in '72—has maybe 18,000 today . . . a good challenger to your Galveston, lads.

The Scotsman pulled several draws on his pipe, wondering how to say his next thoughts so he could make his listeners understand what he felt. And what means this to you and to me? What's going to happen to South Texas? What's going to happen to Galveston? We're the big city now, aren't we? Most of the state's population has been in South Texas, and for a score of

years, maybe three score, the people of Texas have looked to the
Old Lady by the Sea—Galveston—for commerce and culture and
the news. That's us lads, the *News*. But the balance is swinging
to the north. In ten years, maybe 20, there are going to be more
people in North Texas than around here. And some day, lads, if
we don't mind ourselves there's going to be a bigger paper in
Texas than the Galveston *News*. You know why? Because one
mile to the southeast of this building there starts a peculiar territory called the Gulf of Mexico, and there you have a great population of fish, but they don't read the Galveston *News*. Now listen
to what a man said to me in Marshall this August past, in the
T. & P. depot, a man by the name of William H. Newman . . .
we used to be clerks together in the same office in Shreveport years
ago . . . he's general freight agent in Marshall now. He says we
ought to duplicate the Galveston *News* in North Texas. Duplicate
it . . . print the same paper on the same day in North Texas . . . or
almost the same paper, that is. Do this and the *News* is there a
day earlier than the St. Louis papers, and we grab all their circulation, and we keep growing bigger as the whole area builds up.
And how do we duplicate the Galveston *News* 300 miles away?
By telegraph. Ship the paper by wire. That's Newman's idea. We
write the stories and editorials here, send them by wire, and they
print them there the same night. Of course, the local news would
be different in each city.

Colonel Lowe stopped to let his listeners cogitate the idea a
moment.

Where in North Texas, someone asked, would be the best place
to duplicate the paper?

Newman says Dallas, Colonel Lowe replied. It might be Fort
Worth or Denton or some other place, but Newman says Dallas.
He believes it will outstrip the other towns, and with the railroad
connections out of Dallas you can reach almost any part of North
Texas a day ahead of St. Louis, Galveston, or New Orleans. This
Scotsman says Dallas too.

As George worked his bundles of papers that night, he kept
mulling over the things Colonel Lowe had said. They seemed
probable enough, but to hear Colonel Lowe say, "Some day there'll

be a bigger paper in Texas than the Galveston *News"*—that was something he did not like to believe.

The first week of March, 1881, was occasion for a small celebration by the three Dealey brothers who worked for the *News*. Each got a five-dollar raise in salary: T.W. to 40 dollars a week, George to 25 dollars, and James to $13.85. It was no mere coincidence that the three raises came at the same time. Rather it was incidental to an important development in the history of the company they worked for. With March of that year the old partnership was dissolved and a corporation formed. T.W. was elected secretary and treasurer of the new corporation, increasing his duties and likewise both George and James moved into more responsible work.

A number of reasons had motivated Colonel Belo to organize the corporation. The least material but perhaps the most influential reason was best revealed in an editorial printed at the time:

> **A great newspaper conducted in the spirit of the *News* must absorb or eliminate individualities, because it must itself be a distinct personality, a moral and responsible person. A great newspaper must be serenely indifferent to personal likes and dislikes, personal opinions or prejudices inside or outside of its organization which would interfere with its functions as a faithful collector and disseminator of news; as a voice, an intelligence and a reasoning conscience, to interpret for the reading public the ripest thought and best judgment of the time, touching all questions of public concern.**
>
> **A great and rightly inspired newspaper must sink all personality but its own.**

The colonel believed in impersonal journalism, and with this editorial the policy was declared an article of faith of the *News,* on par with Willard Richardson's "political independence but not neutrality." The creed of the *News* was rounding out.

Another important reason motivating Colonel Belo to establish the corporation was centered in a short but highly important provision of the charter: ". . . [this corporation is formed] for the purpose of printing and publishing one or more newspapers in the City of Galveston and at other points in the State of Texas." Specifically, Colonel Belo was thinking of the duplicate paper in North Texas. The idea that Colonel Lowe had brought back from his travels and the proposal expressed by the railroad freight agent in Marshall named Newman had taken root with the colonel. After more than a year of exploring the idea, writing letters to individuals in position to gauge the soundness of the undertaking, and calculating the expenses involved, Colonel Belo had taken the first preparatory step. It was a step toward one of the most notable journalistic ventures of the era.

Though George Dealey, in March of 1881, scarcely gave a second thought to the far-reaching implications of the company's new charter, a year and a half later when Colonel Belo would take the second step toward this daring venture, it would start George on the road to a career far different from anything he had dreamed of.

But more than the new corporation and duplicate papers and such, the great concern to George in the spring of 1881 was his personal lack of a good education. It had gradually become apparent to him that at 21 years of age his education was sadly lacking. He and James were now sharing the "bindery room" together, and this new close association with his younger brother had brought his personal problem into sharp focus. James had already long passed him in the matter of education. James had continued his schooling after the family came to Galveston, but George had dropped out after a few irregular periods. James was 19 and ready for college. He was constantly talking about the professions that would open up if he could find a way to go off to school. This talk spurred George, and a great desire to improve his education seized him. The little he could do about it at the moment was to enroll in the night classes of the Island City Business College. This he did and quickly poured himself into his studies.

He became a creature who lived mainly during the hours of darkness. His day started with the 6 o'clock evening classes : bookkeeping, mathematics, and letter writing; after 10 :00 P.M. he would return to the "bindery room" to prepare his assignments for the next evening, pushing to get them done before the presses started at 3 :00 A.M. By dawn the papers would be loaded on the trains, and then for another two or three hours he would prepare the mailing lists for the next issue. It would be late morning before he went to bed.

By the spring of 1882 George felt he was making good progress at his studies. Professor Bemish told him that he showed unusual aptitude in his business courses. Professor Joss encouraged him to add two courses in classical studies. Professor Joss' descriptions of his *alma mater* in Scotland, Aberdeen University, fascinated George. Making friends with a young lawyer named W. B. Lockhart, a graduate of the University of Virginia, George learned all he could about the university founded by Thomas Jefferson, and he obtained a catalogue of courses from the school. James became interested in Brown University in Providence, Rhode Island. But how could they go off to college? By their calculations it would take several years to save the money.

On Sunday morning, May 14, 1882, George finished dispatching the papers about 5 :30, but he stayed at the depot another hour to watch the arrival of the special train bearing the Missouri Press Association delegation—150 strong. Though the hour was early, all the bigwigs from the *News* were waiting on the station platform, and the mayor of Galveston, Colonel W. L. Moody, dressed in his most formal welcoming attire, was on hand.

That afternoon George trimmed his narrow mustache carefully and put on his best suit. He had a well-formed physique and clean-cut face, and when he groomed himself he was quite a handsome young man. At 5 o'clock he went to the Tremont Hotel Pavilion, where a concert and dance were being given for the Missouri delegation. On the pavilion the band was playing and couples were dancing. George scanned the group and saw two young ladies seated on a bench with an elderly gentleman. George introduced himself . . . he worked for the *News* . . . his pleasure to help enter-

tain the guests . . . would Miss Allen or Miss Shields care to
waltz?

Neither of the girls danced, but George had found a damsel in
distress. Miss Allen had lost the key to her trunk and was forced
to wear the dress she had traveled in, now soiled and wrinkled.
What would she do tomorrow? How could she go to the formal
reception at the Cotton Exchange? She would miss the dinner tomorrow evening at the Garten Verein—and looking so terrible, so
terrible she couldn't possibly make the boat excursion—just think,
to come all the way from Missouri and then to have this happen.

Some time later that Sunday evening George drove a reluctant
locksmith to the Tremont Hotel. If he could get a locksmith to
open her trunk, Miss Allen had promised to go for a buggy ride
on the Strand with him the next morning—in company with Miss
Shields of course.

By Monday morning the Gulf, whose omnipresent spirit hov-
ered eternally over the island, sometimes a ruthless, raging savage,
sometimes a docile sleeping giant, seemed in a charming mood,
rolling the waves far up on the gleaming sand, cradling the gentle
swells with tender care. Miss Allen and Miss Shields told their
companion this great expanse of water frightened them. How high
did the waves get in a storm . . . wasn't it dangerous to live on an
island . . . there was nothing like this in Missouri.

George hitched the horses to the post outside the *News* building,
and said follow him, he would show them how they printed the
best paper in Texas. Here was the counting room, there was the
desk he used when he was office boy; come on and see the new
web-perfecting press; it printed faster than the eye could see. Here
was the mailing room . . . his hangout. This was the new addressing machine . . . saved a lot of time. Two years ago he showed
President Grant how to work it . . . that was in March of 1880
when the general visited Galveston on his trip around the world
. . . sure, General Grant shook hands with him . . . no, he wasn't
excited . . . the general looked just like Galveston's mayor, Colonel
W. L. Moody, the man they saw at the train Sunday morning . . .
both the general and the mayor always had a cigar.

George took the party through all four floors, and before they left, the young ladies signed the guest book: *Lizzie Shields* and *Olivia (Nellie) Allen.*

The "collation at the Garten Verein" was scheduled to begin at 5:30 in the afternoon, and by 4 o'clock George was quite impatient to be on his way. This Miss Allen was a pretty thing, small and slender, bright eyes, brown hair done up in a fashion like his older sister, Nora, did hers—but Miss Allen couldn't be more than 17 or 18. George thought of several things he wanted to tell her that evening. He already knew where he could get a mocking bird to send to her mother if she really wanted one. The press party was going on to San Antonio, and they were sure to visit the Alamo; he would tell her the famous story—about Travis and Bowie and Crockett.

Dinner on the lawn by the clubhouse pleased everyone. Miss Allen told George that in Missouri no one had ever heard of redfish chowder and oyster roast. She was fascinated by the Chinese lanterns and worried for fear the strong breeze would cause them to catch on fire. They watched the Gulf; after dark it sounded fierce, Miss Allen said. But when the moon rose she said it seemed to make the water grow calmer . . . she didn't know the moon could be so bright and reflect so much in the water.

The Missouri party went on to Houston the next day, visited San Antonio Wednesday, and Austin on Thursday. Each day the *News* carried a telegraphic story of the party's activities, and George read every line. Of course Miss Allen's name wouldn't be mentioned, he knew, but the stories did tell him what she was doing, whom she saw, and the speeches she heard. It filled his head with dreams. He was pleased that he had told her about David Crockett because the Austin correspondent wrote that the governor in addressing the Missourians alluded to the Crockett motto —"Be sure you're right, then go ahead." The newspaper men of Texas, the governor said, had real "goaheaditiveness." George liked that idea.

Friday evening George started a letter: "My dear Miss Allen: Only four days have elapsed since you left behind you the roaring Gulf and at least one faithful friend, but to that friend it has seemed an age . . ."

CHAPTER THREE

1882 = 1885

As THE SUMMER GREW HOTTER, THE THOUGHT OF CONTINUING to do night work, especially the monotonous mailroom job, became more and more unbearable to George. He vacillated in his plans. At times he would be sure that a clean break with the *News,* burning all bridges behind him, was the thing to do. Or should he ask for a different job within the organization? He would stand motionless for minutes rehearsing to himself what he would say to Colonel Belo . . . how he was 23 and still just a mailing clerk . . . he wanted to make more money so he could save enough to go off to college or perhaps he might get married.

Should he mention this last reason? George wasn't sure. This marriage idea was new and vague . . . many uncertainties about it. With each letter he wrote Olivia Allen, and with each reply he received, the oftener he thought she might be the girl he was looking for. True, she still maintained a reserved tone in her letters, but there was something about the way she said things . . . yes, surely she liked him. But these were really idle thoughts. How could he see a girl two days and think of marrying her? Oh, why did he have to find a pretty girl who lived 900 miles away!

There was something in the wind, T.W. told George one day in July, regarding the North Texas duplicate paper, and it might

call for an extra traveling agent soon. They agreed that this
would be a good job with more future, more possibilities, more
business experience, and he might possibly go as far north as the
Indian Territory . . . halfway to Missouri . . . half the way to
Olivia Allen! He asked Colonel Belo for the job immediately.

August 7, 1882, was his last day in the mailing room, and then
life became an adventure. Colonel Belo kept him several days in
Galveston going over instructions. This assignment, the colonel
told him, was one that the company would ordinarily send an old
head to accomplish. Not the traveling part—that would be routine
enough—but the survey of North Texas to determine circulation
possibilities for the new paper—that assignment called for mature judgment. But the mailing room experience would stand him
in good stead, in fact, it probably made him the best fitted man
in Texas for the job. The survey was important to the company
. . . very important.

The colonel walked over to the large railroad map of Texas on
the wall of his office. Here, George, he said, pointing to the
juncture of the Red River with the Arkansas boundary, here is
the northeast corner of the territory. Everything from here south
to the 32nd parallel . . . west to the 100th degree of longitude . . .
and up that line to the Red River, which forms the northern
boundary. That's North Texas, roughly from Arkansas to Abilene running east and west, and from the Indian Nation to Waco,
north and south. What the company wants to know is how much
circulation can the *News* get if a duplicate paper is established
somewhere in North Texas. Circulation should probably be
calculated town by town . . . visit every town and city of any size
in that whole territory.

It made George's thoughts race as he watched Colonel Belo run
his finger over the map and define the territory by latitude and
longitude. What a great expanse of territory! New land that
some day would have millions of people!

The colonel's stance before the map was soldierly. North Texas,
Colonel Belo continued, is in itself much larger than the country
of Austria, and far richer in good fertile soil. People say Texas

is an empire. Then here is an empire within an empire. Go investigate it, George, and come back and tell us how to conquer it.

Now, where to locate the duplicate paper? Colonel Lowe says Dallas is the place. But there's a letter that raises a question . . . perhaps Fort Worth should be the city . . . or perhaps it would be wise to look to the day when Texas will have a great manufacturing industry centered around the coal mines in Palo Pinto and Stephens counties. There's the job, George . . . make the survey with an open mind . . . select the best city.

Before the interview was over, Colonel Belo took two letters from his safe for George to read. The letters were remarkably enlightening, particularly the one from the vice-president of the Texas and Pacific Railway:

Executive Office

TEXAS AND PACIFIC RAILWAY COMPANY

275 South Fourth St.

Philadelphia, Pa., Feb'y 11, 1881

Personal

A. H. Belo, Esq.
  Galveston, Texas.

Dear Sir:

I am in receipt this morning of your letter of the 4th marked "Personal and Confidential", asking my opinion as to the best place to establish a newspaper similar to the "Galveston News" in Northern Texas. My own opinion is that Dallas has got such a start, that it must necessarily retain relatively its position as the most important city in Northern Texas. It is the center of a rich agricultural country, and the lines of road constructed, will always secure to it cheap freights and make it a central distributing point for business of all kinds.

The fact that Dallas has practically today or will have within the calendar year, three independent lines to Galveston, two to New Orleans and two to St. Louis, secures to it advantages that no location farther west would probably enjoy for many years to come. Fort Worth will naturally crowd it somewhat, and I think Fort Worth a better point for a large city in some respects, notably for its elevation, being built upon a ridge instead of in a prairie. This elevation, I think, makes its drainage better and it has, I understand, a better water supply, and it is a little nearer to the coal, although that will not make so much difference; but I doubt if in the race it will ever overtake Dallas, nor do I think its competition will materially injure Dallas, but on the contrary I believe that any increase in the business of Ft. Worth will correspondingly add to the prosperity of Dallas, although it may alter the character of business by changing its retail dealers into wholesale dealers.

Of course I give you my views frankly as you have asked for them, but I do not claim that they are infallible. If the country was unsettled, geographically and topographically speaking, I should locate the central town in Northern Texas somewhere in Palo Pinto or Stephens County, as near as possible in the centre of the coal region, and I think that an important town will grow up there eventually, as the cheap fuel will give to it great advantage for different kinds of manufacturing business.

I am very glad to know that you contemplate establishing a newspaper in that section of the country. I think one is greatly needed and that it will do a great deal of good, and I believe that once started, it will be pecuniarily a success, as much so as has been the Galveston News under your able administration.

If it should be in my power to aid you in any manner to carry out your purpose, I shall be very glad to do so. Meanwhile, I remain,

Yours very truly,

Frank S. Bond
Vice-President

The second letter was written by ,William H. Newman, the man who had suggested to Colonel Lowe that the *News* "ship the papers by wire to North Texas." It substantiated the opinions of the T. & P. vice-president, and Newman was even more certain that Dallas was the best location for the North Texas paper.

For the next few months George lived out of a suitcase . . . a hotel tonight, a rooming house tomorrow, a Pullman occasionally. Towns . . . towns . . . towns . . . on the Missouri, Kansas & Texas from Waco to West, Abbott, Hillsboro, Itasca, Grandview, Alvarado, Burleson, Fort Worth, Roanoke, Argyle, Denton, Mingo, Aubrey, Pilot Point, Collinsville, Whitesboro, Beaver, Pottsboro, Denison, Bells, Whitewright, Leonard, Kingston, Greenville, Lone Oak, Alba, Mineola.

Towns . . . towns . . . towns . . . on the Texas & Pacific making Texarkana, Sulphur, Green City, Wayne, Kildare, Jefferson, Woodlawn, Marshall, Hallsville, Longview, Gladewater, Big Sandy, Lake Fork, Grand Saline, Edgewood, Wills Point, Elmo, Terrell, Lawrence, Mesquite, Dallas, Arlington, Fort Worth, Benbrook, Aledo, Weatherford, Millsap, Brazos, Sparta, Gordon, Strawn, Ranger, Eastland, Cisco, Putnam, Baird, Clyde, Abilene.

Towns . . . towns . . . towns . . . back to Fort Worth and up the north line of the T. & P. to Sherman, Savoy, Caney, Bonham, Dodds, Honey Grove, Lookout, Brookston, Paris, Blossom Prairie, Bennett, Bagwells, Clarksville, Annona, Douglas, De-Kalb, Whaley, Texarkana.

Towns . . . towns . . . towns . . . across to Jefferson and on the M-K & T again to Lassater, Hughes Springs, Daingerfield, Pittsburg, Leesburg, Winnsboro, Sulphur Springs, Black Jack (Cumby), Greenville, Farmersville, McKinney, Dallas, Letot, Farmers Branch, Carrollton, Lewisville, Denton.

And still more towns . . . towns . . . towns . . . on the International & Great Northern, on the Fort Worth & Denver, on the Houston & Texas Central, and on the Gulf, Colorado & Santa Fe.

Never had he met so many people. He numbered friends now from one end of the state to the other, and had made scores of acquaintances within that nomadic fraternity of *bons vivants* called the drummers. These drummers were a sharp and hearty lot, and as George learned one night on the northbound Santa Fe out of Brenham, they could carry a practical joke to a cruel extreme. On this particular evening there were six drummers on the train, all together in one coach, and they had been greatly annoyed by a new and smart-aleck salesman from Meriden, Connecticut, who boasted of his ten trunks of the world's finest cutlery. Have you made the city of Milano, one of the old-timers asked the man from Meriden. No, should he? The remainder of the ride to Milano was carefully sprinkled with just the right

amount of "chance remarks" of the good business to be had in
the "thriving city of Milano." At 1 o'clock in the morning, George
watched the porter and three of the drummers help the man from
Meriden unload his ten trunks at Milano, where he was soon to
discover there was no hotel, no store, not even a rooming house,
just a depot that served the junction of the Santa Fe and the
I. & G. N. railroad lines. And worst of all, there wasn't another
passenger train until 1 :00 A.M. the next night.

Never had George done work that was so satisfying. Although
it wasn't a great feat to look over a town and estimate the potential circulation, still it required a special knowledge of a sort.
Never had George felt so much alive. Never had he dreamed that
the world could challenge a man so. He wrote letters to Miss Allen
that flowed with enthusiasm . . . If she could only see this wonderful land, he told her, she would love it . . . rolling hills to the
east with beautiful tall pines . . . rich prairie land to the west . . .
plentiful streams lined with willow and oak and pecan and cotton
wood . . . a great variety of crops, cotton, wheat, corn, beans,
sugar cane, whatever the farmer pleased . . . and next June he
would send her peaches and plums a month earlier than Misssouri-
ans were accustomed to taste them.

By January of 1883 the survey was finished. It was long, page
after page containing the names of all towns in North Texas, with
estimated circulation for each . . . several pages describing the
newspaper competition to be faced . . . and other aspects. George
had never prepared anything so lengthy before. From beginning
to end it was written by hand, not the neatest handwriting in the
world, but bold and clear. He was proud of it. The night before
he turned it over to Colonel Belo, he got somewhat panicky at the
thought that the building might burn down, and no one would
ever see the report.

His conclusion was that the North Texas paper could start
with a circulation of about 5,000 and should reach 15,000 in a
reasonable period. Dallas was his choice for the city. Colonel
Belo, Mr. Jenkins, Mr. Hand, and T.W. were complimentary of
his work, and their praise made him feel good inside.

Having gotten his fill of traveling for a while, George wel-

comed a two months' assignment to Austin, the capital of the
state, where his principal task was to sell a subscription of the
News to every member of the Eighteenth Legislature, which con-
vened in Austin on January 9. Although it was somewhat disillu-
sioning to get acquainted with the ways of the State House, to
hear the rantings of such as Rutabaga Johnson and his breed, it
was a valuable experience for George.

From Austin he went to Waco as agent and correspondent.
Handling the local circulation came natural to him, but his first
attempts at news gathering and reporting were more arduous
and called for more training than he had ever suspected of a reporter's job. Each day he had to telegraph to Galveston about a
stickful on the local happenings, and send additional material by
mail. Usually how dull!—"A young lady attending the Methodist
female college here fell from a seesaw plank today and seriously
sprained her arm." . . . "the weather continued hot" . . . "the
northbound passenger train was late" . . . Only occasionally something exciting or interesting . . . an elopement, a shooting, a band
concert, or a public speaking.

George soon discovered, like all reporters, that he took an im-
modest pride in seeing his own stories in print. His best dispatches
he would clip out and send to Olivia. It was no longer "Miss
Allen," but "Olivia."

Many of the long hours in his lonely room on the top floor of
an empty and almost dilapidated three-story building were filled
penning the details of his daily life to "the most interesting young
lady in Missouri." Letters, he found, could be better than parlor
conversations. For a time he kept her amused with the doings of
the "darky waiter" at the Pacific Hotel, his favorite eating place.
"Here is the latest one on Sam," he would begin.

"Yas-suh, what'll it be tonight, boss?" Sam asked a fat man
who sat down at a table. The man said, "Eggs." Sam said, "Raw
or cooked, boss?" The man said, "Cooked." Sam said, "Fried or
scrambled, boss?" The man said, "Fried."

"One side or two sides, boss?"

"One side."

"Which side, boss?"

In September, George was transferred to Dallas. He had been at the new post long enough to set up office in the rear of the Hickox & Hearne Drug Store, near Main and Lamar, to renew acquaintances made the previous fall and to establish his daily beat for collecting the news when his first big news story broke.

A few minutes before 11 o'clock on the morning of October 6, he was sauntering down Main Street, nothing particular on his mind. A bicycle rider brushed by on the board walk, and he wished there was a law to keep the bicycles in the street. He saw the editor of the Dallas *Herald* approaching. "What's the news?" he asked.

"Not a damned thing," rejoined the *Herald* editor.

At that very moment the fire bells began to ring. A few blocks away two fire wagons crossed Main Street racing north. In the direction of the W. C. Howard Co. grain elevator, the black smoke was billowing up and spreading out on the strong southeast wind.

At 1:00 P.M. George filed a wire to Galveston, but the fire was just getting started good:

> DALLAS, Oct. 6, 1 p.m.—Probably the largest and most destructive fire that ever occurred here is now raging. At 11 o'clock this morning a fire broke out in the engine room of W. C. Howard & Company's elevator, and soon after the flames spread rapidly and soon the cottonyard of the City compress, occupying one block of ground, caught fire and was rapidly consumed by the devouring element. A strong breeze is blowing from the southeast and the heat from the burning district is frightful. At 12:30 the elevator fell with a crash. A brick building adjoining it . . . is a total loss. The flames rapidly spread and soon the cotton around the City compress caught and is being rapidly burned. At 12:45 the fire is still raging, going

in a northerly direction, and has just
caught and wiped up the electric light
works and a livery stable.

Shortly after noon a special train
from Fort Worth brought over a
steamer, two hose carriages and fifty
men, who immediately went to work
with a vim. . . .

The fire wiped out a large part of the business section of Dallas,
and damage was estimated at 1,000,000 dollars. About 4000
bales of cotton were destroyed, and hundreds of the bales continued to burn and smolder for more than a week, making an
acrid smell that permeated the city. But the fire boys were "invited
to the city hall, where a royal time was had, with speeches by
Colonel Elliott, Mayor Cabell, and others."

After the fire, life in Dallas settled back to routine, and George
had time again to write Olivia. In the space of a year and a half
he came to confide his innermost thoughts and aspirations and
dreams in these letters. She in turn, though more slowly, entrusted her confidences to him. George contemplated a bold step.
Should he ask Olivia to marry him? He hesitated. Did he really
know Olivia Allen? It was strange, the emotion he felt when
reading her letters. How could he be so interested in the little
things of this person's life? Just to read that she had picked a
basket of autumn leaves, or that Lexington's first snow of the
winter had fallen and she had gone sleighing . . . these little details somehow fascinated him. What was the mysterious charm
this girl had for him? George wondered. He wondered too if a
girl ever married a man on such a courtship as theirs—two days
together and 200 letters!

What brought the issue closer to a decision was another unexpected transfer for George. This time he was to be manager of
the branch office in Houston and to give his entire attention to
building up the circulation of the *News* in that city. Thinking
over the work and responsibility involved in the new assignment,
he knew it was either go to see Olivia between jobs, or wait another year or more.

By the first week of 1884 affairs in Dallas were turned over to the new correspondent, and early on a cold January morning George boarded the train to Kansas City, which would put him within a few miles of Lexington, Missouri. In his vest pocket was a small velvet-covered box, and in the box was a diamond ring . . . just in case Olivia should say "Yes."

A week later, when George returned south, heading for Houston, ready to commence his new duties, the diamond ring was no longer in his pocket. George felt triumphant. It was a wonderful trip. Olivia was prettier than a painting. They went to the Presbyterian Church together, and she wore a most becoming dress . . . not that he noticed dresses particularly . . . but he remembered hers. It was blue and gold . . . velvet mainly . . . bright and elegant. The skirt almost touched the floor.

Everything between them went smoothly. Even the date for the marriage was set—to be April 9, when he would arrange to return to Lexington for the wedding. He liked her family. Mrs. Allen seemed alternately solicitous of his welfare, then anxious at the thought of Olivia's going so far off to Texas to live. She seemed to think Texas was only half-civilized.

Mr. Ethan Allen was cordial and agreeable. He was copublisher of the Lexington *Intelligencer,* and had published the Lexington *Caucasian* before merging with the *Intelligencer.* He took George to see the office, and they talked shop for hours. Mr. Allen was extremely proud of the several generations of newspaper men in the Allen family. The first of the line was Ebenezer Walbridge Allen of Middlebury, Vermont, who published a newspaper in Middlebury around 1800 and after, but the name had been forgotten. His son, Anson Hall Allen, followed in his footsteps, publishing *The Old Settler* in Keeseville, New York. Anson Hall Allen was the father of Ethan Allen and the grandfather of Olivia.

"Like his paper, my father was known as 'The Old Settler,'" Mr. Ethan Allen had related to George. "He once fought a bear with nothing more than a knife for a weapon. There's a song about it, and one verse goes:

" 'Oh, Lord,' he cried in deep despair,
    'If you don't help me, don't help the bear.' "

The bear story impressed George. Olivia had shown him a painting that hung in the parlor entitled "Allen and the Bear." The bear stood upright, with jaws wide open, and Anson Hall Allen was about to thrust a young sapling down its throat.

February and March dragged interminably, while George waited for the time to go back to Lexington. But the ninth of April eventually came, and George and Olivia were married in a church wedding. The train trip to Houston sufficed as a honeymoon. Then there was the usual round of visiting for the newly married couple . . . a quick trip to Galveston for Olivia to meet the Dealey in-laws . . . an evening with the Duvernoy quartet, in which George was second tenor . . . weeks of searching for a nice apartment with a low rental . . . more weeks buying furniture, equipping the kitchen, and setting up housekeeping.

As the year progressed, George became busier and busier. The competition with the Houston *Post* was more of a circulation war than he had anticipated. At his suggestion the *News* engaged a special train to speed the papers to Houston each morning before daylight. This was the first time in America that a newspaper had engaged a special daily train for circulation purposes. It made much talk in the "exchanges," and George was proud of his feat. He organized a corps of carriers and laid out circulation routes just as if the *News* was being published in Houston. His goal was to have more circulation in Houston than the *Post* itself had.

When the year 1885 rounded the corner, it appeared that the *News* might be winning the circulation battle, but George had his troubles . . . a family matter. A baby was on the way. Weeks before the baby was born, he would rub his forehead at the thought of diapers and a crib and boiled water and walking the floor. He knew nothing about taking care of babies, and he was afraid Olivia didn't know either. February 6 came and the doctor was at their apartment for hours. When it was all over, the doctor said the mother and baby were fine. George silently thanked God. "Annie" was the name they selected for the little girl. For the

first few weeks of the baby's life, George wondered at times if
he were a normal father because the baby's crying annoyed him
extremely and he seemed lacking in the so-called paternal instinct.
But this love developed with time, he discovered, from day to
day, and came with abundance when the baby began to smile and
gurgle.

CHAPTER FOUR

1885

"BOUND TO LIKE DALLAS." THE DALLAS
MORNING NEWS IS BORN. A SPECIAL
NEWS TRAIN TO FORT WORTH. THE DAL-
LAS *HERALD* ACQUIRED.

CASUAL READERS OF THE GALVESTON *NEWS* ON SUNDAY, MAY 24, 1885, might have noted that a cattle drive would leave Columbus, Texas, shortly with 6000 head bound for Colorado, and the top story on foreign news reported that in Berlin Bismarck was negotiating with a British envoy regarding interests in Egypt. There was a comment on Henry Ward Beecher's latest sermons on evolution, and a story with an Arizona dateline said the Apaches were on the warpath. These items were interesting, but the news that got the most notice throughout the state was contained in the *News'* own special announcement carried on the editorial page:

> On the 1st of October proximo, or perhaps earlier if arrangements can be perfected, the *News* will establish a branch office of the publication in the city of Dallas, where it will be printed and published simultaneously with its issue at Galveston. . . . The *News* enters locally the great field of Northern Texas not as a stranger, but as an old

> friend. ... The movement ... is a for-
> ward effort ... to overcome time and
> space in the matter of distribution,
> and to hold for all time the great field
> of Texas journalism.

Reaction to the announcement was vigorous in many quarters. In Dallas it was something of a sensation. The city as a whole could hardly have been more pleased had Charles A. Dana said he would move the New York *Sun* to Dallas. Dana himself was interested and had told Colonel Belo in a conversation in New York that the experiment "would be well worth watching" because it hit at an unsolved problem in journalism: Could a chain of newspapers be successful?

Reaction in the press of Texas saw expression in more than 150 newspapers. Wrote the Texas *Farmer:* "This movement is in keeping with the usual enterprise of the *News* and fully illustrates the truth of the following paraphrase:

> " 'Tis not birth, nor wealth, nor state,
> But git-up-and-git that makes men great."

Not so approvingly the San Antonio *Express* said: "The *News* people have the cheek, the brazen effrontery to announce that the whole state will be covered by its two editions. ... Its supreme arrogance and assumption have become intolerable and need a rebuke." Though a few newspapers objected, the great majority hailed the undertaking as a forward step in the interest of Dallas, the state, and Texas journalism.

There was reaction too in the business and personal affairs of numerous individuals. Ten printers in Chicago would come to live in Texas. A man named Hughes would shortly build a three-story brick building in Dallas on Commerce Street between Lamar and Austin. A representative of the Edison Incandescent Lighting Company would come from New York to Dallas to sell an electrical plant. The Dallas *Herald* would order a new press, but never install it. A fly-by-night printer would start a newspaper called The Dallas *Daily News* in an attempt to grab the name and sell it at a high price. Fifty Dallas businessmen would buy 25,000 dollars' worth of stock in A. H. Belo & Co. The publisher of the Dallas *Evening Times,* William Greene Sterett, would leave his own paper to work for the *News.* Frank Doremus would quit as Washington correspondent of the Dallas *Herald* to rejoin the *News* staff.

And George B. Dealey was another whose business affairs and personal life would soon be affected. Following the May 24 announcement, George pleaded both in person and in correspondence for the management to send him to Dallas, and in June he was notified to proceed there to assist Colonel Lowe and T.W. in the preparations.

"Think of it," he said to Olivia, with pride and excitement, "I'm to be the business manager for the branch paper at Dallas!"

But how would he know what to do, Olivia asked. He had never been a business manager before. It made George wonder a little. But he had not been asleep during the last 11 years. He had worked in or closely observed every operation in the publication of a daily newspaper. He felt an inner confidence that he could do the job.

Dallas in 1885 . . . What was it like? . . . What of the people? They were good people with a touch of refinement but also the ruggedness and uncouthness of pioneers, pioneers but with the keen eye for a dollar that marked good merchants, good merchants but too stingy to pave the streets, stingy but with a soft heart and a full cup for charity, charitable but never foolish enough to give Fort Worth an even break.

Spreading in a disorderly fashion along the east bank of the Trinity River was the business district, and hovering in a semicircle around the business district was the residential area, abruptly ending to the north and south along the flood line of the Trinity bottom. Five railroad lines chopped through and around the city in an awkward pattern, and several creeks sliced across it to the river. On the west river bank there was nothing but farm land.

Fully half of Dallas' 18,000 citizens had settled there in the last five years, a part of the great westward movement. Covered wagon trains still slogged through the environs heading west, and it was a tradition for the older Dallas residents to carry food baskets to the wagon camps. The new opera house seated 1500, and traveling companies could usually anticipate a full house. Dallas men folk were noted for the quantities of hard liquor they drank—attributable, they said, to the lack of pure drinking water. Even the Grand Windsor Hotel served raw water from the Trinity, easily detected by the tinge of red silt that came from the soil of the north prairies. In the summer heat men were sensible enough to shed their coats and carry black umbrellas, but fashionable wives attended household duties in long morning gowns that swept the floors. Reading circles were popular, each lady taking a turn at the book while the others knitted or crocheted. Breakfasts at the hotels were hardy and *table d'hôte* . . . thick slices of smoked ham, platters of eggs, butter brown biscuits, peach and plum and pear preserves, corn fritters, doughnuts, pots of coffee, and twice a week—fried chicken!

"Ollie, you're bound to like Dallas," George wrote his wife, who remained in Houston with the baby until matters in Dallas were more settled. He told her he had seen the driver of the mule-car on Main Street stop in the middle of the block, get out, and carry a lady's baby from the sidewalk to the car. That was so the lady could hold up her skirts to keep them out of the mud.

Construction was being pushed on the three-story brick building at 509-511 Commerce Street, but in June and July it seemed to George that too many things remained to be done to start publication by October 1. Colonel Lowe and T.W. were spending more time in Dallas than in Galveston, and Jno. J. Hand was in Chicago buying printing equipment and hiring printers. They were all working feverishly, but behind schedule.

George's work was a mass of details and dozens of persons to see each day. Where a month ago he had shied a bit at Ollie's question as to how he would know what to do, now he only wondered how he would get it all done. There were employees to hire for the counting room, two managers and 20 carriers for circulation, 5000 subscriptions to be sold in advance—a goal he felt to be a personal obligation in view of his estimates from the North Texas survey. There was a regular weekly payroll, even though publication of the paper was still weeks off. The mail had to be opened and attended daily, the bookkeeping to be started, office equipment to be purchased, bills to be paid, and most important of all, as October approached, advertising had to be solicited and local copy prepared for the composing room. By working from early in the morning until late at night and seven days a week, George managed to keep his head above water. About 10:00 P.M., when his eyelids felt heavy and rough, he would weight down the jumble of papers on his desk, blow out the smelly kerosene lamp, and lock up his temporary headquarters at the Hickox Drug Store on Main Street. His route to the Windsor Hotel never varied. On Lamar he would turn the corner at the fire station and city hall building, and the next 50 paces west on Commerce would put him in front of the new building for the *News,* where he invariably paused to check the progress.

As yet the new building was a gaunt, simple structure with yawning unfinished windows that looked black in the moonlight. More than once late at night as he stared at this empty building, he thought how a newspaper was an odd kind of factory, which turned out neatly folded packages each day . . . and these packages were carried and mailed to thousands of people scattered over the city and for hundreds of miles around . . . and these packages were perishable and had to be fresh daily.

Soon another month had slipped by and the summer melted into September, and finally the deadline was upon them. The next day would be October 1—the day for the first issue. Would they make it? From his "sanctum" on the second floor, Colonel Belo was issuing orders and calling for last-minute reports. Donaldson C. Jenkins, now carrying the title of editor-in-chief of both papers, was on hand to direct the news coverage and supervise the telegraph dispatches from Galveston. The new eight-page web-perfecting Bullock press was oiled and primed. In the middle of the afternoon the Dallas Brewing Association sent word that "all attachés of the *News*" were invited to the bar next door for one on the house—a toast to the success of the first issue. The loud cheers of the 25 compositors on the third floor spread the invitation instantly to all parts of the building. Work was stopped completely for at least 15 minutes.

By nightfall George had his affairs in order and not too much to do until the presses rolled. He took off time enough for the first real supper he had eaten in weeks. That Wednesday night the Grand Windsor was serving its usual wide selection, but George filled up on black-eyed peas, corn bread, and spare ribs —first of the hog-killing season. The combination had never tasted so good. When he returned to the office, there was a large crowd of curiosity-seekers in and around the building. Judging by their remarks, they were more intrigued with the incandescent lights than with the idea that a newspaper was about to be born. These electric lights were news, and there was a story about them for the first issue:

> The Dallas *Morning News* office displays nightly 100 Edison incandescent lights. Each lamp consists of a pear-shaped glass globe, exhausted of air, and containing a filament of carbonized bamboo slightly thicker than a horse hair, which, becoming incandescent by the passage of the electric current, emits a beautiful, soft mellow light, absolutely steady.

Between 9 and 10 o'clock, George went over city circulation matters with F. A. Wilmans, the city circulator. Mr. Wilmans said several carriers were sick, but Arthur Allen would take their routes. George counted the subscription lists again, but the circulation still didn't quite stretch to 5000. Mr. Wilmans promised it would be more than 6000 in a week or two, "as soon as the people could see the paper."

By midnight most of the several hundred spectators had gone home, and the remaining hardy souls had hied off to nearby saloons. Outside the night air was chilly. The hours dragged on ... 1:00 A.M. ... 2:00 A.M. ... 3:00 A.M. George caught several short naps on a mailing room table. Finally about 4 o'clock word went out that everything was ready but the starter plate. The two top floors of the building emptied quickly, with all the employees attempting to get inside the pressroom on the ground floor. Patrons and bartenders from all saloons close by filed in, summoned by two of the printer's devils who had gone shouting from door to door in Paul Revere fashion.

"Are all heads of departments on hand?" yelled out the greasy ink-besmattered figure at the big Bullock press.

"Who cares?" someone piped.

"Let 'er roll," said the pressman.

George looked at his watch. It was 4:15 A.M.

Slowly the rollers began to turn, and neatly folded eight-page papers began to stack up. The first dozen papers were quickly passed around.

"Whoa!" shouted the pressman, stopping the machinery. "We got a bum plate on Number 8 cylinder."

An unnatural calm prevailed for a few minutes while a new impression of page 8 was being made on the third floor in the stereotyping room. One of the spectators—a small man named Pat O'Keefe—pushed his way up to the pressman. "What's wrong with this copy?" he asked.

"It's got a bad impression, Pat," the pressman said, pointing to the outside middle of the back page. "Here, give it back to me, and we'll give you a good paper in a moment."

"Oh, no," said O'Keefe, pulling back and heading for the door. "I'll keep it. The first impression of an Irishman is always bad!" And out he went with the first copy of the Dallas *Morning News* to leave the building.

Soon the new plate was on, and the press was ticking the papers off at 100 a minute. George rolled up his sleeves and lent a hand in the wrapping and mailing. It seemed like old times to him . . . it had been more than three years since he had handled the mailing room work for the Galveston paper. For the next two hours he clocked the push cart to the railroad stations. They were making each train departure nicely. At 6:12 one more batch was

needed to catch the southbound Santa Fe, leaving the station at
6:30. Unexpectedly the presses stopped.

"Something missing," the pressman said. "Had to pull the
switch."

"Can't you let us have just two hundred more, Mr. Dowell?"
George pleaded. "We've got to have our records clear."

Grunting, Mr. Dowell pushed the switch. The 200 rattled off at
half-speed in four minutes. At 6:19 the loaded push cart started
for the Santa Fe station several blocks away. It made the southbound train with minutes to spare.

The Dallas *Morning News* was born. George rolled down his
sleeves. It was broad daylight.

"Let's go to the Windsor for breakfast, Mr. Gordon," George
said to the mailing clerk. "Then I'm going to the barber shop and
get a bath even if it is only Thursday morning."

"May Aladdin's lamp be thine." This poetic felicitation was on
a card tied to the large basket of flowers on the front counter of
the business office. It was the second day of publication, and a
Mrs. McKee had sent the flowers over by her yardboy. George
overheard two reporters making sport of the phrase, and he was
annoyed. Appropriate or inappropriate, the sentiment implied
good will, and that was what counted.

Many incidents, some important and some trivial, were long to
be remembered from the first days of the new paper. All in all,
the first week went off well. Of course some kinks remained in
the complicated operation. The editors were concerned about increasing local coverage. The urgent business problems were mainly
in distribution. Train schedules going west were missing three
important connections in Fort Worth, and the paper was one day
late in reaching the large region west and north of Fort Worth.
If they could correct this situation, the paper would probably pick
up a thousand circulation in a year's time. George was impatient
to do something about it. Following the pattern of the *News'*
Galveston-to-Houston special train, he recommended to Colonel
Belo that the company run an early-morning train to Fort
Worth. Reluctant to bear the expense, Colonel Belo delayed the

decision. George puzzled how to bring the colonel to action. There was a limit to the number of times one dared prompt the boss for an answer. Then an idea occurred to him. On the editorial page, where the publisher's notices customarily preceded the first editorial, George inserted the following:

> The *News* is now perfecting arrangements whereby its distribution will be promptly effected. In the west and northwest . . . there have been some difficulties within the past week, but it will not be long before the reading public will find the *News* a prompt daily visitor.

It worked. The colonel read what his own paper said, and there was no choice but to support the claim. The colonel and George called on officials of the Texas & Pacific Railway, and after several days of negotiation, the *News* was able to announce that beginning October 25 there would be a daily Texas & Pacific passenger train leaving Dallas for Fort Worth at 5:55 in the morning. Not one to hide the *News'* light under a bushel, George wrote the announcement as follows:

> . . . the special train would have been the less expensive to the *News*, but the latter [a regular passenger train] was adopted for the double reason that it served the purposes of the *News* just as well as a special train and it gives Dallas an advantage that the whole community, especially the traveling public and the business interests, will fully appreciate. The whole expense of extending the passenger train . . . is borne by the *News*.

Such feats as this, together with news and editorial superiority and a favorable public reception far and wide, led to the demoralization of at least two of the other newspapers in Dallas.

Already there was an agreement with W. G. Sterett, part owner
and editor of the Dallas *Evening Times*, whereby he would soon
join the *News*. George had a feeling he was going to like Sterett
when he heard the man's quip that he was down with the dengue
fever, which some friends of his had sent to him in a letter from
Fort Worth.

The other newspaper suffering from the effects of the *News'*
immediate success was the Dallas *Herald*. Rumor had it that the
Herald could be purchased at a price. Being a morning paper, it
was the main competition, and George was eager to see it acquired by the *News*. More than anyone's on the staff, his work
would be benefited. George discussed the case repeatedly with his
superiors. If the *Herald* folded, the *News* would have unchal-
lenged supremacy in both city circulation and advertising. He held
that the *Herald* would sell out cheap. He knew that its new press
was still at the depot, never having been unloaded. Colonel Belo
and others of the executive staff were equally enthusiastic for
the purchase. Besides the business reasons, there was prestige in
the *Herald's* date of founding—1849. The merger would make the
News a continuation of the oldest paper in Dallas.

In November the *Herald* owners were approached with an offer,
and on December 1, the *News* acquired its morning rival. Forty-
five years later, George Dealey was to recollect, "from that day
on for many years we had it pretty much our own way in Dallas."
Had the *Herald* remained in the morning field, all the hard work
and enterprise of the *News,* and in particular that of the business
manager, quite likely would have been stripped of much of the
handsome profits enjoyed during the early years.

CHAPTER FIVE

1885-1895

AT THE THACKER HOUSE. "A SMALL
PIECE OF CHAGRIN" WITH A BIG ADVER-
TISER. THE SECOND BABY. "GEORGE" BE-
COMES "MR. DEALEY."

NEAR THE END OF OCTOBER, OLLIE AND THE BABY MADE THE
move from Houston to Dallas. It seemed hardly any time since
they had gone through the troubles of setting up housekeeping.
Ollie readily agreed that a boardinghouse in Dallas would be a
relief for a while. At the Thacker house, on the corner of Wood
and Akard, the roomers were friendly, if a bit nosey, and the
front porch was a gossip mart, where small topics were preferred. Major J. B. Scruggs was the autocrat of the dinner table.
He had a reputation as a raconteur, and his favorite story was
how the lightning bug had clogged up the Thacker house telephone. The instrument was one of the latest type, and had a
lightning-protector device, which was a little brass plug that could
be pushed in during electrical storms to break the connection with
the outside line. A new boarder one day reported that the telephone was out of order, and summoned a repair man to fix it.
Immediately the repair man discovered that the brass plug had
gotten pushed in, and he remarked, disgustedly, "It's only the
lightning plug." The new boarder misunderstood, and that evening at the dinner table he expressed great surprise that a tele-

phone could get clogged up by a lightning bug. Major Scruggs never let the man live that one down.

George was fascinated at the major's unfailing ability to get a laugh from the crowd. He felt that he himself did not have the knack, but he saw good humor in lots of things that happened at the office. Everyone liked his account of how they sold Mr. Rosenberg, the dry-goods merchant, an advertisment two columns wide by 20 inches deep—on one condition: only if it ran at the top of the page. Gladly, they told him. Mr. Rosenberg never afterward mentioned, if he noticed, that there was no way to run a 20-inch ad other than from the bottom of the page all the way to the top, because the page was exactly 20 inches deep.

After hearing the story, Major Scruggs told George that what he had was an English sense of humor. The remark touched a responsive chord. George took pride in the fact that he came from England, but he had never thought that there might be capital in having an English sense of humor. That was something to cultivate.

After some months at the Thacker house, George and Ollie decided to leave, the main reason being that George took a tumble down the stairs while carrying the baby one dark night. Annie was unhurt, but George sprained his ankle and had to use crutches for two weeks. They were convinced that the stairs were too steep and dangerous, and shortly moved to the Ardrey house, on the northeast corner of Akard and Cadiz Streets, later the location of the Federal Reserve Bank building.

It was here at the Ardrey house in the summer of 1886 that Annie took sick. The illness hung on, and it became apparent that their troubles stood to get worse before they got better, because in October there would be another baby in the family. George and Ollie had never before experienced the anxiety and the nervous and physical strain that they now faced. The doctor came almost daily to their room to see Annie, and he finally concluded that her trouble was "cholera infantum," an illness that frequently proved fatal. It was a lingering malady. Sometimes the baby appeared to get better, but then she would relapse again. One medicine after another was tried, but nothing seemed to cure her.

Ollie was soon worn out with day-and-night vigils by the baby's bed, and George had to take over the night duty, although he continued to work long hours at the office, rarely less than twelve hours a day. Near the end of the summer Ollie grew desperate. She decided to go to Lexington, Missouri, where her mother could help. The baby had recovered some strength, and the trip was made.

Trouble at home, trouble at the office. That was a saying George had heard and now he believed it, because there was trouble at the office too. One of the paper's biggest advertisers was being extremely difficult. It was a man named Keating, who owned the largest farm implement store in North Texas, and who was a local political figure of considerable influence, having the backing of the Knights of Labor and the Farmers' Alliance. Also, Keating owned a few shares of stock in A. H. Belo & Co. He had gotten deeply involved in the fight over the selection of the site for the new state fair grounds in Dallas, and he was trying to use his influence as an advertiser to get the *News* to back his side. Keating's faction demanded that the city locate the grounds in North Dallas. The opposing group were equally insistent on an East Dallas site. Editorially, the *News* was staying neutral, merely reporting the day-to-day developments. At length each faction prepared to stage a separate fair on its own chosen site, and Keating asked the business manager of the *News* see to it that the paper supported the North Dallas fair. George demurred, for independence of advertisers had always been a keystone in the code of the *News*. Keating next wrote an angry letter, demanding the paper's support or else.

"Under no circumstances will the *News* swerve from its set course," George replied.

Keating canceled his advertising contract, and ordered the *News* to insert a classified ad offering his five shares of A. H. Belo & Co. stock for sale at 50 cents on the dollar. Now George's ire was up. Colonel Belo was out of the city, so George consulted by telegraph with Colonel Lowe in Galveston, the next in command of the two papers. "When you're right, give them no quarter," the Old Scotsman replied. This was the support George

wanted. He saw to it that Keating's classified ad not only got
published, but that it ran on the front page. And for Mr. Keating,
the *News* had an editorial on which George and the editor collabo-
rated :

> ... The *News* is desirous of aiding the
> Keating Implement and Machinery
> Company in finding a customer for this
> stock. This is a small piece of chagrin
> growing out of "the two fairs imbro-
> glio," to which the *News* is perfectly
> indifferent.
>
> A point has been reached, however,
> where the *News* management deems it
> necessary to say that it is master of
> its own business and will submit to no
> dictation at the hands of anyone. . . .
> The *News* is here to stay. This fact the
> Keating Implement and Machinery
> Company may rest assured of, for the
> *News* will be doing business in Dallas
> long after the Keating Implement and
> Machinery Company and all connected
> with it are dead and forgotten. Mean-
> time, the heavy "block" thus rushed on
> the market is not likely to "bear" the
> stock of the A. H. Belo & Co. to any
> considerable extent.

The management of the *News*—and George—could afford to
feel confident, because the Dallas paper was rounding out a very
successful first year. In the issue of October 1, 1886, the accomplishments were acclaimed :

> . . . To say that the success of the
> *News* has been phenomenal is not
> drawing upon the imagination in the
> slightest particular. . . . At the end of
> the first year the *News* has attained a
> circulation three times as great as any
> morning newspaper ever before pub-

lished in Dallas, and greater than the
combined circulation of all morning
newspapers heretofore published in
North Texas.

A circulation victory was George's victory. He was the one
who had made the North Texas survey in 1883 and laid the
groundwork. He was the man who had hired the solicitors and
worked with the carriers all year long.

In the same editorial, the *News* said:

> This success could not have been
> done . . . unless its policy was over and
> beyond the "shriveled localism" that
> would have confined it to the city
> limits. In reaching out, the *News*
> reaches out for Dallas. . . . The
> advancement of Dallas is the advance-
> ment of the *News*. The one is insepar-
> able from the other. . . .

Here was evidence of the sagacity of Colonel Belo in matters
of policy. A paper could be no bigger than its scope of interests,
a city could be no larger than merited by the market it served.

At the end of the first year, George had hoped to get a raise.
The $31.15 a week he was making was being painfully stretched,
especially since Annie's illness. No raise, however, was forthcoming. Colonel Belo possessed a hard shell when it came to salary
matters, and he was primarily concerned with retiring the first-
mortgage bonds which the company had floated in raising the
80,000 dollars to get the Dallas paper started. But for George
there was good news in the making. A telegram dispatched from
Lexington, Missouri, on October 14, announced: ANOTHER
DAUGHTER. OLIVIA AND BABY DOING WELL. ANNIE IN GOOD
HEALTH.

With 1887 the years in George's life began to go by with an
ever-increasing tempo, and they began to show, on the one hand,

a sameness which at times dismayed him, and, on the other, an unending panorama of change, progress, and development that stimulated and prodded him.

Year after year there were the same contract renewals to negotiate, the same special editions to work up, the same-looking advertisements to lay out, the same unceasing struggle for more and more circulation . . . to 7000 to 10,000 to 15,000. Year after year several new faces appeared in the ranks, and a few departed. Year after year Dallas politicians promised what they never seemed able to fulfill. Year after year the Trinity overflowed its banks and separated Dallas and Oak Cliff with a valley of water for days and sometimes weeks.

But these were the exciting years, too, when Jim Hogg was the idol of the common people of Texas, when the Dalton brothers were the terror of the Midwest, when James J. Corbett knocked out the great John L. Sullivan, when John D. Rockefeller's Standard Oil Company battled Congress and defied the courts, when the shot was fired that set off the Indian Territory Land Rush and Oklahoma City and Guthrie and other towns were settled overnight, and when Henry W. Grady was giving inspiration to the New South, and stirred the hearts of 10,000 people in Dallas with the ringing words, "Fellow Citizens, I salute the first city of the grandest state of the greatest government on earth."

These were the years when the *News* started its daily train to Denison, and named it the "Cannon Ball," and drove the St. Louis papers from North Texas . . . when George was raised to 37 dollars a week and became second only to the editor-in-chief in earnings . . . when two typewriters were purchased for A. H. Belo & Co. and the first carbon copies of business letters were made for the files . . . when the *News'* own artesian well was brought in down in the basement of the *News* building and an outside fountain installed for use of the general public . . . when the front page was run in two colors on the opening date of the 14th Annual Texas Press Association Convention in Dallas . . . when the first linotype machines were installed in the *News'* composing room, and a saddened printer was moved to write:

When the machines are going
And the cases all "unload"
Many a "comp" will be counting
The ties upon the road

CHORUS:
After the "flank" is over
After the "flank" is made
Many a "print" will be saying:
"Oh, why could I not have stayed?"

Oh, baby, I now must leave you,
The chance for work is thin,
For the ten machines are clicking
And the final "flank" is in.

These were the years when George's parents moved to Dallas, and shortly thereafter Father Dealey "passed from life to death" . . . when James Q. Dealey made his mark at Brown University in Providence, Rhode Island, with a bachelor's degree, a master's, and a Ph.D. in quick succession, and George was proud of his brother, "the Professor." These were the years, it seemed to George, when at home Ollie was always coaxing a baby to eat, and the high chair was never empty. Before Annie was ready to give up the high chair, they had to use it for Fannie, then Walter, then Ted, then Maidie.

Walter Allen Dealey, the third child, was born September 11, 1890, when the family was living at the corner of Harwood and Polk at the head of Wood Street (later to be the site of the Masonic Temple). This was the cottage they built on the lot owned by T.W., and the furniture in it was bought with money borrowed from Ollie's father. It was a nice house, but the neighborhood was so noisy George could not sleep at night. The "kids" for blocks around were attracted to the new concrete sidewalk in front of the house—a sidewalk of concrete being a rare and modern innovation in Dallas—and they made a din of racket. When they stopped, noise from the Turnverein across the street began to pick up volume in the usual sounds that came from a beer hall and bowling alley in 1890. Shortly after Walter was born, the family moved to Oak Cliff, remaining about a year in the new residential section west of the river. But needing more room and a more convenient location to the *News* building, they moved back across the river in 1892, buying a doctor's former home at 195 Thomas Avenue. It was here in the two-story brick house on Thomas Avenue that Edward Musgrove (Ted) Dealey was born on October 5, 1892, and Mary Dealey (nicknamed Maidie) was born on March 15, 1895. Five children completed the family. Time was when George and Ollie could live comfortably in one room in a boardinghouse, but in the space of ten years they came to need a house with four bedrooms and two baths.

These were the years of transition, ten hard-packed years . . . from day to day much of the same . . . but from year to year much in development. These were the supererogatory years when the effort and time and loyalty given A. H. Belo & Co. measured above and beyond the call of duty, and when the personal remuneration was slow to increase . . . years when an inborn faith in the self-reward of "sticking to the job" sustained George in his zest for work and in his constant fidelity to an employer's interests. The unencumbered young man who went to Lexington, Missouri, to take a wife in 1884 was markedly different from the George B. Dealey of 1894. At the end of ten years, he was a man of family, a property-owner, a taxpayer. At the end of ten years with the Dallas *Morning News,* he was clearly the business mainstay of the paper. As responsibilities came along for this growing newspaper in a growing city, he shouldered them one by one. The employees, from editor-in-chief to printer's devil, took it for granted that the company would never fail to meet a payroll— George Dealey would see to that.

At the beginning of these ten years, most of the employees of the *News* had known him as "George." At the end of these years, most of the employees knew him as "Mr. Dealey." "George" had become "Mr. Dealey." That was the symbol and key to the transition that had taken place.

CHAPTER SIX

1895

THE *NEWS* FAMILY CELEBRATES. THE
FIRST AND ONLY SPANKING. TWENTY-
ONE YEARS WITH THE *NEWS*.

"THE *NEWS* FAMILY" WAS A PHRASE OF LONG USE BY STAFF MEM-
bers of the two Belo papers, and there was considerable tradition
behind it, going back to the days of Willard Richardson. But in
1895 it could be said that in the memory of the oldest employee no
occasion ever brought the *News* family as closely together and
added to their *esprit d'corps* as did the wedding feast in celebration of the marriage of the only daughter of Colonel and Mrs.
Belo, which took place on January 8 of that year.

In the fall of 1894 the colonel and his family did not return to
Dallas as they ordinarily did after spending the summer at their
cottage at Saranac Inn, a mountain resort in the Adirondacks of
New York State. With the approach of the date for the wedding
of Jeannette Ennis Belo to Dr. Charles Peabody, it proved opportune to plan to have the wedding in New York City. As the Belos
were known to a fashionable crowd of Easterners who congre-
gated at Saranac Inn, and as Dr. Charles Peabody was a professor
at Harvard University and the brilliant grandson of the famed
George Peabody, the British-American philanthropist, the event
assumed a rank of some social note in New York City.

Although the wedding would take place far from Texas, Colonel
Belo wanted it properly celebrated in Dallas and Galveston, and

early in December he instructed by letter that a wedding feast should be arranged for the staff of each newspaper office.

In Dallas, at 3:00 P.M. on Tuesday afternoon, January 8, all outside doors to the *News* building were locked. The banquet was timed to coincide with the wedding in New York. Excitement was running high. By 3:15 all but two employees were seated around the temporary banquet tables, which had been set up in the composing room on the third floor. Hiding the stones and type cases were rows of palms and evergreens. Seventy glasses of sauterne wine and numerous flower arrangements added color to the tables. All the banqueteers were men, except the society editor and the business manager's secretary. They were the only two women on the staff.

Last to enter the banquet hall, by prearrangement, was Mr. Donaldson C. Jenkins, the old white-haired editor-in-chief. He was met and escorted to the seat of honor at the head of the table by the managing editor, Frank Doremus, toastmaster for the occasion. As a matter of office protocol, Doremus and Dealey shared two seats side-by-side at the foot of the table.

"To our editor-in-chief," said Doremus, raising his wine glass. The response was quick and loud, and many glasses were drained to the bottom.

"Eat, drink, and be merry," responded Mr. Jenkins, and the crowd wasted no time. Seldom if ever had a banquet spread for a newspaper staff been more sumptuous . . . oysters on the half-shell, ox-tail soup, fried oysters . . . sauterne with the fish and claret with the meats . . . turkey, tongue, ham, and corned beef . . . lobster and chicken salad, celery, olives, assorted cakes and fruits and imported cheese . . . to top it off, ginger ale and champagne . . . and finally, coffee and cigars.

When the speech-making began, Mr. Jenkins made the first toast to the couple being married that day in New York City. Then the banquet orator, Judge Otis Eaton, junior law counsel of the *News,* spoke for 20 minutes in mellifluous phrases and with pure eloquence.

At the foot of the table, Dealey listened with a mixed feeling of admiration and a twinge of mental pain. He admired and envied the young judge for his fluency of speech. But it only served to remind him how disheartening his own attempts at public speaking had been. He had spoken a few times before Y.M.C.A. and church groups, and each time he had to think out carefully beforehand just how he must express his thoughts. Even today at the wedding feast he had his toast written out on a card and tucked away in his pocket for the appropriate moment.

As the banquet progressed, the toastmaster called for more toasts to the honored couple in New York City, and each department head was asked to speak for his coworkers. The toastmaster's eye fell on Charley Martin, and he asked if the party would entertain a toast from the oldest newspaper worker in Texas.

"A toast from Charley! A toast from Charley!" The merrymakers clamored in unison.

"I will propose the health of our chief, Colonel Alfred H. Belo," Charley Martin began, "whose absence is forced through honorable wounds received more than thirty years ago while battling for the cause of the Confederacy."

A hush fell over the hall. Charley Martin was speaking from his heart.

"Let us hope that he will soon be restored to usual strength and grand energy. In the battles of the cause that was lost, he was always found among the foremost in the front, and when the war had ended and the smoke of battle had cleared away, leaving this beautiful Southland a scene of desolation, he applied in the field of industry the same splendid courage and energy that had won him fame on the battlefield as the youngest Colonel from North Carolina, and today the Galveston *News* and the Dallas *News* are monuments to his success."

The crowd was electrified. The cheers shook the glass panes in the windows, and the noise drew a large crowd in the street below to the front of the building.

The wine had flowed freely all during the banquet, and when the toastmaster called on Mr. Florer to express the sentiments of the mailing room, the amiable chief clerk of the mailing room

stood up, braced himself, and said, "For the first time in my life,
I am too full for utterance."

The hands of the clock were pointing the hour of 6 when Doremus announced that the business manager would make the final
toast of the party.

"We are here in the chapel of the typos—the holy of holies,"
Dealey responded, "and everyone who enters these sacred precincts
has got to bring his card. I have brought mine. [Out came the
card on which his toast was written.] It is a wish from the business office. Here's to the joining of hearts and of hands of the fair
daughter of Texas and the learned son of Massachusetts, the union
of the South with the North, the West with the East. May their
lives be happy and useful ones and their success equal to that of
the *News,* that 'double-ended whizzer,'* pride of the bride's father.
May their influence be for good and as extensive and healthy as the
circulation of the *News.* May their position in life continue 'top
of column,' and as they are of literary turn, may it also be 'next
to reading matter.' And may the general turn of their lives be as
smooth as the rails over which daily glide the three special trains
of the *News.*"

In reporting the celebration in the next morning's paper, five
full columns were used, and the story concluded: "It was the happiest occasion with which the *News* building was ever enlivened."
In writing Colonel Belo about the wedding feast, Dealey enclosed
extra tear sheets containing the story from Wednesday's paper,
suggesting that the colonel might want to show his New York
friends how weddings were celebrated in Texas. At the same
time Dealey sent extra copies to the newlyweds, who had started
on their wedding trip, which was a field expedition on horseback
in the western part of the United States in search of archeological
remains of early American Indian tribes. If at this moment anyone had prophesied to Dealey that this blithe young lady whom
he had toasted the day before would one day, 30 years later, be
the key person to decide whether he, George B. Dealey, would

---

* "Double-ended whizzer" was an allusion to Governor James S. Hogg's current anathema for the *News*—"the double-ender."

attain the goal of his most cherished dream in life, he would have laughed at such a fantasy.

During this period, first noticeable about 1895, Dealey in his own mind began to magnify the handicap which he felt in his lack of a college education. All during his later life he was to reveal a certain deference to the man with a degree tacked to his name. At 21 he had begun a serious effort to bolster his few earlier years of formal education by attending night school in Galveston, but this ended two years later when he started the survey trip through North Texas, and it was more than 12 years later before he again attempted to broaden his knowledge in a systematic way. His new plan was simple. He resolved to spend two or three hours each night reading selected books. In a year's time, he calculated, he would be able to read about 50 books, as well as keep abreast of leading periodicals.

As people occasionally asked him if he were familiar with any of the places in England mentioned in Dickens' books, Dealey thought it would be a good idea to make a study of the famous author's novels. Ollie had read most of Dickens, and she recommended *Oliver Twist* or *Great Expectations* to start with. He chose the latter and immediately had a great liking for Mr. Pip and a sympathetic understanding of Mr. Wemmick.

But it took weeks for him to finish the book. Somehow work and children conspired to reduce his spare time to almost nothing. Annie, the oldest daughter, was ten now; Fannie going on nine; Walter was five; Ted going on three; and this was the time when Maidie was merely "weeks old." It was the spring of 1895. Although Ollie managed the children entirely, still when he came home a little early in the evenings, the children contrived to prevent his reading until they were sent to bed, and then there were calls for glasses of water, coughing spells to stop, and occasional crying or fighting to be quieted. When he wasn't too tired or nervous, he played with the children, but usually at the end of 30 minutes he was herding them up the stairs and keeping them in step to the tune of a ditty he remembered his mother would sing when he was a small boy in England:

"Tramp, tramp, tramp, the boys are marching;
Cheer up, the bobby's at the door;
If you don't let him in, he will knock the door in,
And you'll never see your Daddy any more."

One evening three-year-old Ted outdid himself in starting fights
with the other children and in aggravating his father. The trouble
started when Dealey settled down to eat his supper. He usually ate
alone because he seldom got home before 7:30 or 8:00, and his
supper was kept warm on the stove. Before eating he first took a
teaspoonful of a powder called Croupon in a glass of water, a
medicine for his chronic dyspepsia. At the moment he was mixing
the Croupon, Ted dashed into the dining room, chased by Walter,
and, without warning, leaped on his father's back. Croupon went
all over the place, but mainly on Dealey. The boys were ordered
out of the dining room and upstairs to bed. They started, but Ted
managed to provoke several more trying incidents before getting
to the stairway. This was too much for Dealey. Although he had
never before spanked any of the children, there was always a first
time. He hustled Ted up the stairs and into the nearest bedroom.

About three blows had been struck with a handy bedroom slip-
per when the door to the room popped open. Ollie stood in the
doorway, holding Maidie.

"George," she said, in a voice so determined that it startled both
father and son, "leave that child alone. When the children need
punishment, I will punish them."

That ended the spanking, and it was the first and last time
Dealey ever spanked any of the children. Ollie was right, he reflected. He left the responsibility for rearing the children entirely
in her hands, and it followed that he should leave the punishment
in her hands too.

Earlier than usual on the morning of Saturday, October 12,
1895, Dealey hurried out of the house to the stable to "work out"
on the punching bag. Calisthenics of some kind had been a daily
practice for several years, and he was being quoted in Saturday's
paper on the value of exercising.

"A business or professional man in good physical condition can do twice as much work in a given time as one who is run down," the testimonial read. "Therefore two or three hours a week regularly spent in the Y.M.C.A. gymnasium will prove a time-saver. I speak from experience."

He felt unusually exuberant on this morning. This October 12 marked 21 years he had served the *News,* 11 with the Galveston paper and 10 with the Dallas paper. Of the Dallas staff, only Mr. Jenkins outnumbered him in years of service. In Galveston, several had served longer, notably T.W., his older brother, and Colonel Lowe, the Old Scotsman.

As he walked in the front door of the *News* building, every member of the front office staff turned to greet him enthusiastically. Something odd going on, he thought. Instantly he saw the reason. On his desk there was a silver tea set—a teapot, sugar dish, and a spoonholder.

Mr. Geen, the bookkeeper, Mr. Florer, the mailing-room clerk, Miss Maynard, the one and only lady secretary in the office, and a dozen other persons gathered around as he picked up the three elegant pieces of silver and admired them.

"It's not often Colonel Belo gives away silver," Mr. Geen remarked wryly.

They asked Dealey to read the letter which accompanied the gift:

Saranac Inn, New York
October 2nd, 1895

Mr. G. B. Dealey
Dear Sir:

On the 12th inst. you will complete your 21st year with the "News," and accompanying testimonial is intended to commemorate the event. It affords me great pleasure to assure you that all of our relations have been of the most satisfactory character. I have watched your career with much interest and you have won your place by your own merit. Your close identification with the "Dallas News", as business manager, from its beginning to its present very prosperous condition, is the best tribute to your ability.

It is very gratifying to me to testify to your unswerving loyalty and devotion to the "News".

With assurances of highest regard, I remain,

Yours truly,

A. H. Belo, Pres.

By noon Dealey was impatient to get home to show the set to Ollie, but the run-sheet on advertising was incomplete. He couldn't leave the office until it was decided whether to order in a 20-page paper for Sunday or a 16. If 16, it would be too tight to accommodate all the advertising without cutting out some important features. Deciding the size of the paper was always a headache. Shortly before 1:00 P.M. word came to release a full-page advertisement that was being held up.

"Make it twenty," he shouted to Mr. Geen as he hurried out the door for home, with the silver service under his arm.

Ollie loved the silver. After lunch, at her suggestion, he took the set back to the office to christen it. The tea party turned out to be one of the brightest memories of his life. Among the numerous office friends who dropped by the mailing room after 5:00 P.M. for tea and wafers was Mr. Jenkins. For a quarter of an hour, much to the amusement of the group, the white-haired editor-in-chief and Dealey swapped reminiscences about early days in Galveston. Dealey said it was on the day Colonel Belo hired him that he first met Mr. Jenkins, and the thing that awed him about Mr. Jenkins was how matter-of-factly Mr. Jenkins regarded his prerogative to approve or disapprove of whatever President Ulysses S. Grant happened to be doing on that day, which, as he recalled, had to do with a trip the president was making through the Indian Territory to North Texas.

The next morning was Sunday, and after taking the children by Sunday school, Dealey went to the office to attend to the usual circulation matters, and, on this particular Sunday, to write a letter of appreciation to "My dear Colonel."

... The gift is a handsome and a lasting one, but I value the letter much more. ... It is very gratifying to me to know that my work on the *News* has been so pleasing to you. I have done my best and since I reached manhood and learned the meaning of *responsibility*, it has been my aim always to do the work assigned me with as much fidelity as if I owned the property.

CHAPTER SEVEN

1895-1899

**MANAGER OF ALL DEPARTMENTS. PRO-
MOTING CIRCULATION. A SICK SPELL.
THE FAMILY GOES FOR A SUNDAY RIDE.
MOTHER DEALEY RELATES THEIR AN-
CESTRY.**

As THE END OF 1895 DREW CLOSER, CERTAIN SIGNS INDICATED that Colonel Belo's health was growing slowly worse. "Office talk" had it, in the event of the colonel's early death, that authority in Dallas would probably pass to Managing Editor Frank Doremus. In due time, of course, the colonel's only son, Alfred, Jr., would assume charge, but in 1895 Alfred was still attending Yale. As for Mr. D. C. Jenkins, the elderly editor-in-chief was generally conceded too far along in years. In Galveston the accepted leaders were R. G. Lowe and T. W. Dealey. Colonel R. G. Lowe, the Old Scotsman, was vice-president of the company and second in charge over both papers. Although Frank Doremus and George B. Dealey had been with the Belo papers practically the same length of time, Doremus appeared to many to have the inside track in Dallas. He was a relative of Mrs. A. H. Belo, and he made more of a show as spokesman for the paper. He was a dark, slender man, weighing less than 120 pounds, and always wore a cutaway coat with long tails that reached to his knees. As a writer, he was capable, but as a managing editor, too impulsive and excitable. It was a common sight, when a big story broke, to see Doremus racing about the second floor chewing up the little black cigars which he constantly "dry-smoked" and spatting the bits in every direction.

In December of 1895 Colonel Belo wrote from New York issuing an order that the word "business" was being dropped from Dealey's title, and henceforth he would be "manager" (of all departments) of the Dallas paper. The action came as a surprise to many in the organization. Why the colonel chose at this time to elevate Dealey and not Doremus was never set forth.

Dealey's own reaction to his new title and extended authority produced no outward signs. He attended to the job of business manager the same as ever, and for months, insofar as anyone could observe, he showed no inclination to give orders to heads of other departments. In fact, the exact extent of his new authority was never specifically outlined. What it eventually became seemed to evolve. From the day of the promotion, however, Dealey himself sensed the possibilities. The colonel had paved the way for him to rise to the top. Instinctively he kept a tight rein on any feeling of elation or overambition. He knew he had yet to prove equal to the job. He understood, too, without being told, that his real authority as yet did not extend to the editors or to editorial policy. Hands off there.

This intuition was soon confirmed when William Greene Sterett, the popular Washington correspondent of the *News,* made it known that, the new "manager" notwithstanding, as far as he was concerned he was still taking orders from Doremus. "Doremus is on top in Dallas, sure," Sterett wrote to Colonel Lowe, "and he will be the power when Belo leaves." Bill Sterett was an explosive character who "talked rough" but wrote with a warm heart and the pen of a master. In age, he was 12 years Dealey's senior. He had joined the *News* staff in 1885, but had spent most of the intervening years in the nation's capital as Washington correspondent of the *News.* Consequently, in 1895, Sterett and Dealey were little more than acquaintances.

Fortunately for Dealey, he had no quarrels with Sterett during this formative period. Colonel Belo continued to live for several years more—and made the important decisions on editorial personnel and policy.

But even without the worry of the editorial department, the new manager had more than enough to do. Among the jobs which years earlier he had appropriated to himself was that of promotion of the newspaper, and with the approach of the nation's general election of 1896, he grew promotion-conscious. Great interest had been building up in the presidential race. It was "William McKinley and sound money" on the one hand, and "William Jennings Bryan and free silver" on the other. The state political race was hot too.

"Do you realize the great importance attaching to next week as far as paper sales are concerned?" Dealey wrote to all circulators of the *News*. There were several hundred of them scattered over Texas and in Southern Oklahoma. "Never in your life have you experienced an occasion like next week will be, provided the result of the election is at all in doubt. What do you think of this idea: Get a lot of colored tickets, and on these tickets have printed or written: GOOD FOR ONE COPY OF THE DALLAS *NEWS* ON NOV. 4th."

So great would be the demand for the *News,* only those with tickets would be sure of getting a copy of the paper, because "the election reports in the *News* will not be eclipsed by any paper in the United States."

Enterprise like this was in character for the *News,* but so rare among Texas newspapers that not only did the *News* sell thousands of additional copies on November 4, but hundreds of new subscriptions poured in, pushing the total circulation to 18,682 before the end of November.

In the field of journalism, this was the beginning of something bigger still. When it came to circulation battles, Dealey adopted the motto of the Confederate General, Nathan Bedford Forrest: "Get there fustest with the mostest." The *News* must get out first with the most election news. The trick was in the rapid collection of results from all over the vast state. No other Texas newspaper had anything to compare with the far-flung army of correspondents and circulators and traveling agents of the *News,* and Dealey made the most of these facilities. This was the forerunner of the Texas Election Bureau, established more than two decades later, an enterprise in which many newspapers would cooperate and whose services the public would take for granted, as if it were a part of the machinery of democracy that had always existed.

During 1897 the fever of war spread like an epidemic over the nation. The jingoism which Hearst's New York *Journal* and Pulitzer's New York *World* were breeding daily was highly contagious, and even the conservative newspapers which preached caution editorially were unable to resist filling their columns with news of atrocities and oppression in Cuba. The *News* in Dallas was in the conservative camp and had warned its readers repeatedly that war was unnecessary. "In Texas there is much sympathy for the Cuban patriots," said the *News* in a typical editorial on December 14, "but the people believe that Davy Crockett's maxim—'Be sure you're right, then go ahead'—applies to the United States in this emergency with much force."

But after the blowing up of the battleship *Maine* on February 26, there was no holding back the tide. By April 25 the country was at war, and the *News* bowed to the inevitable and about-faced its editorial stand.

While this mad war dance had keyed many newspaper men to a new emotional height and to unprecedented journalistic enthusiasm, it produced a heavy depression on Dealey's spirits. But added problems brought on by the war forced him to work longer and harder than he had ever worked before. During the first half of the year, because of the uncertainty of the times, business everywhere slowed down, and both the Dallas and the Galveston papers suffered in revenue, while the costs of publishing increased. Colonel Belo became critical of the failure to curtail expenses, especially in Dallas.

"Every year expenses increase at Dallas," Colonel Belo wrote on July 4, 1898, from New York, "and the question is whether the best and most economical arrangement is in force . . ." The colonel was pressing forward with plans to build a larger building in Dallas, and this objective made the drop in revenue all the more serious.

In the same letter, that of July 4, Colonel Belo added in a more pleasant vein, "I hope Mr. T. W. Dealey can make a satisfactory

deal for the Garlington property * so that the board of directors
will approve its purchase, as it is undoubtedly the best location for
us. If there is any falling off in expected revenues, owing to de-
crease in advertising, I can arrange the financial part, but I hope
with the downfall of Cervera's Fleet, the ocean lines between
Galveston and New York will resume and business soon become
lively with you."

Dealey believed that some of the *News'* troubles were due to
failures at Galveston. In the course of the continuous correspondence which he maintained with Colonel Lowe in Galveston, he
wrote in the summer of 1898: "I have carefully noted your remarks with reference to the Houston *Post* and its work and am
very glad indeed to see that you now fully realize the situation
as it is. . . . As you put it, 'The *News* has been practically routed
out of the southern territory.' There is only one thing to do now,
and that is to reduce the price below what the *Post* is now offering
its paper for and to enter the fight to a finish . . . I would make it
so hot for the *Post* that they would wish in six months they had
not been born . . . I have talked to Colonel Belo about this matter
on a number of occasions but he never did seem to realize that it
was necessary that such action as I have outlined be taken."

Troubles, troubles, troubles . . . newsprint was running low . . . a
new train schedule meant an earlier press time . . . advertising rates
had to be raised . . . calculations had to be made for the purchase
of a new press . . . a printer was drunk on the job . . . somebody
was "leaking" confidential advertising information before the ads
appeared.

"Mr. Campbell," he wrote in regard to the leak on advertising
matter, "at various times attention has been called, as you know,
to the necessity of the strict enforcement of the rule preventing
advertisers from entering the ad alley. This rule is again being
violated. Possibly there are some new men in the room who do
not understand the rule and the necessity thereof. Will you please
explain it to all . . . GBD."

---

* The Garlington property referred to was located in Dallas at the corner
of Lamar and Commerce Streets and adjoined the then-existing *News* building.

If it wasn't one thing, it was another. Every day somebody had to be prompted to do the things that he was supposed to do. Hours and hours were consumed in just putting things to order. Dealey often asked himself why should he have to spend so much of his time correcting the failures of others? It was frustrating and nerve-wracking.

Every man has his physical and nervous limitations, and at the end of 1898 Dealey became sick. For more than two weeks he was seriously ill, and Ollie watched him anxiously. The symptoms were confusing to the doctor, but Ollie knew that her husband's trouble stemmed, more than anything else, from sheer nervous exhaustion and overwork. She feared that he was having a nervous breakdown.

Soon Ollie herself was near exhaustion. Taking care of a sick husband, five children, and a big house was too much. To add to the general discomfort, the weather was cold and wet. Things might have gone from bad to worse, but Mother Dealey was available in Dallas, and she moved in temporarily to help with the nursing and the family chores. Although 70 years old, Mother Dealey was in good health and active, and she had a lovable, placid nature and truly enjoyed helping people.

Once his fever was gone, Dealey began to recover rapidly. Rest and relaxation were the medicines he needed most, and Colonel Belo sent instructions for Dealey not to return to work for at least another two weeks.

The period of recuperation afforded Dealey more time with the children than he had ever had before. Maidie, the youngest, was nearly four years old, and it seemed to Dealey she had grown right out of babyhood without his knowing it. It couldn't have been more than a few months back, he thought, when she was a little baby and they started calling her "Pud." The nickname had come about in an interesting way. In the wall between the kitchen and dining room of their house, there was a small opening for serving dishes. It was the practice for the cook to push the dishes through the opening from the kitchen, and Dealey or Ollie would place the dishes on the dining table. One evening when the meal was almost over, Dealey called to the cook, "Pass in the pudding."

To the delight of the family, the cook pushed in Maidie, who was at the crawling age. From then on, Maidie was "Pud" to the family.

On the first good-weather Sunday in January after Dealey had recovered from his illness, the family prepared to resume the regular Sunday afternoon buggy ride. The destination on this Sunday was to be Cole's Pond, in the north outskirts of the city, later the site of the North Dallas High School. As soon as the horse was hitched to the surrey, Ted, who was six, and Walter, eight, raced to get the outside seats in the back of the surrey. When Dealey climbed in, the boys were scuffling on the floor, getting their new blue serge suits dirty.

"Get up!" he shouted to them.

The horse lunged forward, thinking the command was for it, and the quick movement sent Dealey sprawling against the back of the seat and nearly over it. The buggy ride almost ended right there.

Order was restored, and Ollie and Maidie joined the group. Neither of the two older girls cared to go, as they preferred to spend the time with playmates in the neighborhood. Ollie looked charming in her brown woolen skirt and cape to match. The full skirt was especially useful on the Sunday rides . . . as a cover for Maidie after they were seated in the carriage. Her brown hat had a suggestion of a boat shape, and billowed fully ten inches above her head. Dealey wore a dark gray suit, bow tie, black derby, but the feature that best marked him as a father and businessman was his bushy dark mustache.

Although Dealey handled a horse with ease when riding in the saddle, he was usually tense when driving the family in the surrey. The continual shifting about of the children kept him nervous for fear one would fall out. As the ride progressed this Sunday, Ted directed a stream of questions at him that made him more nervous than usual. Finally, having answered all the questions he thought he could stand, Dealey asked Ted to stop and not talk any more until they got home.

"Just one more question," Ted pleaded.

"Yes, but hurry up."

"Well, Papa, if I were to eat up all the houses and all the trees and all the sidewalks and all the things around us, would I bust?"

That was the last straw. Dealey turned the buggy around and headed back home, and he said in no uncertain terms that he did not want another single question the remainder of the day.

On January 24, 1899, a few days before Dealey returned to work, he received a letter that put the final rout to any unhappy worries that might have been lurking in his mind. It was a letter from Colonel Belo, who was in Galveston presiding over the annual end-of-the-year meeting of the board of directors. Dated January 23, 1899, the letter read:

> During the past year many men have become heroes in the Army and Navy, but there are also heroes in civil life, and your conduct when the crisis of the war came, with its many problems in our business, in standing firmly at your post, with cool head, although your physical condition was on the verge of collapse, entitles you to unqualified praise, which you justly earned.
>
> As a testimonial of our appreciation, enclosed please find s/d No. 10621 on Galveston National Bank for One Thousand Dollars.
>
> Rejoicing that your health has been fully restored and with renewed assurances of our highest regard, we are
>
> Yours truly,
>
> A. H. Belo, Pres.

The praise gave Dealey an inner glow. Praise was his elixir. But oh that One Thousand Dollars! How the Dealey family needed the extra cash at this time! As he reread the letter, Dealey had to smile. There was a saying attributed to an old Missouri publisher that he sometimes quoted to others who worried unnecessarily: "I'm an old man and have had many troubles, but most of them never happened." It applied to himself too. From January to July, it had been worry, worry, worry for fear the year would show a loss. Instead it turned out the best year ever.

In another way, too, his misfortunes brought a good consequence. Dealey resumed his daily exercises, which of late he had thought he was too busy to take. Never again would he get too busy to take care of his health. Never would he neglect the little things, which, if attended to regularly, accumulate strength, but if neglected, undermine the body. Among his firm resolves, he decided he would drink eight glasses of water each day, and to insure that he drank them with the regularity that would increase the benefit, he instructed the office boy to hand him a glass of water each hour of the day no matter what he was doing or to whom he was talking. This resolution would hold firm for 47 years.

One evening in the spring of 1899, Dealey and Ollie drove the surrey over to Mother Dealey's house. After some pleasantries over tea and butter cake, Dealey took a seat at his mother's little writing desk and asked her to relate everything she could recall about her parents and grandparents. He had been thinking that the interesting accounts his mother told occasionally had better be put down in writing or they would some day be lost forever. Pleased at the request, Mother Dealey settled down with her knitting in her favorite straight-back chair, and commenced to tell all she could remember. As she talked, Dealey made full notes in pencil on a sheaf of newsprint copy paper which he had brought along.

"Now, I was born in Clones, County of Monigham, Ireland, on August 26, 1829, and christened Mary Ann Nellins," Mother Dealey began. "My father was William Nellins, and he was born in Dublin and educated at Dublin University. He stood five-feet-five-inches tall, weighed about one hundred forty pounds, and had blue eyes. Your grandfather was a soldier, and proud of it. He fought against Napoleon at the battles of Toulouse, Waterloo, and one other I don't recall. He had a medal showing him to be a Quartermaster Sergeant and that he served under Wellington."

Dealey stopped his mother to ask if her father ever said anything about the Duke of Wellington.

"Oh yes, he used to remark, 'The Duke was a brave general, but a hard man on the poor soldiers.' Once when passing through some valley in the Peninsular Campaign, my father told how they found wine running through the streets. One soldier stooped down

and filled his canteen, and the Duke ordered him shot for doing
this. It was said the enemy placed the wine there."

"When did Grandfather marry?" Dealey asked.

"After the wars. He returned to Ireland and met and married
Jane Johnstone, daughter of James Johnstone, freeholder of Granshaw. Now, the Johnstones of Granshaw, as they were widely
known thereabouts, were of the land-owning gentry. Most of the
town of Granshaw was their property, and the head of the clan,
old Grandfather Johnstone, looked and acted the part of an eight-
eenth-century gentleman."

"Did you ever see your Grandfather Johnstone?"

"Yes, indeed. I remember him clearly. He was a rather small
figure of a man but impressive in his knee breeches, buckle shoes,
light coat, and buff waistcoat. He wore his hair long in the fashion
of an older day, always carefully parted in the middle."

"Didn't you tell us that your mother and father acquired some
land from the Johnstones of Granshaw?" Dealey asked.

"That is right. But my father never tilled the land himself. He
rented land to six cotters, who in payment worked three days a
week for him. We had two house servants too, and they were
needed, for there were five sons and seven daughters in our family.
Then, when I was seventeen, my father died, and the family was
soon on hard times. In the latter part of 1847, I went to visit relatives in Liverpool, and there I soon met a Mrs. Sale, who was
distressed on account of her husband's illness. I went to live with
them and to help in their shoe business. Shortly Mr. Sale died. As
the shoe business had to be carried on, Mrs. Sale advertised for a
foreman."

Dealey stopped his mother and remarked to Ollie, with his
tongue in his cheek, "Here's where the Dealeys come in, showing
the importance of newspaper advertising." He had heard the story
related before.

"Yes," Mother Dealey said solemnly, unsuspecting that a bit of
humor was being passed at her expense. "The man who answered
the advertisement was George Dealey. If you want to know about
your father, he was born in West Derby, Liverpool, England, on
January 20, 1829. That's the same year I was born. He was the

fifth son of Thomas and Leonora Quayle Dealey, and like my
parents they had twelve children in all. Leonora Quayle was the
daughter of James Quayle, who held the rank of Master Mariner.
The Quayles were from the Isle of Man. Now, Thomas Dealey
was for a time a steward of the Earl of Derby's estate. But he had
a fuss with Lady Derby and refused to beg her pardon and resigned. After that he was a land agent. Also he was connected with
the building of the Mersey Docks, and it is said that he handled
and paid out all the money used in building those docks. He was
well fixed financially, and he had a friend named Bannerman, a
merchant, and that's where you, son, get the Bannerman in your
name."

"And did you and this George Dealey who answered Mrs. Sale's
advertisement get acquainted?" Dealey asked, winking at Ollie.

"We most certainly did. We were married in 1851 on February
10, in St. Judes Church in Liverpool, by the curate, the Reverend
Joshua B. Lowe."

The time was growing late. Dealey would have liked to pursue
the family history further, but Mother Dealey was showing fatigue, and so a halt was called.

As Ollie and Dealey drove the surrey back home, Dealey made
sure he had the packet of 12 folded pages of notes securely in
his pocket. He was glad this information about the family history
was down on paper. He had heard the stories before, but could
never remember the details. He must send this account to James
Quayle, his brother in Providence. James would appreciate it. It
was good to know about one's forebears. It took just a little of the
mystery out of life. But in America it did not greatly matter who
one's ancestors were.*

---

*For a more detailed study of the ancestry of Dealey, see Appendix A,
pp. 299-301.

CHAPTER EIGHT

1899

EDITORIAL POWER SHIFTS. THE "CLEANER
DALLAS LEAGUE" TAKES CHARGE OF THE
CITY. DEALEY EVOLVES A CAMPAIGN FOR-
MULA. NEW PRESTIGE.

AMONG TEXAS NEWSPAPERS THE LEADERSHIP OF THE *NEWS* HAD
not been challenged since the Civil War, and at the turn of the
century its pre-eminence had never been greater. This was the day
when the newspaper was king—no picture show, no radio, no tele-
vision with which to share the public. There was awesome power
in the press, and where there was power, there was bound to be
an undercurrent of struggle by the able men at hand for control
of that power.

For many years on the *News* the struggle was quiet. The power
had been held firmly in the hands of Colonel Belo and the few men
who were charged with the editorial direction: D. C. Jenkins, R.
G. Lowe, and, to a lesser though important degree, T. W. Dealey,
Luther W. Clark, William G. Sterett, and Frank Doremus. But in
1899 signs of shifting power became evident. The change was
only natural, for with each passing year Colonel Belo spent less
time in Dallas, Mr. Jenkins was aging and no longer worked a full
day, and before 1899 was half gone Frank Doremus was dead.
New and younger men were assuming certain editorial responsibilities: D. Prescott Toomey, Tom Finty, Jr., Hugh Nugent Fitz-

gerald, and Alonzo Wasson. Alfred Belo, Jr., was learning the
business, preparing to take his father's place.

As some of the older heads withdrew, the editorial power they
released was bound to gravitate to other hands. In 1899 the unsettled question was, To whom and how much?

When Dealey was promoted to manager in 1895, he had shown
little inclination to involve himself in matters of editorial direction. Gradually, however, he acquired a position of influence in
the editorial department . . . at first a business control over the
number of news-editorial employees, their hours of work, travel
expenses, and the like. Then more and more he enlisted news-editorial support behind city-wide activities and promotions of the
businessmen, and also for social-welfare projects in which he was
interested—the Buckner's Orphan's Home, the Y.M.C.A., and the
Christmas charity of the public schools. By 1899 Dealey saw his
job as manager in broader scope.

In recent months something important had focused his thoughts
on editorial direction. During the period of his recuperation, following his recent illness, he had read a formidable stack of magazines, newspapers, and books . . . more than he read ordinarily;
and the current journals were full of the aftermath of the war
with Spain. He was particularly interested in accounts of the
methods used to fight yellow fever and malaria. There was some
belief that these diseases were spread by mosquitoes, and by rigid
enforcement of sanitary laws, the United States Army had eradi-
cated the insects from the Cuban cities and quickly brought the
epidemics under control.

He was inspired by the army's experiments in city sanitation.
Something should be done about the filthy conditions in Dallas!
Most American cities were filth-ridden, but Dallas was worse than
average. Its refuse-laden alleys, stinking privies, garbage-glutted
back lots, acres of malodorous dump yards, and endless swarms of
flies were enough to make hygienic-minded individuals despair.
Nearly every year the doctors of Dallas made some effort to
awaken the city to the threat to public health in the insanitary
conditions. But nothing ever came of it. The *News* ran occasional

editorials warning of the seriousness. But the people never gave
the advice a second thought. The trouble was in the lethargy of
the people.

The more Dealey thought of it, the more certain he became that
if the newspaper were determined and persistent enough, it could
arouse the people of Dallas. It could make them want to clean up
the city. Also, he was sure it was the newspaper's duty to do it.
Customarily this sort of project originated with the publisher
or the editors, not from the business side. However, the business
side of the newspaper, Dealey reasoned, held a distinct interest in
a cleaner city. If Dallas was cleaned up and kept clean, people
would flock to live there. The city would grow and prosper, and if
the city prospered, so would the *News*.

As early as February, Dealey had definite ideas in mind as to
how to wage the campaign to clean up the city, but he felt no
assurance that the editors would carry out his proposals. He was
thinking in terms of a campaign such as Dallas had never seen
before, a campaign that would go on for days and days . . . certainly something bigger than the usual one-shot editorial and fol-
low-up news stories.

Colonel Belo was receptive to Dealey's ideas and readily approved the project, but on the question of how far Dealey should
enter into news-editorial direction, the colonel held back. This was
a question of policy. He would think it over.

On March 15, 1899, Dealey had the colonel's answer—in writing. It was no ordinary office memorandum, but a promulgation.
RULES PROMULGATED BY THE *NEWS'* MANAGEMENT, the document
was headed. In the years that followed, it came to be regarded as
one of the important statements of organizational policy of the
institution.

Actually the new set of rules changed nothing about the *News*.
It merely clarified existing practice. Dealey was glad to have the
rules in writing, but in one particular he was not altogether
pleased at first. The document not once mentioned the position of
manager; it did, however, define the authority of the "business
manager." Dealey questioned whether the *business manager's* priv-

ilege in news-editorial matters was strong enough. Paragraph 8 read:

> The Business Manager will also be expected from time to time to make suggestions to the editorial council regarding matters which from his contact with the public he may think it advisable to take action upon, and to suggest news features, topics of interest to be treated, etc.*

After due reflection, Dealey conceded the wisdom of the meaning and the wording. "To suggest" was power enough for the business manager. The paramount interest of the *News* was its public service and not its commercial ambitions. If at any time the interests of the business manager should conflict fundamentally with the public service aims of the paper, the editor in charge should have the final say. Actually, that was the existing practice of the *News,* and it had been so as long as Dealey could remember.

In the clean-up drive Dealey had in mind, there was no conflict between business interests and editorial interests, but there was the matter of Dealey's assumption of editorial and news direction in order to carry out his plans. On instruction from Colonel Belo, the managing editor and the editorial council were told to cooperate fully with him as long as the campaign continued.

During the week preceding March 20, Dealey made elaborate preparations. He held conferences with city aldermen, city engineers, and the city sanitation officer. He wrote letters to Dallas city officials, to doctors, to businessmen, to civic leaders, asking each: "What should be done to clean up the city and keep it so?" He sent queries to officials of other cities. How was Chicago cleaned up? New York? Kansas City? In a memorandum addressed: "To Every Employee of the *News,*" he outlined the coming campaign and asked for slogan ideas.

In the issue of Monday, March 20, the campaign broke, but rather quietly. It was a contest announcement, in a two-column x 11-inch space on the back page offering ten dollars in gold to the first person to submit the correct five-word sentence about sanitation composed from these letters: YPLNHETCIE KHEAEPLCET.

---

* For complete document, see Appendix B, pp. 301-302.

Each successive day other phases of the campaign began to unfold.

TUESDAY—City council meets, promises thorough "spring cleaning" for Dallas . . . will enforce sanitation ordinances . . . to patch up old crematory so that all flesh can be burned. Two aldermen excoriate the closet nuisance.———WEDNESDAY—*News* reprints all city ordinances on sanitation. Chief Sanitary Inspector begins serving notices on all violators.———THURSDAY—Alderman Lincecum tells "What Should Be Done to Clean Up the City and Keep It So." New York City official tells how New York keeps clean.———FRIDAY—Terrible stench emanating from river bottom. *News* reporter finds 37 "decomposed and putrid" hogs in the Trinity River.———SATURDAY—*News* warns of disease from filth. Raw sewage empties in Trinity River below Oak Cliff Bridge. Ten doctors tell "What Should Be Done to Clean Up the City and Keep It So."

The contestants for the ten dollars in gold mobbed the *News* building on the morning for submitting the five-word sentence on sanitation. They broke the glass pane to the front door, and the police had to be called to keep order. Master Archie Harris, a ten-year-old lad who had stood in line since 5 :00 A.M., submitted the first correct entry : HELP KEEP THE CITY CLEAN. This was adopted as the campaign slogan, and it was placed in the ears of the *News* with the notice that it would stay there until the city was cleaned up.

By the end of the first week all Dallas was talking sanitation. Even the editors and reporters were impressed. Dealey was producing news faster than they could write it up. Alderman Lincecum stated publicly, "The *News,* which is the greatest public educator in the state, is doing the city a splendid service by its timely articles on improved sanitation."

During the second and third weeks the stream of news, feature articles, and letters on sanitation continued without let up.

For the fourth week Dealey had a surprise. The campaign needed a shot in the arm. As yet, there was more talk than action, and Dallas was far from being cleaned up.

On Saturday, April 8, the first public trash can ever to be seen on a sidewalk in Dallas was placed at the corner of Commerce and

Lamar Streets, just outside the door of the *News*. It was painted
a bright red, and on the front and back it carried the sign: HELP
KEEP THE CITY CLEAN—AND BE A PUBLIC BENEFACTOR. On the
side of the can it read: No. 1—FROM THE NEWS EMPLOYEES.

"Who'll be next?" asked the *News* editorially.

Three days later a Number 2 can was donated by the employees
of A. Harris & Co.

"Who'll be next?"

By April 16, Dallas had 26 public trash cans, all uniform in size
and painted bright red in color, and they hadn't cost the city a cent.

In the latter part of April the campaign seemed to lag. There
was still much talk, and some cleaning up had taken place, but it
was only a start. Dealey searched for a new angle. How to move
the average citizen to do his part? It was win or lose on the average citizen. The idea he thought of was revealed in the story that
broke in the *News* on May 4:

A SANITARY MASS MEETING

We, the undersigned, desire to express our unqualified approval of the
great sanitary movement lately inaugu-
rated in Dallas, and now extending
throughout the state.

We therefore call upon the good
people of Dallas, especially the ladies,
to assemble in mass meeting at the city
hall auditorium at 7:45 p.m. Monday,
May 8, to devise ways and means of
creating wider interest and cooperation in this vital matter. Also to consider the advisability of organizing the
Cleaner Dallas League.

[Signed by fifty leading citizens]

In an atmosphere of stirring oratory and military band music,
on May 8, the Cleaner Dallas League was duly organized. Alex
Sanger was elected president, and George B. Dealey became first

vice-president. The clean-up campaign was rolling forward again. Soon the League was joined by the Federated Women's Clubs of Dallas. Next the civic and commercial clubs. Next the teachers and school children of all the city schools. There was no stopping it now.

For three months the League took charge of Dallas—city government and all. The League's executive committee met every day. What it demanded, it got—new street sprinklers, better crematory facilities, better dumping ground supervision, sidewalk cuspidors for tobacco chewers, more sewage extensions, more paved streets, a new city garbage collection department, more sanitation inspectors. All over the town the alleys were emptied, yards were cleaned, ponds were drained, weeds were cut, and garbage went into regulation cans.

Each day the *News* covered the activities and reported the progress. Ward by ward and block by block, Dallas began to show a new and clean face. Before the summer was over, Dallas was, by 1899 standards, a clean city.

Who had cleaned up Dallas? In the final analysis it was the work of the average citizen. But it took the Cleaner Dallas League to make the average citizen work. But nothing would have worked if Dealey hadn't started the campaign, directed the publicity from start to finish, and coordinated the efforts of the various groups ... and, above all, kept at the job every day.

Though he had improvised the plans as the drive developed, he had evolved a success formula for public campaigns. Many times in the future he would follow the same pattern. It was: Start something good, call in the city leaders, let them take charge, support them with the *News,* give them the credit, play the role of coordinator, and keep working at it.

In March, before the clean-up drive, the businessmen and professional men of the city thought highly of Dealey, but he had no real rank as a city leader. After the campaign—the biggest, most prolonged activity ever undertaken in Dallas up to that time, involving practically everyone, from city officials to the youngest school children—Dealey emerged as a dynamic city leader, a man who could organize and get things done, a man who wielded the power of the *News*.

Among the staff members of the *News* there was a new respect for his ability and opinion, too. Before the start of the drive he had been uncertain about his part in the editorial direction of the *News*. Five months later he understood more clearly what his real editorial power was. It was equal to his ability to use the *News* for public service.

With the clean-up drive a *fait accompli,* he was ready to turn his attention to other civic matters. His *Memo to the Editorial Council* dated July 29, 1899, spoke with the new assurance and the new prestige:

> For a great number of years objections were very generally urged against The News because of its lack of interest in local affairs. I always contended that this avoidance of discussion of local affairs was a great mistake. Anything regarding the municipality of Dallas is of interest not only to the people of Dallas, but to every town in Texas. Since the sanitary agitation commenced, this feeling against The News is beginning to disappear.

> Now I want to suggest this: At a recent meeting of the city council the fund appropriated for the support of the public schools of Dallas was reduced from 25% to 23%. Many people believe this is illegal and that the council has no right to reduce it. They also have changed the age from 7 to 21 years, as at present, to 8 to 18 . . . I believe from what I can hear that both actions on the part of the city council are very unpopular and the consensus of opinion is that they have no right to meddle with public school affairs, which should be left entirely in the hands of the school board. There is a good deal of talk on the subject; it is of grave importance, and I would suggest the advisability of publishing a large number of very brief interviews from people on the council action, perhaps getting expressions from leading lawyers, and that it be discussed editorially.

Dealey's influence was steering the *News* to a greater interest in city affairs than it had ever had before. And it was all being done by suggestion. To suggest was power enough for Dealey.

CHAPTER NINE

1899-1900

**A NEW BUILDING AND A NEW CENTURY.
COLONEL BELO REAFFIRMS THE LINE OF
AUTHORITY. ALFRED'S WEDDING FEAST.
THE GALVESTON STORM.**

A NEW BUILDING WAS DESPERATELY NEEDED BY THE *NEWS*. CIR-
culation had jumped from 17,000 to more than 24,000 during the
Spanish-American War period—an increase of almost 42 per cent
in one year. Advertising likewise had bounded upward with the
war boom. Fortunately, the *News* was in position to expand. With
his customary foresight, Colonel Belo had bought up all the buildings on both sides of the original *News* building and owned a solid
stretch of property 100 feet deep on Commerce Street from Austin
to Lamar. The corner lot at Commerce and Lamar, where the old
city hall and fire station had been, was hard to come by, but
Dealey had negotiated the purchase personally for Colonel Belo
for the sum of 25,000 dollars.

In the spring of 1899 the management decided to build a new
plant on the corner at Commerce and Lamar, facing 100 feet on
both streets. Before leaving for an extended stay in the East,
Colonel Belo turned the building problems over to Dealey, with
a few clear-cut, simple directions: "Build it fireproof. Plan it to
suit the convenience and comfort of the employees, and make it
an ornament to the city."

Although Dealey was preoccupied with the clean-up drive and

all that it entailed, as well as carrying on his regular duties, some-how he managed to sandwich the building project into the day's work. One of the first steps was to hire an architect. A classified ad brought in a youngish-looking man named Herbert M. Greene. Dealey liked the way Greene said he would open an office across the street, watch every brick laid, and refuse all other work until the building was completed. That was the kind of architect the *News* wanted.

"But aren't you rather young for such a big job?" Dealey asked.

"Not as young as you think," said Greene, taking off his hat to display a bald head.

Greene got the job, no further questions asked.

Before the plans were drawn, Greene and Dealey made a hur-ried trip to St. Louis and Chicago to inspect the plants of the newspapers of those cities and to gather ideas for the new building.

Everyone in the *News* organization followed the progress of construction almost as closely as did the architect himself, and as a topic of conversation, the new building topped even the weather. One morning on the sidewalk opposite the *News,* a group of the employees gathered to watch the placement of several extraordi-narily large steel girders. Dealey was among them.

"Must be the largest girders ever used in a three-story build-ing," one member of the group commented. "How come, Mr. Dealey?"

"Need them to support the heavy artillery of the editorial de-partment."

Truth was that seven or eight additional floors were planned for the future, but his retort was bandied around the building, got into print, and was destined to outlast both the building and the steel girders themselves.

Construction on the new building continued through the re-mainder of 1899 and into the next year.

As the new century opened—the wonderful, new twentieth century—men all over the world, from emperors to home-town statesmen, dedicated themselves to many causes and predicted great changes.

Kaiser Wilhelm of Germany said in his New Year's Day address: "The German Empire will soon be in position to win the
place which it has not yet attained."

The Dallas Commercial Club passed a New Year's resolution in
favor of the Isthmian Canal [in Nicaragua].

A prominent New York financier said: "No state in the Union
has within it greater possibilities of industrial development than
Texas."

The *News* in its January 1 editorial peered into the crystal ball
and said:

> **Great things have been accomplished.
> It is not easy to see now how as much
> can be done during the next century.
> Still, we cannot tell. We may yet learn
> to see by phone with a glass eye, to
> work while we sleep, to fly from city to
> city, to soar the ocean over. Some
> humorist may yet spring a new joke,
> albeit nobody expects man to work
> miracles.**

Too busy to prophesy, Dealey dedicated himself to work. With
each successive year his work grew more complex, particularly
now that he was taking a hand in news and editorial matters.
Scarcely a week went by that Dealey didn't attend to several minor
editorial details. He revised the rules for handling opera notices,
he banned Jewish jokes, he moved the book reviews from the
woman's page to a page of general interest, he urged more copy
be contributed to the struggling Associated Press, and he initiated
the printing of résumés of Sunday sermons. Several times he had
to settle libel suits which careless reporters and editors brought on
the paper, and this led him to set down written policies for the
guidance of *News* men when handling libelous material. This was
a job for an experienced hand, because the laws on libel were not
yet clearly defined, and the current interpretations posed a serious
threat to certain freedoms of the press.

Whenever editorial matters went begging for attention, Dealey
stepped in.

Just at this time a far-reaching change occurred in the editorial hierarchy of the *News*. D. C. Jenkins, the old editor-in-chief, was 76 years old, and he deemed it time to quit. He had served the *News* since 1873. To fill his place, Colonel Belo designated a veteran editorial writer, Luther Clark, as the new editor-in-chief, but supervisory powers passed into Dealey's hands.

In a memorandum dated January 30, 1900, Dealey established an important new editorial department procedure:

MEMO TO CAPT. WALTER, MANAGING EDITOR

Beginning tomorrow I wish you would start a daily conference between yourself and other members of the editorial department.

Would suggest that this conference take place in your office at 3 P.M. sharp each day, to be attended by yourself, city editor and his assistant, artist, and also any other members of the department who are present and desire to attend the conference.

I feel confident that a conference of this kind each day will be productive of good. Its object first of all should be to briefly discuss the news events on hand for the day, the features to be looked after, and if possible the size of the paper should be then determined. In this connection would say that the management does not desire the weekday edition to be arbitrarily established as a ten-page paper. Where you can get along with eight pages do so and save the additional expense. Where you think the necessity exists for a larger paper than ten pages in any specific instance you can discuss it with me.

GBD, Manager

With methods, policies, and ideas, Dealey helped fill the vacuum that Mr. Jenkins had left. Perhaps it was this assumption of authority or perhaps it was other circumstances that soon led to an incident which cautioned Dealey, if he had not realized it before, that authority had to be held with a firmness if a man was to keep it. The incident occurred at a special meeting of the editorial council on April 13, 1900, with Colonel Belo taking part in the proceedings. R. G. Lowe came to Dallas from Galveston to attend. Luther Clark, Captain Walter, and H. N. Fitzgerald were present, as well as William G. Sterett. "Bill" Sterett, the "Washington

pro-consul of the *News*," had recently been brought back to Dallas
to serve as associate editor. Dealey was not present as it was not
the custom for him to attend meetings of the editorial council.

Various matters were discussed at length, and as the meeting
was about to break up, Sterett asked Colonel Belo to rule on a
question concerning his new position on the editorial staff. He
had discussed the matter with Colonel Lowe, Sterett said. He
could see the advisability of his making trips around the state
and possibly out of state to write up special matters or special
events. How much initiative might he exercise in this regard?
He would like to have the authority granted to him to perform
this activity.

Bill Sterett wanted to be his own boss, and Colonel Belo knew
it. Now was the time to set the record straight. The colonel believed in the military pattern of organization—a definite line of
authority.

"Gentlemen," the colonel said sharply, standing up, "my answer
to Mr. Sterett's question applies also to Messrs. Lowe, Clark,
Walter, and Fitzgerald. The organization in this office is thorough
and complete. Mr. G. B. Dealey, as manager, has control over
all departments. Mr. Clark has charge of the editorial page. Now
whenever Mr. Sterett has any ideas he wishes to submit with
reference to taking a trip, they can be submitted to the manager
of the paper, who will decide the matter after conference with
the managing editor."

The following day, the colonel, still somewhat riled, related the
incident to Dealey. On Dealey's suggestion, an appropriate record
of the colonel's dictum was made and signed. More than once
Sterett would test the line of authority in the organization. There
was something about taking orders from a younger man that
Sterett did not like. But Dealey understood Sterett's nature, and
in his quiet way he resolved to try to find ways of keeping Sterett
in harmonious accord with the organization.

Alfred Belo, Jr., only son of his father and heir to the *News*,
was getting married in June, and of course this was occasion for
a celebration and a wedding feast like the one given the employees

of the two papers when Jeannette, Colonel Belo's daughter, had married in 1895. As before, the plans were left entirely to Dealey, and Dealey saw how to make the party serve several purposes. It came just at the right time to be the house-warming for the new building. Except for the installation of equipment and furniture, the new building was ready for occupancy.

Shortly before 8 o'clock on the night of June 13, 103 employees gathered around long tables set up in the otherwise empty composing room on the third floor of the new building. On the east wall was draped a great American flag. Modern incandescent lights overhead "yielded a brilliancy scarcely unsurpassed by the sun at noon." A string orchestra of six pieces furnished music.

"Ladies and gentlemen," said official spokesman Dealey, precisely as the clock on the wall showed 8:00 P.M., "at this hour, perhaps at this moment, Alfred H. Belo, Jr., the promising and only son of his honored father, is being united in marriage to Miss Helen, daughter of Mr. and Mrs. W. A. Ponder, a prominent citizen of Denton."

The party for Alfred was the equal of the party for Jeannette, but there was one notable difference—no wine and no champagne. Too many good men had been too much in their cups when the 1895 banquet was over, and Dealey did not care to have the performance repeated.

Dealey's public speaking had improved in the five-year interval between the two wedding feasts. "It has been my privilege to know Alfred Belo from his childhood," Dealey said that evening, without the aid of notes. "I can speak from my own knowledge of his genial spirit, of his lovable nature, of his sterling character, and of his ability . . . Alfred Belo spent many years away from home. A graduate of Yale, he has been an extensive traveler, and I have no doubt he has met many charming women. But it was left for the arrow of a Texas Cupid so to hurl a dart as to find a resting place in the vital part. So again I say, 'Hurray for Texas!' "

The toastmaster for the program that night was Associate Editor Bill Sterett, and Sterett proved to be a witty and charming master of ceremonies. He cajoled the newly appointed managing

editor, Hugh Nugent Fitzgerald, into giving an impromptu
speech on "The Tractable Irishman," and, to the amusement of
everyone, he got the first speech of his life out of Alonzo Wasson
on the topic "Why Night Editors Fall Easy Victims to Dan
Cupid's Darts." There was not a dull moment for anyone, and
Sterett thoroughly enjoyed himself. It was Alfred's party, but
Sterett held the spotlight. There were more ways than one to
"manage" important editors.

"My dear George," Colonel Belo wrote Dealey from Massachusetts, where he had journeyed immediately after Alfred's wedding, "the report of the wedding banquet last Tuesday night has
just been read, and I desire to thank you heartily for the perfect
manner in which you carried out my wishes to give them all a
good time, making it in reality a happy wedding feast. Your
speech at the beginning was especially touching to me, and I hope
the friendship between Alfred and yourself will constantly grow
and bind you together in pleasant ties. It is such occasions as these
which bring out the latent feelings of good will and fellowship,
taking off the rough edges of the daily routine, and let us see how
we are deeply interested in the common purpose of making a
complete newspaper every day."

Few summers would be filled with as much happiness and good
fortune for Dealey as the summer of 1900. Alfred's wedding had
set a happy keynote. Things were going right. Times were prosperous, and business for the paper was good. His family was well.
But, as the summer ended, calamity was not far off. It would not
be a personal calamity for Dealey, but he would be profoundly
affected.

Saturday, September 8, 1900, was a warm day in Dallas, but
the wind was erratic, coming in hard gusts, and peculiar clouds
such as never seen before flurried low over the city. It was ominous and awe-inspiring. For three days people had followed the
news of an equinoctial hurricane off the Gulf coast. Each day it
had grown worse and had advanced across Florida to Louisiana,
doing considerable damage.

In the *News* building at 3:00 P.M., the *dit-dit-dit* of the tele-

graph key spelled out bad news from Galveston. Within the space
of a few hours half the Island City had been covered by tide-
water. The velocity of the hurricane had increased alarmingly.
In Dealey's office a little group gathered, discussing the seriousness of the news, and Dealey recalled incidents from the storm
of 1875, when the sea water got up into the Galveston *News*
building. He remembered poignantly, he said, the plight of a ten-
year-old boy named Willie Blount. The boy was with his grandfather, a Dr. Peete, at the quarantine station house on the
breakwater. A boat was taking the people at the station house to
safety, and Willie and his grandfather expected to take the boat
on its last trip. But the boat was unable to return for them. Willie
Blount and his grandfather were never heard from again . . .
washed out to sea.

"That could happen to the whole island," commented someone
in the group listening to Dealey. Galveston was no more than 12
feet above sea level at the highest point. An argument ensued
about the vulnerability of the island. Just at 4:30, when City Editor William O'Leary was proving by the map in Maury's *Geog-
raphy* that destruction of Galveston by tropical storm could not
happen because of the contour of the coastline and other geographical features, the telegraph editor called down from the
second floor to report to Dealey that all wire and telephone connections with the island had gone dead.

After a few hours had passed, the continued silence from "The
Old Lady by the Sea" made the waiting excruciating to those
members of the *News* staff in Dallas who had close ties with the
parent paper and with individuals living in the Island City. Especially was Dealey alarmed. He had hundreds of friends in Galveston, and T.W. and his family lived there.

Nothing but conflicting rumors of Galveston's fate were
received in Dallas for the next 24 hours. Then on Sunday afternoon the first eyewitness account of the catastrophe began to
come in on the wire from Houston. It was a story by Richard
Spillane, a Galveston newspaperman, one of the few men on the
first boat to make the mainland after the storm had subsided.

"The wreck of Galveston," Spillane reported, "was brought

about by a tempest so terrible that no words can adequately describe its intensity, and by a flood which turned the city into a raging sea. . . . During all this time the 40,000 people of Galveston were like rats in a trap."

A Captain Timmins was another of the few men to reach the mainland on Sunday, and his account told the same dreadful story.

"I saw houses piled up like dry-goods boxes," he described the scenes of horror, estimating 4000 houses destroyed. "Women and children were crowding into the Tremont Hotel seeking shelter, and all night these unfortunates were bemoaning their losses of kinfolk and fortunes. They were grouped about the stairway, in the galleries and in the rooms of the hotel."

Timmins estimated the dead at 1000, but the days that followed would prove his estimate to be several thousand short, and it was never actually known how many bodies were washed into the Gulf.

As soon as the news definitely established that Galveston had suffered a catastrophe, Dealey turned his thoughts to getting relief for the helpless city. Taking one of the reporters aside, he dictated an appeal to be run on the front page the next morning:

> As told in the dispatches appearing this morning, there are thousands in South Texas today who are destitute that a few hours ago were prosperous. There are scores of homes that have been darkened by death that were places of happiness. It is an old saying that charity begins at home. That it is not necessary to teach the people of the great Southwest how to apply this adage, the *News* is confident.
>
> Therefore it takes this method of announcing that it will receive contributions for the needy and suffering at Galveston and other places visited by the terrible cyclone. The contributions may be either cash, clothing, or provisions, for all are needed. . . .

The dire need for relief became more apparent as details of the destruction were accumulated and reported on Monday. By Tuesday night the *News* had collected 2153 dollars. In the Wednesday morning issue the names of the first 49 contributors were printed, and the name heading the list was "G. B. Dealey—$25." Newspapers in every part of the country took up the plea, and thousands of dollars poured in. The New York *Herald* quickly raised 20,000 dollars and called on the Dallas *Morning News* to use the money to make purchases and dispatch them to Galveston. Dealey assumed charge and called in the mayor of Dallas, Ben Cabell, and County Judge Kenneth Foree to help administer the funds with him. On Wednesday, they expended the first 500 dollars for ten carloads of lime, desperately needed for sanitation purposes. All day and much of the night on Thursday and again on Friday, Dealey's relief committee worked tirelessly, dispatching two carloads of food and wearing apparel . . . 27 dozen ladies' knit skirts . . . 14 dozen children's reefers . . . 314 men's shirts . . . and 10,196 other articles. Much of the material Dealey selected personally, and he insisted that a hard bargain be made with every purchase. It was the least they could do for the sufferers.

Each day Dealey watched the death lists coming from Galveston. For several days he feared that many of the Galveston *News* staff might be among the dead or missing. On Tuesday, three days after the storm had ended, the first direct wire news from anyone on the Galveston *News* came from Colonel R. G. Lowe, whose message was endorsed by the mayor of Galveston as an official appeal to the nation for help:

A summary of conditions prevailing at Galveston is more than the human intellect can master. Loss of life cannot be computed. No lists could be kept and all is simple guesswork. Those thrown out to sea and buried on the ground wherever found will reach the horrible total of at least three thousand souls. [Lowe's estimate was at least 2000 short by later calculations.] . . . The necessities of those living are total. Not a single individual escaped property loss. The property on the island is wrecked, fully one-half totally swept out of existence. Whatever our needs are can be computed by the world at large from this statement much better than I could possibly summarize them. The help must be immediate.

Fortunately, nearly all members of the Galveston *News* staff and their families were saved. Those who had stayed in the newspaper plant during the storm found it one of the safest places on the island. Many buildings equally as large had been damaged or swept away, but the Galveston *News* building had such little damage that only 50 dollars was later spent on repairs.

By the end of the month Dealey and Mayor Cabell and Judge Foree had directed the expenditure of more than 100,000 dollars toward relief of the storm victims. Even the governor called on them to purchase supplies for the state militia, which had moved in to administer relief.

Of the voluntary drives to raise funds, one of the largest sums was raised by the *News*. It amounted to $28,052.33 at the end of three weeks, and the names of the contributors filled six columns of type. Dealey's 25 dollars was not the largest donation, but it was the first.

CHAPTER TEN

1901

COLONEL BELO DIES "AT THE ZENITH."
DEALEY AND OLLIE BUILD A 13-ROOM
HOUSE ON MAPLE AVENUE. THE "ACAD-
EMY OF IMMORTALS." TED EDITS A
NEIGHBORHOOD PAPER. "PAPA" ROUTS A
BURGLAR.

IN AND AROUND DALLAS, THE SPRING WAS APPROACHING ITS PEAK
of delightfulness. It was the middle of April, 1901. The weather
was cool and refreshing, and the foliage grew lush and green. Like
most young Southwestern cities, Dallas was spread thin over a
wide area, and within the city proper there were long stretches of
vacant lots and even whole tracts of land yet uncleared of trees
and virgin underbrush. The profuse bloodweed and abundant
willow scented the air in every direction, and early in the morning
and late in the evening the city had a country-lane and creek-
bottom smell. It was pleasant and relaxing.

To catch an extra breath of the invigorating atmosphere,
Dealey was glad to leave the office early the afternoon of Friday,
April 12. He was on his way to the Belo residence on Ross Ave-
nue, paying a call on the colonel before the latter departed for the
East the next day. Of late the colonel had not come to the office
with any regularity, and Dealey felt apprehensive about his health.

As he walked up the sidewalk to the colonel's magnificent brick
home, he scanned it carefully for ideas which he and Ollie might

incorporate into the house they were planning. Just two and a half weeks earlier, on March 25, he had signed the papers for a lot on Maple Avenue, in the new bon-ton addition at the north edge of town, and they hoped to get a house built within the next few months. What a relief it would be to have enough rooms for everyone in the family. He would like to make it brick, like the Belo mansion, but the colonel had told him his brick cost ten cents each. They were shipped from St. Louis. That was too expensive for a man who had to borrow the money to build, as he did.

Alfred Belo met Dealey at the door. The colonel was feeling so-so, Alfred said, a little more spirited perhaps at the thought of visiting the old home place and relatives in North Carolina. This was what they had hoped the trip would do for him. Alfred said he and Jeannette and their mother had urged the trip on him. They were all going along. Dealey found the colonel propped up in a chair in the parlor. He was pale, but full of conversation. What was the news?

"Oil," Dealey said. The whole state was going wild over the Beaumont gushers. The railroads were running special trains from Houston, Galveston, and even from Dallas and Fort Worth to the oil fields so people could watch the geysers blow in. Talk was that around Spindletop a gusher came in almost every day. The excitement made business good for the paper. The oil-stock advertising was starting to roll in. The next day's paper would carry nine columns, and the run-sheet for Sunday already showed 30 columns of oil-promotion linage. Mainly it was half-pages and full pages, not much composition, and very profitable. The coming week looked like the biggest week of business in the history of the *News*.

"The biggest week?" the colonel asked. "Well, George, some men would think it a good time to die. At the annual meeting in January we closed the best year on record. Now the biggest week ever. Old men have to go some time, and it's best to go at the zenith." [1]

The conversation turned to Colonel Belo's early days in North Carolina. If he felt like it, the colonel said, he would try to visit some of the old battlefields where he had fought during the War

Between the States. There would never be men more courageous than his Forsythe Rifles at Gettysburg. They were a part of the 15,000 men under Hill and Longstreet who marched straight into the storm of canister shot and shell and bullets.

"I was within earshot of General Armistead," the colonel related. "I heard the general shout when he leaped the stone wall in that final assault on Cemetery Hill. He was waving his hat on his sword, and he shouted, 'Give them cold steel, boys!' An instant later he was shot and fell with his hand on a smoking cannon. And a few moments later I caught a piece of canister that did me in."

That Friday evening was the last time Dealey would see Colonel Belo. The next morning the colonel and his family left for North Carolina. One week later, on Friday, April 19, at 4:00 A.M., he died in Asheville, North Carolina, his birthplace.

When Dealey arrived at the office on the morning of Colonel Belo's death, the sad news had already spread through the building and work seemed to be at a standstill. He hurried up to the second floor to confer with the editors. Mr. Fitzgerald, the managing editor, asked if it would be proper to have a black border around the front page. Dealey said he could remember very well when Mr. Richardson died in 1875, and he recalled that they turned the column rules on the editorial page. The same should be done for Colonel Belo. He thought also that some time during the day or on the following day the employees would want to gather in a body and express their feelings. This ceremony had been done for Mr. Richardson, and it was an occasion which he remembered vividly to this day.

On Sunday afternoon at 4 o'clock, more than 100 employees were present in the composing room. Mr. Fitzgerald called the meeting to order. After announcing that the interment would be in North Carolina and that Colonel R. G. Lowe and Mr. T. W. Dealey of the Galveston paper would represent the employees at the funeral, Mr. Fitzgerald proposed that Mr. G. B. Dealey be elected chairman to conduct the meeting. Muffled voices of assent were heard, and Dealey stood up before the group.

"We are gathered today to pay a tribute of respect to our departed chief." Dealey found his throat tight and his voice weak. "As I am the oldest attaché of the paper, I may be pardoned for making a few personal remarks. I went to work for Colonel Belo when a boy of fifteen and have been connected with him for nearly twenty-seven continuous years. For the past sixteen years I have known him intimately. During all that time I received perfect kindness at his hands. He was like a father to me—the best friend I ever had—and it seems that a part of my life has been taken away. I loved him dearly. And now he is gone. I can say no more. May God bless those he has left behind." [2]

After Colonel Belo's passing, it was a month or two before Dealey fully realized the way that he missed Colonel Belo the most. The business ran along as usual, but he found himself still thinking in terms of "Would Colonel Belo want it done this way? Would Colonel Belo approve this action?" Colonel Belo had nearly always approved whatever he did, but to have the colonel's judgment back him up had been more important than he had realized. Too, he missed the ready word of appreciation which the colonel dispensed whenever an improvement in the paper was effected or a job done well. During the week after the colonel's death he had occasion to write Alfred Belo about an improved system for the filing of mats which he had helped to develop, but as he dictated he thought that the colonel would have appreciated this matter more than Alfred would. It was not that Alfred lacked his father's virtues, but Alfred was still a beginner at the business. Alfred had much to learn yet.

During the summer months while the new house was under construction on Maple Avenue, Dealey hoped he would be able to let a few things at the office go so he could give some attention to the house. There were a thousand decisions somebody had to make . . . which way to swing the cabinet doors, how high to make the mantels, how deep to put the cistern, where in the parlor to place the combination gas and electric light fixture. Unless he or Ollie were constantly on hand, the contractor would invariably make the wrong decision. At least it seemed that way. But matters at the office had a way of coming up unexpectedly and being too important to let go. Sterett was going to quit the paper and run for Congress, and that meant hiring a new writer and shifting the editorial staff around. Rural mail delivery was being started out of the Dallas post office, and if he acted swiftly, he could tie up the mail carriers as agents for the *News*. The president of the United States, William McKinley, would stop in Dallas on his tour through the South, and of course the head of the *News* had to be on the reception committee, and that meant committee meetings and planning work. Every matter was time-consuming, and there was little time left for him to see about the new house. Ollie spent as much time as she could with the workmen, but it was difficult for her to get over to Maple Avenue from Thomas Avenue.

But the work got done somehow, and by late August the house at 157 * Maple Avenue was finished. Dealey and Ollie were proud of it. It was two stories, large and roomy. It had 13 rooms and a big rambling attic with two gables. Two identical galleries, one for each story, ran across the front and completely across the east side, and the round pillars and fancy bannisters added handsomely to the appearance of the house. The lower story had a clapboard exterior painted white, and the upper story was sided in brown-stained shingles and trimmed in white frame. The two-tone color, together with the three red brick chimneys, gave the house a bright, livable appearance.

Inside the front door a vestibule opened to a large hallway. Off the hallway to the right were the parlor and dining room, to the left were the living room and library, and to the back was a large kitchen. When the fold-away doors between parlor and dining room were pushed back, a spacious effect was achieved. In these rooms the wallpaper was light blue, and there was a matching blue carpet in the parlor, and lace curtains for every window. For the dining-room floor, Ollie selected a practical covering of linoleum, which had a hardwood-floor design. She said she had no intention of putting a rug in the dining room until the children grew up and stopped spilling things on the floor.

---

* Renumbered "2519" nine years later.

From the vestibule a two-landing stairway led to the second floor, which contained five bedrooms, a sleeping porch, and two baths. Three bedrooms had glazed brick fireplaces with carved wooden mantels, and there were three fireplaces downstairs, making six in all. The furniture was more of a practical style than of high fashion; however, an upright Steinway piano graced the parlor, and there were several stylish chairs in the sitting room. Dealey's favorite chair was a broad-armed, sturdy wicker chair, and Ollie's favorite was the all-leather upholstered easy chair that stayed to the left of the fireplace in the living room. Ollie liked this chair especially because the seat was low enough that her feet rested solidly on the floor.

The whole family loved their new home place. Annie and Fannie, 16 and 15, respectively, could hardly wait until they could have a slumber party, and show off the new house to their friends. Walter and Ted made time in the new stable and big back yard. They used the loft of the stable for a clubhouse, that is, for the club's known headquarters. Secret headquarters was in a cave they dug in the back yard. It was reached only by a circuitous tunnel, which went under the fence to a secret opening in a vacant lot. The only girl ever to see the inside of the tunnel and cave was Maidie Dealey, who was six years old, and she had to smoke a Cubeb cigarette to obtain this singular privilege.

Dealey's pride in the new house centered in the library, which had the walls lined around with Globe-Wernecke bookshelf sections. He began to fill the shelves with books of all sorts . . . a set of Dickens, the works of Mark Twain, some volumes called *The World's Greatest Classics,* a two-volume set entitled *Gladstone and His Contemporaries,* a copy of *The Autobiography of David Crockett,* and many others. Also into the library went copies of current magazines, and among them were issues of *The Philistine,* the work of Elbert Hubbard, that genius of The Roycrofters of East Aurora, New York. Dealey was a "Life Member of the American Academy of Immortals" . . . meaning simply that he was enrolled in Elbert Hubbard's book club. Also, "exclusive to life members of the American Academy of Immortals," he held

a "Thirty-Third Degree Membership of The Roycrofters," which
had cost him 100 dollars. In return, he was promised:

> ... at once, ten three-quarter levant, hand-tooled Roycroft books;
> and we will send you without further payment, one copy of each
> and every book that The Roycrofters issue for ninety-nine years.

If The Roycrofters were gambling on subscribers having short
lives or short memories, here was one "Immortal" named Dealey
on whom they were going to lose on both counts.

Despite a penchant for the flamboyant, Elbert Hubbard had his
moments of brilliance, and his "Message to Garcia" was then at
the height of its popularity. Dealey was especially fond of it, and
also he liked the mottoes and dogma about good work and good
living which *Fra Elbertus* issued in a continuous stream from the
presses at East Aurora. They were printed on three-by-five cards
with bright colored borders and initial letters, and Dealey kept
dozens of them in his desk drawer at the *News*. The more appropriate ones he posted on the walls of various offices and work
rooms around the building. Among his favorites, which he put on
the wall of his own office, were: "Responsibilities gravitate to
the person who can shoulder them," and "Power flows to the man
who knows how."

One of the first books to go into the library, and one which
Dealey valued most highly, was *An Editor's Retrospect* by Charles
A. Cooper, long-time editor of the Edinburgh *Scotsman* in Scotland. The book was sent to him from Galveston by Colonel Lowe.
Being Scottish to the core, Colonel Lowe admired all things from
the "auld countra," and in commending the book to Dealey, he
wrote: "Read the book through and through, and carefully. There
are some splendid business points enumerated." After reading it,
Dealey agreed with Colonel Lowe that it was splendid and that
the similarities between the Edinburgh *Scotsman* and the *News*
were most striking, even to the point of each paper being the first
to start a daily newspaper train in its own country. Dealey found
many of the author's ideas on newspaper-making coinciding with
his own, and particularly he liked a passage in Chapter XVIII

which summed up in a nutshell the very way he thought a newspaper should be run :

> It has been a feature in The Scotsman office for the last thirty
> years, and probably more, that no sharp line has been drawn be-
> tween the Editorial and the Business Management of the paper.
> I do not mean that the Business Manager directs the policy to be
> adopted, nor that the Editor helps to keep the books. There is no
> interference of any kind with the Editor, and no interference with
> the Business Management; but there is the closest association and
> interchange of views between the two departments. It may be
> thought that there is nothing of much novelty in all this; the people
> who think so know little about newspapers.

Now that he had the kind of library he had wanted for years,
Dealey took renewed interest in reading books. Many nights the
stroke of midnight found him still reading in the library.

There were two bathrooms in the new house, and they were a
great convenience to a family with seven members. Now that they
had this convenience, Dealey decreed, there was no reason why all
the children could not get to breakfast punctually and henceforth
the entire family would be expected to have breakfast together and
arrive at the table on time. For a few days the new rule was
obeyed but by the second week the children were back at their
old habits of straggling in one at a time, and the late ones usually
had to bolt down their breakfast so they would not be late for
school. They always had some kind of an excuse. Next a ticket
system was tried. Each child arriving at the breakfast table on
time received a ticket bearing Dealey's initials. On Saturday the
children redeemed the tickets for an allowance. A full quota of
tickets got the full allowance. For each ticket less than the quota
there was a penalty of five cents. The ticket system wasn't perfect,
but it produced a definite improvement in breakfast punctuality.

Much to the amusement of the older members of the family,
Ted, who was nine, started "publishing" a little newspaper, which
was circulated among the younger set on Maple Avenue. It was
named the Dallas *Evening Globe,* and there was only one copy
per issue, but it got around. It had four pages, seven by eight

inches in size, and its columns were filled mainly with news clipped
out of old newspapers and pasted on. But the cartoons were
original, and there was usually a sprinkling of incomparable want
ads and lost-and-found items, which were handwritten. The following were typical:

> **WANTED—Customers wanted at the
> Dealeys Bazaar to buy him out of his
> candy.**
>
> **FOR SALE—One gasoline double-
> headed peanut roaster.**
>
> **LOST—A green parasol with silver
> hinges. Finder will please return to
> J. M. Coalman.**
>
> **WANTED—A good-sized dog. Our
> sausages will be out 1 day after we get
> the dog. Apply to Mark Soper Meat
> Market.**

The Dallas *Evening Globe* was inclined toward sensational
news and climaxed its period of existence with a lurid murder-
suicide story in the issue of September 29, 1901. Following that,
the *Globe* was discontinued, and a more conservative and literary
publication named *The Little Chronicle* was issued by the young
editor, and there is ample evidence that the demise of the *Globe*
and the high tone of its successor were considerably influenced by
the young editor's father.

Shortly after moving to the Maple Avenue residence, the family
acquired two new members. One was Sawmill Billie, a cat, who
just appeared one day, and stayed. At first he was named just
Billie, but he purred so much like a sawmill that he came to be
called Sawmill Billie. The other new member was a stray dog who
also "took up" with the family. Arriving at a time when the
Uncle Remus stories were being read aloud to Maidie, with Ted
and Walter usually listening in, the dog was named Brer Purp.
It was later discovered that the animal should have been named

"Sister Purp," but in spite of the mistake, she remained Brer Purp all her life.

One cold night during the first winter in the new house, there was an uninvited guest who caused much commotion for an hour or so. Dealey had just dozed off to sleep some time after 1 :00 A.M. when he was awakened by a shadowy figure coming in the door of the bedroom.

"Who's there?" Dealey yelled. The figure vanished through the door, and Dealey leaped out of bed and gave chase. Down the back stairs leading to the kitchen they both went, hitting two steps at a time and making a startling racket. Dealey's red flannel nightgown with large black polka dots was billowing out, and he looked much larger than he was. The burglar dashed out the back door, and Dealey followed. A moment later the wind blew the door shut and it locked. Outside it was bitter cold and there was a light snow on the ground.

Inside the house the whole family was aroused by now, and they all gathered in the upstairs hall, together with two young ladies who were spending the night with Annie and Fannie. They waited in fear and trembling, and after several minutes had passed, the front door bell rang.

"It must be Papa!" someone said. But what was Papa doing at the front door? He went out the back. Nobody wanted to go unlock the door.

Finally a shivery voice shouted, "Somebody come let me in!"

It was Papa all right, and when the door was opened, he was shaking with cold and trying to knock the snow out of his bedroom slippers.

Back in the house, Dealey put on a wrap and proceeded to get the household organized for defense, in case the burglar should return. There being plenty of kids, he posted sentries on all sides of the house. Each sentry was stationed on his knees by a window with the shades drawn down within an inch of the window sill. The moon made enough light outside to show up the approach of any marauders. With the watch set up, the lights inside the house were turned out. After a few minutes Ted, who had been assigned alone to the kitchen, slipped hurriedly to the front room where his father was.

"It's too dark in the kitchen," Ted whispered excitedly.

This broke the morale of the sentries, and they all appeared quickly in the front room. Disgustedly, Dealey sent them upstairs to bed, and said he would stand watch himself. But no more burglars showed up that night.

CHAPTER ELEVEN

1902=1905

STEP BY STEP DEALEY HAD COME UP IN THE COMPANY . . . FROM
office boy, 27 years ago, to "Manager of All Departments." Now
—as of January 28, 1902—he was a member of the Board of
Directors. He was fourth in the two-paper organization, but he
was in complete charge at Dallas. Two of his superiors, Colonel
Lowe and T. W. Dealey, devoted their time entirely to the Galveston paper, and Alfred Belo, his other superior, was too new at
the business to assume control yet.

The news-editorial side, of course, was run by the editor-in-
chief and the managing editor with the independence accorded by
the broad general policies of the institution, but Dealey exercised
an ever-increasing influence in editorial matters. He had a way of
studying out a question until he knew the background better than
anyone else, and then when he presented his proposals to the editors, they usually carried them out.

His latest effort affecting the news side was a move to take
the advertisements off the front page of the *News*. He believed it
was news more than advertising that sold the paper. Therefore it
was illogical—taking a typical day's paper—to allow advertisements about ladies' shirtwaists and silk neck ruffs to pre-empt the

front page and force the latest cable reports on the Boer War and Senator Joe Bailey's speech on the Oleomargarine Bill to inside pages. Moreover, for a number of years there had been a trend toward all-news front pages by the more progressive newspapers of the country, notably since 1895, when the Hearst-Pulitzer newspaper battle in New York City boosted the popular appeal of the all-news front page.

But Colonel Lowe and T.W., "the conservatives" in the management, opposed the change. The *News* had always carried advertisements on the front page, and there were a good dozen reasons why it should continue.

Methodically Dealey set about preparing the evidence to overturn the arguments of "the conservatives." He began compiling two lists of leading newspapers—List Number 1 showing those with front-page advertising, and List Number 2 showing those without front-page advertising.

"The attached data," he wrote in a formal letter addressed to the Board of Directors, "will show that the papers which can be compared with the *News* and who run advertisements on the first page, are decidedly in the minority."

It was seven against 52.*

Obviously he had a good case. But before he could press the matter with the Board of Directors, there happened one of those little unanticipated incidents which, though insignificant in themselves, can completely upset the best-laid plans. On April 1 and 2 a number of local merchants devoted space in their regular advertisements in the *News* to publicizing a piano concert to be given at the fair grounds by Ignace Paderewski, the celebrated Polish pianist. This free publicity rubbed Dealey the wrong way. His pet aversion was free publicity for circuses, tent shows, and traveling entertainers. To each of the merchants Dealey sent a polite but stern note:

> Gentlemen:— We wish to call your attention to the fact that under your contract for space it is not your privilege to advertise anything but such as pertains directly and wholly to your own business.

---

* For complete lists of the newspapers, see Appendix C, pp. 303-304.

This letter is occasioned by your advertising the Paderewski concert in your ad of yesterday and today. It passed through without being noticed. A similar letter is being sent to other firms who did the same under a misapprehension.

Very truly yours,

A. H. Belo & Co., Pubs.,

By G. B. Dealey, Manager

If Dealey thought that was the end of the matter, he had not reckoned with the Messrs. Sanger Brothers of the big department store at Main and Lamar, the paper's largest and oldest advertiser. Their reply came back before noon on the same day, delivered by messenger boy:

Messrs. A. H. Belo & Co.
City.

Gentlemen :— Your note of today surprises us. We thought it was generally known that we were subscribers to the guarantee fund to bring Paderewski to Dallas, surely not for the benefit of a piano player, but wholly and solely to bring a crowd to Dallas, and, directly and indirectly, benefit our business. Shall you, then, deny us the right to pay for the privilege of making that fact known to the people of Texas through the columns of the *News?* We have, in days gone by, advertised in a similar manner the "Texas State Fair", the "Fourth of July Celebrations", "The Kaliph's Parade", etc., etc. . . . We believe that so long as we do not violate our postal laws, the space we have contracted for can be used to print an essay on Ancient History, to reproduce a poem from the New York *Herald,* and last, but not least, compliment the *News,* just as occasion requires, or we can fill a page and simply say "Sanger Bros." In other words, your point is not well taken.

Yours very respectfully,

Sanger Bros.

Before Dealey had finished reading Sanger Bros.' reply, his right eye was twitching, a sign that he was about to "explode" on somebody. His rebuttal, dictated the same day and dispatched by messenger, was three pages long:

... There is no objection to your puffing a 4th of July celebration because that would simply be done to bring people to Dallas. There is no charge for admittance to the gates of Dallas, so no one in particular would be benefited.

But when it comes to your advertising a concert at the Fair Grounds, wherein you specify that Mr. Paderewski or Mrs. Smith is going to have a big concert out there, and in which you specify the prices of admission, state where tickets are on sale, etc., we most emphatically insist that you have no right to do this and cannot do it under your contract for space in the *News*. . . . If we permitted you the right to advertise anything you pleased, we would be in a pretty predicament. Mr. Martinez across the street could make a dicker with you to advertise his business, paying you 4 cents a line, whereas he would have to pay us 15 cents a line if he came to us with his ad. . . .

Normally Dealey was the soul of tact, adroitness, and patience, and usually managed to avoid getting at loggerheads with people. But when differences arose involving a matter of principle in which he felt he was right, he would hold stubbornly to his point; and it made no difference who opposed him—not even the paper's largest advertiser.

In this instance Sanger Bros. acquiesced. Apparently each party had vented its spleen by the end of the day, and the matter was never mentioned again. But the effect of the incident, nevertheless, was to delay Dealey's plans to remove the advertising from the front page of the *News*. He decided this was no time to abrogate a privilege which Sanger Bros. had used practically every day since the paper was started. They might think that the new rule was put in to spite them, and that would never do.

It would be four years later before he could return to the problem and accomplish his objective.

After the Paderewski incident things at the office ran smoothly for a few months, but in July troubles began in the editorial department when the managing editor took to the bottle—*again*. Dealey reported the situation in a letter to Alfred Belo, who was summering in the Adirondacks at Saranac Inn, the summer retreat his father had loved so much:

July 24, 1902

Dear Alfred:

Poor —— has fallen by the wayside. Experience has taught me to be somewhat apprehensive of this whenever his wife goes away. He says he started drinking on the Sunday morning of the Texas State Fair fire. It continued along quietly, but he was at work every day. But on Friday he failed to report for duty. . . .

In accordance with his promise to you and me if it ever happened again, he has turned in his resignation. . . .

To fill the managing editor's job, Dealey had the pick of several able staff members—William G. Sterett, Tom Finty, Jr., DeWitt McMurray, Alonzo Wasson, E. B. Doran, or D. Prescott Toomey. If prestige was to be the deciding factor, Bill Sterett merited the promotion, but Sterett was much too headstrong to suit Dealey. He preferred Toomey over them all. Toomey was his protégé. He had raised him "from a pup." Toomey was just a kid when he started to work in the mailing room, but he was talented and versatile, and Dealey had helped him advance from mailer successively to cartoonist, reporter, city editor, and Sunday editor. Toomey would be cooperative in every way, and he would be understanding of personnel and business problems in a way that Sterett never would.

"Toomey is very loyal, faithful, and always on deck," Dealey wrote to Alfred Belo.

Toomey got the job.

With this appointment, Dealey further strengthened the control he exercised in editorial matters. All previous editors had been Colonel Belo's appointees. Now Dealey selected the editors.

Almost immediately Bill Sterett posed a test of strength for the new managing editor. The controversy developed the day after Mr. Clark, the editor-in-chief, went on vacation. According to the office rules, in the absence of the editor-in-chief, the managing editor assumed responsibility for the contents of the editorial page. That meant that Toomey would have to pass on Sterett's editorials. It rankled Sterett to think that he had to get the approval of this "young squirt." Why, he had owned and edited his own newspaper before Toomey was out of knee pants, and he had been a Washington correspondent when Toomey was a cub reporter. It was too much for Sterett to take passively. His indignation took the form of an editorial criticizing William Jennings Bryan and his "Cross of Gold" speech. But in criticizing Bryan, Sterett knew very well he was violating *News* policy. Since before Colonel Belo's death, it had been the adopted policy of the *News* "to avoid altogether any mention of the free silver question or criticism of William Jennings Bryan, on account of the sensitiveness of a great many Texans on the subject." [1]

When Toomey saw Sterett's editorial, he "did his duty" and asked Sterett to make the editorial conform to the policy of the paper.

"If a word is changed, I will resign," Sterett replied.

Toomey took the issue to Dealey. What were his orders?

There would have to be a showdown, Dealey decided, but the problem was not simple. How to call Sterett's hand but not cause him to resign? After all, by all odds, he was the most popular writer on any Texas newspaper. After several drafts, a carefully worded letter was sent to Toomey, with a copy to Sterett:

August 1, 1902

Mr. D. P. Toomey,
  Managing Editor.

Dear Sir:— Referring to your note of last night, I am persuaded that Col. Sterett is not so unreasonable as to mean what he said, and that his remarks were simply the result of some irritation.

Surely he must realize that on every paper where there are a number of editorial writers, that it is absolutely impossible, from the nature of things, for all of them to have the same ideas on a given subject. Hence, if each one of them were to write just what he thinks without any regard for the policy of the paper, wouldn't it be pretty much of a mix-up? Therefore the absolute necessity of someone to pass upon everything that is written before it goes to the world. And surely no one could rightfully object to conforming to a rule so necessary as this.

The editorial expressions of a paper in political matters, as we all know, are supposed to represent the fixed policy of the paper itself, and not the individual views of any writer, no matter who he may be.

There is only one course for you to pursue in this matter and that is to follow directions.

Very truly yours,

G. B. Dealey, Manager

cc: Mr. Wm. G. Sterett

The editorial was cut, and Sterett never mentioned the matter, and said nothing further of resigning.

The next several years would see little change in staff or in organization at the *News*. The big task for Dealey, and one which was shared by Colonel Lowe in Galveston, was to make a full-fledged newspaper publisher of Alfred Belo. Colonel Lowe summed up the general feeling of the older executives toward Alfred in a letter advising him to spend some time in Austin while the legislature was in session: "You should run down to Austin for some little time and get acquainted with the young men of the state now taking part in its politics. The old set I knew are passing away and the new generation is on the boards. . . . You are the man to look after it. In other words, you are 'next.' " [2]

From 1902 to the end of 1905 was one of the calmest and most profitable periods in the history of the business. Probably the most important decision affecting circulation of the newspaper during this period was whether or not to add a comic supplement. Colonel Lowe scoffed at the idea.

"Don't worry about colored comic supplements," Colonel Lowe wrote in September, 1903, to Dealey and Alfred. "This gag will wear out shortly."

But both Alfred and Dealey were more alert to the significance of the innovation.

"There seems to be a considerable demand for it," Alfred pointed out in replying to Colonel Lowe and Dealey.

Dealey was cautious. "Would it not be better to learn all there is to be learned about it," he wrote to Colonel Lowe, "without deciding anything until we see further developments? The supplement is a nuisance in itself, and the expense is considerable, so it is better to go slow."

It remained for the *News'* agent in Fort Worth to "read the cards" to the management and bring about some action. The Fort Worth *Mail Telegram* added colored comics in October, 1903, and the *News'* agent in Fort Worth wrote to Dealey on October 11:

> The newsboys sold more *Telegrams* last Sunday than they ever did on any Sunday before, and the same today. . . . The dealers say their sales for the *Telegram* doubled. . . . It is true now as it has always been that the *News* sells for its superior news service, but it's also true that there are a great many people that buy Sunday papers that don't keep up with the news. . . . and even our regular readers who have young Americans in their families have to provide them with the papers with the funny page. . . .

The cry of the circulators was heard from all directions, and it prevailed. On Sunday, March 13, 1904, the *News* added two full pages of colored comics. On one page there was a strip called *Muggsy* and another called *Percy Flip and Fatty.* The other page was McDougall's popular full-page cartoon satire on everyday life.

Soon more comics were added, despite Dealey's personal feeling that it was deplorable that a newspaper had to use good white space to carry such silliness.

But silly or not, the "funnies" brought in the circulation. In 1904 alone there was a net increase of 6000 for the Sunday paper, from 40,592 at the beginning of the year to 46,576 by the end of the year, and the daily paper had a similar advance. The increase was equal to the total increase of the previous three years.

Individually, the "funnies" suffered a high casualty rate, and within the first year these strips appeared in the *News: Foxy Grandpa, Leander, And Her Name Was Maud* (Maud being a mule), *Sam, Bugville, Jimmy, Mr. Jack, Little Nemo in Slumberland,* and *Happy Hooligan.* At the end of 1905 the survivors were *Foxy Grandpa, Maud,* and *Happy Hooligan.*

CHAPTER TWELVE

1902-1905

A VISION OF INDUSTRY IN THE TRINITY
BOTTOM. "THEM GUYS" FAIL TO GET A
PARK TAX. SAVING THE STATE FAIR OF
TEXAS.

FROM THE EARLIEST DAYS OF DALLAS THE TRINITY RIVER, AN UN-
pretentious stream winding from headwaters in North Texas, had
been the hope and sometimes the despair of the community. It
was the main source of water supply, and it held forth a dream of
river transportation some day between Dallas and the Gulf of
Mexico, 300 miles away. Normally it flowed in a narrow bed
about 30 or 40 feet wide, but it dominated a wide flood plain and
overflowed so frequently that much of the bottom land was rendered useless for improvements or farming. As Dallas and Oak
Cliff grew on opposite banks, the river became a great hindrance
to their commerce and development. It needed to be controlled.

In October of 1902 workmen began to cut down trees and clear
away the brush from the river bottom between the two cities, a
project designed to abate the floods by speeding the runoff and
preventing back water from piling up. Each evening at nightfall
while the work was going on, the valley presented an intriguing
sight. Big log fires, made by the workmen during the day, gradually burned down to huge beds of glowing coals; and rising curls
of smoke, caught up by the capricious winds of the river bottom,
diffused into the air and spread far out over the surrounding area.

For several weeks all Dallas was permeated with the familiar pungent odor, and it smelled good in the crisp autumn air.

About dusk one nippy evening, while the clearance work was still in progress, Dealey put on his topcoat and walked from his office to the Commerce Street bridge to view the much-talked-about sight of the denuded valley, and to smoke a cigar.

I had nothing on my mind [he related, in a written recollection of the incident recorded many years later]. But while I stood on the bridge, I was immediately possessed with the thought that that vacant land in the bottom, which everybody considered worthless, would some day be available. The thought also possessed me very strongly that I wanted some of that land, notwithstanding the fact that I had no money to buy anything with.

The next day, I went to the courthouse to see if I could ascertain who were the owners of the land immediately west of the river and between Commerce Street and the T. & P. tracks. I didn't want to ask questions because I thought someone might imagine that I knew of some development and would take a hint and beat me to it. But my efforts to find the owners by looking through the records at the courthouse came to naught.

So I called in a friend of mine named Ben Weller, who was then trust officer of the Trust Company of Dallas. I got him to hold up his hand and I swore him to secrecy that he would not divulge any plans which I might outline to him. He promised. I then took him down to the bridge and showed him the land I had in mind and asked him to find out who owned it. He came back in a few days, saying that there was a tract of 17-2/3 acres owned by George W. Loomis, 3 acres of which had been sold to John Barr, leaving 14-2/3 acres. I then asked him to look up Mr. Loomis and find out what he could buy it for, if it was for sale. While he was gone on this mission, during a period of two or three days, I considered how much I would pay for it, and came to the private conclusion that I would pay as much as $500 an acre, but no more. Shortly after, Ben Weller came back saying that he could buy the land for $100 an acre. (So I made $400 an acre right then.) I didn't have a dollar to spare, but raised $100 and told him to go down and close the contract, which he did.

I was enormously impressed with the potential value of the land, and was on needles and pins until the lawyers examined the title and told me it was O.K. I closed the deal on borrowed money, paying cash for the property, and when I went home I told my wife that it meant that some day real wealth would come out of it.

It happened on the same evening when Dealey stood on the Commerce Street bridge smoking his cigar and gazing across the river bottom that he was seized with another inspiration. He saw the possibility of setting aside a part of the valley for a magnificent city park. Now was the time for the city to acquire park land, while it was inexpensive and before it was all committed to other uses, and before all the beautiful trees were cut down. Immediately he had the *News* editorial writers develop a series of editorials on the idea. Stemming from these editorials and also from an article on the subject of municipal parks and playgrounds published in a current issue of *Municipal Journal and Engineer of New York,* Dealey conceived a series of articles designed to educate the people of Dallas to the benefits of long-range park-planning.

While the *News* was running the series of editorials and articles on parks, the St. Louis *Globe-Democrat* was waging a campaign to clean up and beautify St. Louis. Dealey was much impressed by the scope of the *Globe-Democrat's* campaign, and taking his cue from the St. Louis paper, he arranged a meeting early in December with leading citizens of Dallas to discuss the organization of a Dallas chapter of the American League for Civic Improvement. Most of the men who responded were his colleagues from the better days of the Cleaner Dallas League—J. T. Trezevant, E. O. Tenison, M. H. Thomas, L. M. Dabney, A. Harris, Epps G. Knight, Alex Sanger, M. M. Crane, R. E. L. Saner, E. J. Gannon, W. O. Connor, J. B. Adoue, Sr., Sydney Smith, A. V. Lane, G. H. Schoellkopf, Hy. D. Lindsley, G. A. Trumbull, G. R. Scruggs, A. A. Green, Sr., B. M. Burgher, Charles L. Dexter, W. H. Atwell, Barnett Gibbs, Edward Gray, J. M. Moroney, Charles F. Bolanz, and others. These men constituted the nucleus of progressive-minded citizens on whom Dealey could always count for support in civic undertakings and whose names would be associated with practically every major progressive movement in Dallas for the next 20 to 30 years.

Following the strategy he had learned from working with the Cleaner Dallas League, he pressed others to take the lead and assume the offices, while he stayed in the background. He preferred to make his contributions through committee work and through the *News*. He wanted the *News* to be free to criticize, if criticism were necessary.

On December 16, 1902, the Dallas chapter of the American League for Civic Improvement was formally organized, and J. T. Trezevant was elected president.

"Probably in the whole civilized world," Trezevant said in his fiery acceptance speech, "there is no more slovenly community than Dallas. First of all we should stop this continual spitting in the streets. . . ."

At first the Civic Improvement League made a flurry of activity in numerous directions, but after six months of spreading its efforts too thin, the leaders were persuaded by a small group led by Dealey to concentrate the League's efforts in an all-out campaign for a park tax. In one bold stroke they could establish a systematic park program for Dallas.

The "campaign of education" began in July. The keynote avowed at the first public rally was "to make the campaign as hot as the weather."

At the final rally before the election on Monday, August 17, Dealey was sitting on the platform. One of the speakers arrived late, and as all the seats on the platform were taken, Dealey gave up his seat and went down to stand among the audience. After the speeches had been going on for some time, a stranger beside Dealey remarked to him, "I wonder what them guys up there are going to get out of this."

On Monday, the day of the election, the executive committee and other members of the League who had worked hard on the campaign got together in the afternoon at the Commercial Club, which was across the street from the *News*. Nearly everyone was confident of victory, but the weather was as hot and dry as August could be, and very few people went to the polls.

As soon as the polls closed, it was known immediately that the park tax had lost, by 437 to 453.

"When we found out our efforts had failed," Dealey said of the event, "we left the Commercial Club and went across the street to a drugstore, got a soda water, and sadly went home."

For the next 40 years Dealey was to advise against the timing of public campaigns for civic improvement in the hot summertime.

The experience hurt, but fortunately it turned out to serve as a dress rehearsal for a more important public drive. The State Fair of Texas was in financial straits. Since 1886 it had been run on a cooperative basis by a group of private citizens, but the leaders knew in the fall of 1903 that the enterprise could not survive another year under the old plan. What should be done about it? There was little agreement, but Dealey insisted on bringing the situation out in the open.

Almost daily during January and February the *News* asked the question: "How important is the continuance of the State Fair to Dallas?"

"No industrial factor ever known in the history of Dallas has been as potent in developing and advancing the material interests of the city as this Fair," was typical of the hundreds of replies given by leading citizens.

Under the sponsorship of the *News*, a Citizens State Fair Reorganization Committee was created. Oddly, the man chosen to be general chairman, C. A. Keating, was the man with whom Dealey had had a "run-in" during the "two fairs imbroglio" in 1886. But 18 years had smoothed over the hard feelings, and many times since then they had done business together and worked together on civic projects.

The new plan for the State Fair proposed that the city take over the Fair grounds and make it a municipal enterprise. It would cost 125,000 dollars, and the money could be raised by a State Fair tax.

At the March 3 meeting of the Reorganization Committee, the solicitation subcommittee reported it had approached 1474 businessmen of the city and only 25 had said they would not vote for the State Fair tax. A spokesman arose to say that the campaign was as good as won, and they could sit tight and wait for the election.

"It's all very well," Dealey spoke up, "to count on the election carrying, but I have learned to be cautious. Most candidates for public office, because of what people tell them, firmly believe they are going to be elected. But on the day following the election, the defeated candidates realize there are more liars in town than they had ever dreamed possible."

He proposed an intensive city-wide publicity campaign for the State Fair tax. Things were done right this time. The grand finale on the night before the election was a simultaneous street rally in all nine wards of the city. On the morning of the election the *News* climaxed its campaign with a front-page editorial:

> Do you want to see the State Fair held in another city?
> There are others waiting to see Dallas drop it.
> Are you willing . . . for the crowds to pass Dallas by?
> The State Fair is one of the helps that has made the position and reputation of Dallas; and Dallas is not yet big enough to do without it.

It was good news the next day. The State Fair tax had carried by more than 6 to 1.

DALLAS IS ALL RIGHT, the headline shouted.

This step marked the beginning of greater days for the State Fair of Texas. A new Fair on a grand scale was conceived, the grounds enlarged, new buildings constructed, and the landscape beautified. After 1904 the State Fair became a municipal enterprise which all Dallas supported, and in time it would come to rank as the biggest annual state fair in the land.

The saving of the State Fair in 1904 was important to Dallas but equally as important, as time would prove, was the attendant creation of the Parks Board and the small annual park tax. Dallas now had the machinery and the wherewithal for providing and maintaining a city-wide system of parks and playgrounds for Dallas. This was long-range park-planning . . . as proposed two

years earlier in the series of articles in the *News* at the time the
Trinity Valley was being cleared of trees and undergrowth.

Near the end of the summer of 1904—the year everybody was
singing "Meet Me in St. Louis, Louis!"—the seven members of
the Dealey family went to the World's Fair in St. Louis. Dealey
was particularly eager to see the landscaping and general layout
of the grounds, because Dallas had just hired George E. Kessler,
the man given the most credit for the beauty of the St. Louis
Fair, to redesign the State Fair of Texas.

The week's stay at the World's Fair was both a vacation and
an education for the Dealey family . . . amazing sights . . . mov-
ing pictures . . . automobiles with closed carriages . . . an Egyptian
mummy . . . an airship in which the celebrated Brazilian, Santos
Dumont, made aerial flights. Ollie liked the Japanese porcelains.
Walter liked the Electricity Building, and Ted liked Hagenbeck's
Wild Animal Show and the elephants' shoot-the-chute. Annie and
Fannie, who were grown young ladies, talked excitedly about the
"Wedding Car" on the giant Ferris Wheel . . . six marriages had
been performed in it. Dealey and Maidie liked everything.

But what the entire family recalled most frequently for years
after the Fair was the sight of Papa riding the roller coaster.

> That roller coaster was a lulu [Ted Dealey wrote 40-odd years
> after the St. Louis trip]. It was plenty scary. The Boss got on with
> us kids and all the way around he chewed his cigar desperately,
> held his hat down over his eyes, and looked forward with a glance
> of intense dissatisfaction.
>
> When the roller coaster we were riding came up to the loading
> platform after the first round, the Boss stood up and said, "Thank
> God, it's over!"
>
> An attendant put his hand in the middle of the Boss' chest,
> shoved him back in the seat, and said, "Sit down, Mister, we are
> going around again."
>
> It seems that you got two circuits for a dime.

CHAPTER THIRTEEN

1906

"THREE CHEERS AND A TIGER FOR THE EIGHT-HOUR DAY." THE THREE HIGHEST EXECUTIVES OF THE *NEWS* DIE WITHIN 45 DAYS. DEALEY PRAYS FOR STRENGTH.

NEW YEAR'S DAY . . . SHORTLY BEFORE 7 O'CLOCK, DEALEY BEGAN his usual 15 minutes of exercise. While doing knee bends, he wondered what 1906 held in store for him. One thing was sure, it ought to be a happier year at the *News*: the new addition to the building would soon be finished . . . more space for everybody . . . a big headache now, but that was a manager's job—to absorb the headaches.

He put extra vigor in his pushups that morning as his thoughts turned to the trip to Europe for him and Ollie. It was unofficial yet, but Alfred Belo and Colonel Lowe both had notified him the previous week that he could count on the trip for the summer . . . a reward for 31 years with the company. It did not seem that long since he had started to work for Colonel Belo on the Galveston *News*. Alfred Belo was only one year old then.

Dealey called downstairs to Ollie to see if they could have breakfast a little early. He wouldn't be taking the horse out. It was raining. Nothing short of rain could make him forego his 20-minute horseback ride. He would get some fresh air on the porch. Too few people recognized the importance of fresh air, and if T.W. had paid more attention to fresh air and exercise, his health would not be in such a poor state now. The undercurrent of anxiety he had felt about T.W. for some time edged into his mind. The shakiness of T.W.'s handwriting was more noticeable in recent letters. T.W. had always been one of his pillars in life.

Before going downstairs Dealey took a few extra minutes to trim his mustache. He was getting gray, no doubt about it. But a man could expect that at 46. Going down the hall, he rapped on the door of Ted's room. "Time to get up, son."

Ollie called to let the children sleep . . . no school on New Year's Day. No harm done, Dealey replied. It always took three calls for Ted. He passed up Walter and Maidie. Annie and Fannie were in Massachusetts, attending a girls' school.

For breakfast he ate the usual: one piece of toast, one egg, and one cup of coffee. Before leaving he remembered to tell Ollie that he enjoyed his breakfast and that he had experienced no indigestion for several days.

He arrived at the *News* building punctually at 8:30 A.M. but it took more than an hour to get to his office. First he went on each floor and wished every member of the staff in sight a "Happy New Year." In making the rounds, he picked up several bits of useful building gossip. The printers showed him a little story on page 7 of the morning paper:

> Dallas Union printers met at 12 o'clock last night and after discussing prospects gave three cheers and a tiger for the new year and the success of the eight-hour-day movement.

In the editorial department the city editor told Dealey he had heard there was more to the printers' meeting than appeared in the paper. Dealey said they had asked for a 48-hour week, and he was afraid they might be talking about a strike. The union was to have some doings in Waco about the middle of the month, and Reuben Radley, one of the linotype operators, was head of the whole Texas 48-Hour Conference.

"First thing you know you editors will want Sunday off," Dealey said with a wink. On his desk at that moment there was a memorandum from the managing editor proposing a day off on Sunday for the editorial staff. Dealey believed in a six-day week for all the employees, but he hoped there wouldn't be any striking done before the adjustments could be worked out.

He went methodically about the day's work . . . first a thorough perusal of the morning paper. The top story on the first page reported that the "December Uprisings" in Moscow had been crushed. The Number 2 story got closer to home . . . "the New York Typographical Union No. 6 voted 1100 to 400 to demand a 48-hour week . . ." So that was what had inspired the "three cheers and a tiger" from the local printers last night. He hurriedly skimmed the next few pages until he found the "needs of Dallas" story on page 11 . . . a four-column spread of interviews of 288 Dallas businessmen on what they thought Dallas needed most for advancement: "A majority of 288 leading business men agree that paved streets and improved sidewalks are the first concern . . ."

He showed the story to Mr. Benners, the business manager, and remarked that one sure way to get a majority of 288 men to agree on paved streets was to interview them after it had been raining all week.

The telegraph editor stopped by Dealey's office. Nothing much of importance on the wire, he said . . . France was nervous about Germany's intentions toward the Moroccan question . . . a Mrs. Roberts of Dallas had spoken in Austin on woman suffrage. The day went along in the usual fashion. Alfred Belo sent word that he would not be at the office for several days. He was ill with the grippe. There were two letters from Galveston from Colonel Lowe . . . concerned about the cash balance and the dividends, the same as ever. He wondered if he should write Colonel Lowe about the trouble in the pressroom. As yet he could not believe the report that one of the pressmen was tampering with the new press out of spite, but the fact remained that the turning bars and the slitters had been found disarranged several times.

So went New Year's Day, 1906.

A series of misfortunes that were to dog the *News* for 50 dismal days began early on the morning of Tuesday, January 9. Two of the linotype operators of the *News,* Reuben Radley and John

Minor, were trapped in their bedrooms when the Knepfly Building burned. They lived on the third floor. In jumping from the window ledge, Reuben Radley was killed and John Minor was seriously injured.

Unable to get in touch with Radley's wife and children, who lived out of the city, Dealey helped with the funeral arrangements. It was hard for him to realize Radley was dead. Just the day before he had talked to him about the 48-hour week for printers. In the afternoon he went to the hospital to see John Minor. The doctor told him that Minor kept talking about falling down a manhole in the street and saying that was when he got his injuries. After checking into the matter, Dealey was satisfied that Minor was simply delirious. There was a manhole near where he jumped, but it was covered at the time.

The next misfortune to hit the *News* came a week later. On Monday, the fifteenth, at about 11 o'clock in the morning, one of the editors hurried into Dealey's office and handed him a message which had just come in on the wire from the Galveston office:

COL. LOWE DIED 10:15 THIS MORNING.

(signed) K. K. HOOPER

This was a sudden and hard blow . . . to Dealey personally as well as to the business. He had known Colonel Lowe for 31 years, ever since he went to work on the Galveston *News*. Colonel Lowe had been a compositor then, but he had changed to the editorial department, had grown in stature, and soon had become vice-president and general manager of both papers.

Dealey owed something of his own success to Colonel Lowe. In fact, if it had not been for Colonel Lowe, there might not have been a Dallas *Morning News*. The railroad man, Newman, had suggested the idea of duplicating the Galveston paper in North Texas, but it had been Colonel Lowe who sold the idea to Colonel Belo.

Since 1885 Dealey had exchanged hundreds of letters with him, covering a multitude of subjects. Colonel Lowe was a wise counselor on all the problems that a newspaper manager faced. If it was newsprint: "Tie up the contract; we will not see paper cheaper for years to come." If it was politics: "As far as Colquitt is concerned, he is a Jim Crow politician." If it was press trouble: "I think it's better for you to arrange for a color addition to your No. 1." If it was temper: "When a man gets mad, he should take a good night's rest and think about it." Dealey had put in his personal file the letter in which the Old Scotsman had written to him: "On you depends a whole lot. I have now passed the 66 mark."

The wire copy came in about Colonel Lowe's last hours following his heart attack:

> . . . Singing the Scotch songs of his boyhood, conscious to the last, recognizing the members of his family, but with his mind wandering back to the days of his youth, such was the scene attending the death of Col. Robert G. Lowe, Monday morning at 10:15 . . .

On the following day Dealey and Alfred Belo and a few of the older staff members took the train for Galveston to attend the funeral.

While in Galveston Dealey spent some time with T.W. His brother was breaking fast.

Before the end of the week Dealey returned to Dallas, while Alfred Belo stayed in Galveston to direct the reorganization of the business. Alfred hadn't fully recovered from the grippe, but with T.W.'s retirement effective immediately, and with the vice-presidency vacant, the reorganization was imperative.

Dealey had reason to believe he would receive the vice-presidency, but scarcely had there been a moment to think about it when on January 23 he received the following telegram:

> CONGRATULATIONS ON BEING ELECTED VICE-PRESIDENT. MAY PRESENT ORGANIZATION REMAIN UNBROKEN ANOTHER QUARTER OF A CENTURY.
>
> ALFRED H. BELO

A few days later Alfred Belo was back in Dallas and worked at the office February 3, but the next day Helen, Alfred's wife, telephoned that he had suffered a relapse and was quite ill. That same day word arrived that T.W. was seriously ill in Mineral Wells, where he had gone for his health. In a letter to J. D. Lorentz, long-time New York representative of the *News,* Dealey confided his feeling of hopelessness insofar as T.W.'s fate was concerned.

". . . We live and learn," Lorentz replied, "and some of us find what a world of sorrow and suffering sometimes overtakes the strongest, and all that can be done seems of no avail."

On February 15, exactly one month to the day after Colonel Lowe's death, T.W. died. Before leaving for the funeral, Dealey read copy on T.W.'s obituary. It brought back memories . . . their arrival at Galveston Island in the sailing bark *Herbert* . . . the green watermelons piled on the wharf . . . T.W. was 14 and he was 11 and they agreed the first thing they wanted to do in America was eat a watermelon, and they did.

Returning from T.W.'s funeral, he found Alfred Belo had become critically ill. The family had summoned a specialist from St. Louis. Poor Alfred and Helen. This was the couple he had toasted happily a few short years before at the wedding feast in the new building. Strangely, his words came vividly back to mind: *In the language of Rip Van Winkle, "May they live long and prosper."*

Alfred's illness was diagnosed as cerebromeningitis. Was there any hope? Possibly. The specialist from St. Louis said that if any living man could help, it was Dr. C. L. Dana of New York City, the foremost authority on nervous diseases. Then get Dr. Dana! How long might it take for him to reach Dallas? Four days by train. Oh, if only man could fly! Dr. Dana was ready on the telephone. Yes, he would leave immediately. Wire the president of the Frisco Lines in St. Louis.

> PLEASE HOLD FRISCO FAST MAIL FOR DR.
> C. L. DANA. MATTER OF LIFE AND DEATH.

Dr. Dana reached Dallas on the twenty-third, and was with Alfred constantly for almost four days, but it was not the Lord's will. On February 27 Alfred Belo died.

Late that night before retiring for a few hours of fitful sleep, Dealey knelt beside his bed, as he did every night, and prayed to

God, asking that he be given strength to meet the problems that were suddenly thrust upon him.

The next day Dealey spent his time attending to the funeral arrangements. He asked department heads at the *News* to see that every member of the staff be present at the funeral. They would go to the Belo home on Ross Avenue and stand in double rows on each side of the walk. After the casket had been carried to the hearse, they would arrange themselves in two's and march behind it to the cathedral. The order of march was outlined. First after the honorary pallbearers would come the editorial department employees, then the composing-room employees, etc.

As if all nature and the universe were in consonance with the sad event, on the day of the funeral a hard gale was blowing over the city and the sky was darkened with ominous clouds. The foul weather was only a part of a widespread storm sweeping the Gulf states, which brought much destruction and a score of deaths in Meridian, Mississippi. Within the week, the Island of Tahiti was swept by a tidal wave, killing thousands of natives. In Portland, Oregon, the earth rumbled, beginning a vast geological displacement that ended two months later in the great San Francisco earthquake.

CHAPTER FOURTEEN

1906-1907

C. LOMBARDI TO REPRESENT "THE LA-
DIES." TOO MUCH WHISKY-ADVERTISING.
DEALEY MAKES A SPEECH TO THE "MAK-
ERS OF THE *NEWS.*" A CORNERSTONE FOR
THE SCOTTISH RITE CATHEDRAL. DEA-
LEY PROMOTES A PARK FOR WOODCHUCK
HILL.

DESPITE THE DEATHS IN RAPID SUCCESSION OF THE THREE HIGH-
est executives of the *News,* the business appeared to function more
or less the same. But Dealey knew that part of the engine of the
organization had disintegrated, and a new one had to be put together. Who should take over the presidency? Who should fill the
vacancies on the Board of Directors? These and other vital decisions had to be made quickly.

By April 6, the date set for the stockholders' meeting, Dealey
had the new engine fashioned. Mrs. Nettie Ennis Belo, the widow
of Colonel Belo, would be the new president. She had offered the
presidency to Dealey, and there would have been good logic and
ample justification in his acceptance, but he had declined. The
main issue, as he saw it, was guardianship or stewardship of property. He believed that every means of control should rest with the
legal heirs. His sense of property had roots in both an English
concept and in the biblical idea of patrimony as a sacred possession.

In the reorganization, Dealey would continue to be vice-president and general manager, but there would be the addition of another vice-president, and this position would be filled by a Mr. Cesar Lombardi—or C. Lombardi, as he invariably referred to himself. This gentleman was a brother-in-law to Mrs. Belo. In 1900 he had rounded out a successful mercantile career in Houston, Texas, and had retired to live on the Pacific Coast. Colonel Belo, prior to his death, had advised the family that should they ever need someone to look after the family's interests, C. Lombardi could be trusted. The final decision whether to add C. Lombardi to the directorate of the *News* was left to Dealey. One Sunday afternoon in March, after a lengthy conversation in the parlor at the Dealey residence—interrupted several times by the two youngest children, Ted and Maidie, who were consumed with curiosity to see this foreign-looking man with the "General Grant" beard and sideburns—Dealey knew that C. Lombardi was the man of high ideals and good business judgment whom the paper needed. He liked his looks, too, a calm-faced man. He was of Swiss origin, having immigrated to Texas as a youth.

At the April 6 stockholders' meeting, all details of Dealey's reorganization plan were approved unanimously. Although there was no jockeying for votes by stockholders, it was satisfying to Dealey to know that his own 67 shares, which he had gradually built up a few at a time, was the third largest block owned by any stockholder, and that the second largest was in T.W.'s estate, 200 shares, for which he held the proxy. Of course Mrs. Belo controlled the voting majority with the 1851 shares in the A. H. Belo estate. In all, 31 stockholders participated in the meeting.

Within a week after the reorganization meeting, the journalistic ideals of the new Board of Directors were put to the test. The matter involved two whisky advertisements appearing in *The Semi-Weekly News,** the farm edition of the *News,* on Friday April 13. There was nothing wrong with the product, and the price was a bargain—Kellerstrasse X-Old Rye Whisky at $3.15 the gallon, and ten quarts of Rosedale Rye for 5 dollars—but the two ads were so large they dominated the whole issue. Dealey, a

---

* Renamed *The Semi-Weekly Farm News* on October 1, 1908.

teetotaler, lost his patience. He had been trying to reduce the liquor linage to a minimum and had even doubled the rate recently, but it had not "fazed" the distilleries. At a called meeting of the Board of Directors, he proposed the immediate elimination of all liquor advertising in the *Semi-Weekly*. The subscribers of the farm edition lived mainly in areas which had been voted dry, and the whisky advertisements were helping to keep the boozers supplied by mail. It was legal, but it was wrong.

How much revenue would be lost?

About 50,000 dollars a year.

It was not a question of revenue, C. Lombardi commented. He thought the whisky advertising should be stopped. The motion was passed and declared in immediate effect.

The acid test for the new rule came the next day when an order was received from a St. Louis advertising agency to print a full-page whisky advertisement at a cost of 1172 dollars. The ad was returned.

Through the spring, summer, and into the fall of 1906, Dealey gave undivided attention to the paper. During this period there was precious little time for his second love, civic betterment. The storm which the company had weathered in the early part of the year had rocked the boat. Advertising revenue had dropped, and circulation was down to 36,000, about 600 off from the previous year. Nothing in particular was wrong, but Dealey sensed that the good spirit of the *News* family needed a tonic. Tucked away in the back of his mind was an idea of a "something special" for the employees, and the time was ripe to get it started.

By the middle of September the shifting around of departments and offices was completed, and within a few days carpenters were hammering and sawing in the vacated space in the east corner of the second floor. What was going in? The office grapevine buzzed with rumors.

With a knack for making an event serve more than one purpose, Dealey timed the presentation of the "something special" for the employees to fall on October 1, which marked the twenty-first birthday of the Dallas paper. This made it apropos for him to say a few words about the history of the paper, and he had a purpose in mind. Tradition, if recognized and honored, was a powerful force, he believed.

At 5 o'clock on the afternoon of October 1, more than 100 of the employees gathered in the composing room on the third floor of the building. At one end of the room seated on a small platform, which had been built for the occasion, were the eight men of the organization who had been continuously in the employ of the *News* since it was started—William G. Sterett, Harvey M. Campbell, T. M. Rinehart, W. H. Hall, Arthur Geen, A. F. Hess, Arthur M. Allen, and Dealey.

"I ask your indulgence a few moments," Dealey said, calling the meeting to order, "while I revert to the beginning of this paper." After reviewing a few incidents from October 1, 1885, he introduced the seven old-timers around him. Then he marked a few of the milestones of success behind the *News.*

"While not in the least disparaging the advantages of locality," he continued, "to my mind our great success is due in large measure to the wisdom of its founders . . .

"They built The News upon the rock of truth and righteousness, conducting it always along the lines of fairness and integrity, and acknowledging the right of the people to get from the newspaper both sides of every important question.*

"In my judgment," Dealey continued, "no newspaper in this country possesses a force of men in the aggregate equal to those of the *News.* Men of ability, of high ideals, men in every department who love their work and who during strenuous and exciting periods work night and day, work as though they owned the entire plant—such are the men we call the makers of the *News,* and to whom the management owes an everlasting debt."

As a practical expression of its gratitude to the employees, the management had fitted a Library and a Club Room for their use on the second floor.

"The rooms will be opened for use today," Dealey told them, "immediately on adjournment of this meeting."

---

* This statement became the basis for the inscription carved on the front of the new building erected by the *News* in 1949.

A room where employees could enjoy themselves was something new in 1906. A Dallas businessman remarked that this pampering of employees could go too far, but Dealey didn't think so, and before the week was over there would be a reward that would make it all worth-while—a journalistic achievement never before equaled by a newspaper in the Southwest.

Circumstances leading up to the event made it exciting. The time was a period of intense antipathy in Texas toward corporate wealth, particularly oil companies and railroads, being a reflection of President Theodore Roosevelt's trust-busting activities in the nation at large. Late in September of 1906 the president of the Waters-Pierce Oil Company, on the witness stand in a court inquiry, testified that Texas' Senator Joseph Weldon Bailey had served as his attorney in the handling of several large business transactions not involving the oil firm. It was a matter of record that Bailey had endorsed the reorganized oil company's readmission to Texas in 1900, a bitterly fought action. The testimony produced a sensation, and much public anger was turned against Senator Bailey, who was up for re-election. Charges and counter-charges swiftly led to a climax, and during the first week of October a public debate to settle the issue was arranged between Bailey and the leader of the opposition, M. M. Crane, who had been the attorney general of Texas at the first prosecution of the Waters-Pierce Oil Company. The debate was to be in Houston at the municipal auditorium on Saturday night, October 6.

Following the announcement of the date and place of the debate, an inspired plan for coverage of the event caught on at the *News*. Tom Finty, Jr., who had joined the paper in 1897 and had developed into one of its best writers, proposed that the *News* publish a verbatim report of the debate. When the idea was presented to Dealey, he recalled that the *News* had done this sort of thing once before in covering the Hogg-Clark[1] debate in Cameron, Texas, in 1892. He heartily approved the idea.

On Sunday morning, October 7, the *News* carried a 30,000-word coverage of the event, headlined: BATTLE OF THE GIANTS. Included was a word-by-word account of the debate, a general summary of their arguments, and several color stories on the day's activities. Finty had master-minded a reportorial feat. There were no advance copies of the speeches, but by using a relay writing team, most of whom knew shorthand—composed of himself, E. B. Doran, and Alonzo Wasson of the Dallas staff, and about seven from the Galveston staff, including K. K. Hooper, the city editor —they had the last "take" of the 24-column report in the telegrapher's hands 67 minutes after the debate ended, and the whole story had cleared the wire 37 minutes later. Both the Dallas and Galveston papers carried the complete story in their State editions. The *News* family spirit was high again.

During the winter of 1906 and early part of 1907, Dealey gave many evenings to frequent meetings of the Dallas Scottish Rite Cathedral Association. Plans were being pushed ahead so that the cornerstone of the new cathedral could be laid at the annual statewide reunion of the Scottish Rite Masons to be held in Dallas in March, 1907.

Masonry was a comparatively new interest in Dealey's life. He was 43 years old when initiated in the Tannehill Lodge of Dallas on October 12, 1903. He had belonged to other lodges and clubs, but none struck the responsive chord in him that Masonry did. Almost as fast as a member could advance, he had passed from one degree to another. On August 24, 1905, he became a Knight Templar and was made a Royal and Select Master on November 24, 1905. In the teachings, high purposes, and the brotherhood of the Masonic Order he had found something that matched his own beliefs about life.

At 3 o'clock in the afternoon of March 21, 1907, he was in the procession of 250 grand officers and members of the Scottish Rite Order which marched from the Dallas Grand Lodge to the site of the new cathedral at Harwood, Cabell, and Polk Streets. This block had been purchased from Dealey and his brother, T.W. In the transaction Dealey had donated his one-fifth equity to the Scottish Rite Cathedral Association.

The Most Worshipful Grand Master began the cornerstone ceremony. First he placed mortar on the stone, which was a magnificent block of Texas gray granite. Then he scattered a handful of corn upon the top, reciting a prayer which asked that the work-men might never suffer want. Next he poured wine, with the peti-tion to the Supreme Architect of the Universe that there might be the refreshing and the blessing of life to the faithful workers. Last, over the top he poured oil with the supplication that joy might abound and that there might be no lack of those things which go to make the really happy life and the true manhood and the faithful following of the pattern on the trestle board of the master workman.

Dealey thought the ceremony very fitting. He liked the allegory.

Few pleasures in Dealey's life compared with the exhilaration he got on an early-morning horseback ride in the spring, when the trees were first leafing out and the woods took on a deeper shade day by day. Just before 7 o'clock each morning he would hurry out the front door. Merrity, the colored boy, would be wait-ing with Pet, a big black saddle mare.

He could spare only 20 minutes, 30 at the most, for riding, but he knew every twist and turn in the wooded area on both sides of Maple Avenue. Woodchuck Hill, about a mile northwest from his house, was his favorite spot.* It was Pet's favorite spot, too—the place where she got a lump of sugar each morning.

From this wooded knoll the view looked down on Turtle Creek, with its winding course and steep bank on the far side. In the hollows the pecan trees, elms, oaks, hackberries, and gums were so thick they hardly had room to grow. Here the squirrels and birds—especially jays and redbirds and brown thrush—thrived. It was cool and inviting. It smelled clean and free of dust. Down several hundred yards to the southeast, between the hilltop and the creek, encircled by a thick grove of trees and bushes, was a natural open space known as "the Flats," a kind of natural amphitheater, and on the east edge of the Flats was a spring of pure cold water, called Raccoon Spring. Dealey loved the place.

Thirty-odd years later, in writing about his efforts to make a park of the area, he related:

---

* Now the site of Freeman Memorial Clinic, Scottish Rite Hospital for Crippled Children, and the Texas Children's Hospital.

I began a thorough campaign to get the citizens interested in it, first of all, especially those citizens living in the general vicinity. Afterwards we got in touch with the Park Board, and it was my business to take members of the Park Board down to inspect the property. [In the early spring of 1908] I had Mr. Emil Fretz down there, and he was impressed. "Let's go under the Katy track up on Turney Avenue" [later Hines Boulevard] Fretz said, and we made our way there. "Dealey, there is a dandy place for a play park," he said [indicating a smaller tract south of the Cole estate]. The spot he was looking at is now called Pike Park or Summit Park, which the Park Board acquired in 1909, being a result of Fretz's impression and remark on that visit.

Fretz promised to vote for the purchase of the 40-acre Cole estate. But before the negotiations could get under way, the big flood of 1908 came and the property was covered with water for several weeks. It changed Fretz's enthusiasm, and he told Dealey that he was sorry, but he would have to cancel his promise to vote for the park. Dealey countered with the argument that it was his observation that people did not go to parks when it was raining, but it was to be six years later before all the conditions were favorable enough to acquire the Cole estate as a park.[2]

Business had seldom looked better for The *News* than it did at the beginning of the fall of 1907. Through September, earnings had been at an all-time high. Dealey was feeling complacent. And who wouldn't—his portrait was being painted by William Vincent Besser. A fund to pay for the life-sized portrait had been raised by the employees, and they were going to hang the painting in the Employees' Library. To reciprocate, he proposed to the Board of Directors that a large framed photograph of every employee connected with the corporation for 21 or more consecutive years be given a prominent place in the building.

Another reason for his good feeling was that he had finally got all parties agreed on the elimination of front-page advertising. After October 1, the *News* would have an all-news front page and would compare with the best papers in the country.

Then came the third week of October. On the New York market, copper dropped to 12 cents, and the copper industry collapsed.

On October 22 the Knickerbocker Trust Company closed its doors, and the financial panic of 1907 was on. In Dallas mercantile activity slowed down within a matter of days, and immediately advertising suffered. Cotton, the bulwark of Texas' economy, touched the bottom of the market, and hard times gripped the state.

Such was business. Dealey could recall the financial panics of 1890 and 1893. A. H. Belo & Company had weathered those, and they would weather this one; but it would be rough, and the sails would have to be trimmed. It was a lucky thing he had proposed the "calamity surplus" last October instead of this one. Only about half of the 100,000 dollars was in hand yet, but this fund was going to be a life-saver. In December it became necessary to sell 30,000 dollars in railroad stocks in order to pay the newsprint accounts, and the dividends were cut for the last quarter of 1907, and would continue to be cut, even more drastically, for the next four quarters.

CHAPTER FIFTEEN

1908=1909

THE STIRRING IDEA OF A CITY PLAN. A FLOOD INTERVENES. ANOTHER PARK. DEALEY READS A PAPER ON CITY PLANNING TO THE CRITIC CLUB.

PRIOR TO 1900, THE PLANNING OF CITIES WAS SOMETHING GENerally unpracticed in America. It was an old art, however. Washington, D.C., provided an example, and some of the cities of the Old World were noted for the beauty of their planning. But the great mass of people of the United States were too much occupied with settling the vast country and too busy putting in the basic foundations of a civilization to worry with the planning of cities. Cities grew of their own accord, and that was good enough. In the 1890's, however, there was a flowering of knowledge on municipal problems and civic improvement, and the subject became popular in progressive newspapers and magazines. One phase of it was city planning, but until after the turn of the century the idea of the city plan was slow in taking hold.

Dealey was always searching for ideas which the *News* could adapt to the needs of Dallas. Of the hundreds of articles he read, probably the one that had the most effect on him was *The Awakening of Harrisburg,* a pamphlet by J. Horace McFarland, president of the American Civic Association. The day on which he read it —February 28, 1908—he recorded that he was stirred with ideas and wrote immediately for 25 copies to send to some of the more

progressive-minded local citizens. This was the pattern for Dallas
to follow. The situation in the Pennsylvania city was much like
the situation in Dallas . . . about the same in size and with similar problems. Dallas had experienced "awakenings" too—by the
Cleaner Dallas League in 1899, by the Civic Improvement League
in 1902-03, by the "150,000 Club" in 1905—but Dallas always
went back to sleep.

What was it that kept Harrisburg awake? The difference was
summed up in the phrase "the Harrisburg Plan." In 1901 the
Harrisburg Plan was conceived when private citizens raised money
to employ three engineers to study the city's problems and recommend solutions. This work resulted in the drawing up of an entire
city plan which outlined objectives for both the present and future.
From that point on, the progress of Harrisburg had never ceased.

In the case of Dallas, the awakenings had been for limited goals.
There was no great challenge to sustain the people's interest. There
was no long-range city plan.

Dealey was almost ready to launch his greatest undertaking for
Dallas—the campaign for a city plan. The *News* was ready. It had
the power and the prestige for the campaign, and Dealey was in
full control of the *News*. The staff was ready. For ten years he
had been emphasizing to them the paramount importance of city
matters. In Tom Finty, Jr., K. K. Hooper, Luther Clark, Alonzo
Wasson, E. B. Doran, and Prescott Toomey, he had writers who
knew the problems of city government and municipal administration as thoroughly as most of the city officials. The form of city
government was ready. Two years earlier the *News* had led the
movement to uproot the outmoded mayor-aldermen system and
install the modern city commission. All these factors would be
needed for the big campaign ahead.

Dealey's "working philosophy" was ready too. As he later expressed it, with a borrowed quotation, "Nothing else pays so well
as enlistment in some betterment movement. It pays—not in simo-
leons nor in kudos, but in one's right to be on good terms with
one's self, which is about all there is in life anyway that amounts
to a hoot." [1]

This belief had been strengthened by the writings of his younger brother, James Quayle Dealey, who had become a professor of social and political science at Brown University. In 1905 James Quayle Dealey had published his first book, *A Text-Book of Sociology,* coauthored with Lester F. Ward, a pre-eminent geologist-sociologist of his day. The book held forth the thesis that mankind was slowly improving "through a transformation of environment." Dealey needed no book to reveal this social concept to him, but it impressed him to see that he and these two scholars thought alike. He put great stake in scholars, especially in his brother. He agreed heartily with James, too, on the concept of mankind's natural reluctance toward progress. "Social progress," James had written, "is not only a matter of complete indifference to man [except for the most enlightened], but it is for the most part undesired and unintended." [2]

Dealey could say "Amen" with much feeling. From his own experiences with the unceasing efforts of the *News* to get people to do things that would improve their daily lives, he knew that people made it extremely difficult to get good things accomplished. But once the accomplishments were made, it was his observation that most people relished the benefits, and scarcely a man could be found who would admit he opposed them.

Before launching a public campaign, he felt he needed to propagate the city-plan idea with a cadre of leading citizens. Then, after that preparation was made, they should start the drive at a propitious time of the year when little else was on the public mind and the public spirit could be aroused. All was going well when a disaster to the city intervened, beginning on Sunday, May 24, 1908.

All that day a heavy rain fell over the city and surrounding country, but no one expected or was prepared for the avalanche of water that was descending the Trinity Valley. In the upper watershed it had been raining continuously for three days, 15 inches of rainfall. The massive runoff poured down the West Fork and the Elm Fork of the Trinity. At the very edge of Dallas the two swollen streams converged. By midnight Sunday the central valley of the Trinity was an immense and irresistible torrent. Rushing ahead, it was caught in a bottleneck where the valley narrowed to three fourths of a mile between the high ground of Oak Cliff on the west and the high ground of the business district of Dallas on the east.

The water rose higher and higher and began to back up. By 3:00 A.M. Monday it had spread as much as ten miles in width at some points in the west environs of the city. Long before dawn the water reached the city power plant and poured into the basement, leaving the city in total darkness.

It was the worst and most terrifying flood in the history of Dallas.

Shortly after 5:30 in the morning, the night foreman at the *News* sent word to Dealey that water was getting into the basement of the *News* building from the storm sewers. The newsprint was being removed as fast as possible. The river was up to Young Street. At Young and Lamar it was only two blocks from the *News*.

Dealey got to the building just at daybreak. Two lift pumps were in operation, and matters were pretty well in hand. With one of the reporters he walked down Commerce Street to the water's edge, hardly a stone's throw from the courthouse. Already thousands of people lined the banks. Looking across the Commerce Street Bridge, the floor of the bridge less than a foot above water, Dealey saw the wildest and widest torrent of raging water he had ever witnessed in the Trinity Valley. He wondered where his three tracts of bottom land were. The lots must be 40 feet under water. Perhaps it had been a sad mistake to buy the land. How could floods like this ever be contained? How could the Trinity Valley be the industrial district he had envisioned?

But this was no time to meditate the future. There must be thousands of people homeless at this moment, and perhaps the worst was yet to come. It was time to get back to the office and contact Mayor Hay and see what could be done about relief of the flood victims.

About two hours later, around 10:00 A.M., Dealey and others at work in the *News* building heard a great shout of distress come from the river's direction. They hurried out to the sidewalk. Two men were running up Commerce Street.

"The T. & P. trestle went down!" the men shouted. "Lots of people drowned!"

Only four men were drowned, it turned out, but the thousands of spectators on the bank never forgot the horror of seeing the men swept from the falling trestle into the raging torrent.

The flood waters paralyzed Dallas. The state militia moved in to render aid and to patrol the streets at night as long as the city remained without lights. For the 4000 homeless, tent cities were thrown up in various parts of town.

On June 3, ten days after the first onslaught of water, a dozen members of the Citizens Relief Committee gathered on the east bank below the Commerce Street Bridge and boarded the *Nellie Maureen,* a small steam launch. This was their first opportunity to make a safe crossing to Oak Cliff and West Dallas to inspect the flood damage. Dealey was among the group. The little steamer paddled across the vast lake of water which covered familiar land that ordinarily was dry. The captain had to steer around tree tops and avoid telephone wires.

Somewhere underneath the muddy water, Dealey thought, as he watched over the railing, was a roadway that connected the two communities, and he wondered if perhaps the perennial public clamor for a high-water causeway, which followed every flood, might not have a chance to succeed this time. Perhaps, too, they could put over a bond issue to build the river levee, which was often talked about but never accomplished. What Dallas really needed was a city plan. A city plan would solve flood problems along with other problems. For the want of a plan, the battles of Dallas on every major problem were being lost.

The public clamor for a causeway and levee quickly developed. Then July came with its torrid heat, and the river bottom got so dry it cracked all over, and once more the wagons and buggies and the brave new automobiles streamed back and forth on what remained of the gravel road between Dallas and Oak Cliff. A high-water bridge wasn't needed. Soon, as it always happened, the mass meetings stopped and the publicity for a causeway and levee died down.

Perhaps it would have become a dead issue again for an indefinite period, but Dealey made it otherwise, at least as far as the causeway was concerned. In August he went to Kansas City on business, and while there he rode on a trolley that went over a mile-and-a-half long causeway, newly built across the Missouri River. This was precisely the type of bridge needed between Dallas and Oak Cliff. There was no time to inquire about the bridge before departing from Kansas City, but methodically during the next few weeks he searched out, by unrelenting correspondence, the engineer who had designed it, the city leader who had promoted it, and the Boston banker who had financed it, and sapped each one of all the information he could get.

"The viaduct question, as it appertains to Dallas," he explained to Mr. Ira G. Hedrick, the designer of the Kansas City causeway, "is not now up in the public mind, but something will bring it up again, and it is our idea to print pictures of the Kansas City improvement, telling how it was accomplished, financed, etc. . . . We believe the conditions about Dallas are similar to those at Kansas City so far as the bottom lands are concerned."

The project became a challenge to Dealey, and he resolved to see it through. It was going to take much work, politics, promotion, and long-enduring patience. From the idea stage, to the competitive plans, to the bond issue, to the bids, to the contract, and at length to the 14 months of construction, it was a four-year job. But from beginning to end Dealey kept at it, personally and through the *News,* prodding city officials, drumming up public support, and knitting each stage of progress into the next. The way he gave the project his attention even to the last detail came to light in a recollection written in 1945 by the resident engineer of the causeway construction, Mr. E. N. Noyes, who wrote: "Noah Roark was reporter for the *Dallas News* at the time the viaduct was built and he was on the job every day for some time. He finally told me that he had been instructed to watch the job carefully to see if he could find any indication of fraud or poor workmanship."

During the latter part of 1908 Dealey kept postponing the preparations for the city-plan drive. The causeway and other projects diverted his time and energy. Admittedly, they were not as important as the city plan, but each one seemed to be a "bird in the hand" which he could not afford to let get away, as for example, the chance to acquire another park for the city. The land was the little tract near the Cotton Mills in South Dallas, which he and several other citizens had tried unsuccessfully to secure through the park tax vote in 1903. Unexpectedly the land was offered for sale in September, 1908. If it was to be a park, it was now or never.

Dealey corralled the Park Board, and together they went out on the South Belt streetcar. On the way Dealey made the Board members a speech, emphasizing the need for a park in the "tough" neighborhood near the Cotton Mills, where three or four policemen were required to keep order.

"Give these people a park and a good supervisor, and the city won't need so many policemen out there," he said.

After inspecting the property, they got back on the car and started for town. The Park Board members asked Dealey to go up front and talk with the motorman so they could discuss the matter. Just before arriving at the corner opposite the *News* building, the Board members came forward and announced the decision. If Dealey would raise 1500 dollars, the Board would put up the remaining 9000 dollars and buy the property. Fair enough. He would do it. The task took about three weeks, and he had to call on 30 or 40 people, but he got the money, and the property was purchased. It was first named Trinity Play Park, and later changed to Fretz Park, after Emil Fretz, one of the Park Board members who went along on the streetcar ride.

It was January of 1909 before Dealey turned his efforts again to the preparations for the city-plan drive. The immediate task was to write a paper on the need and benefits of a city plan for Dallas, to be read to the Critic Club when it came his time to be host, which was the last Monday in February.

The Critic Club was a new interest in his life, having been started in March of the previous year. The 15 members met for dinner once a month, and the host presented a paper about 30 minutes long on some important subject in which he was personally interested and which he thought would interest the group.

Following the paper, each member would comment on the subject for no more than five minutes. Dr. W. H. Greenburg, new rabbi of the Temple Emanu-El in Dallas, and C. Lombardi had belonged to this type of club on the West Coast, and they persuaded Dealey to help organize one in Dallas.

Dealey had joined on one condition—that he be the permanent secretary and keep the minutes in lieu of writing "learned papers." But when it came his turn to be host to the club, in February of 1909, he had changed his mind about not wanting to present a paper. Now he was eager to do so. The members were all citizens of substantial influence, either city-wide or within certain groups, and they were an ideal group to recruit for the city-plan drive. Judge Yancey Lewis was a power among the attorneys. He had served as a United States judge in the Indian Territory and had been dean of the Law School at the University of Texas from 1902 to 1904. The Reverend M. F. Ham was the Unitarian preacher in Dallas and had a strong following, and Dr. Greenburg was the leader of another religious group. Captain W. P. Wooten of the United States Army Engineering Corps was stationed in Dallas to direct a survey of the Trinity River for flood control and navigation possibilities. Judge M. M. Crane was a former attorney general of Texas and the man who had opposed Senator Joe Bailey in the famous debate in Houston in 1906. Dr. E. H. Cary and Dr. Pierre Wilson were both brilliant physicians of the city and business leaders as well. In addition to these men, all with their "channels of influence," the Critic Club boasted the four men who controlled the only two important Dallas newspapers: E. J. Kiest and H. N. Fitzgerald, respectively publisher and chief editorial writer of the Dallas *Times-Herald* . . . and Dealey and C. Lombardi, the two men most responsible for the direction of the *News*.

The Critic Club meeting at the Dealey home was scheduled for Monday night, February 23. The Dealeys did not entertain often, and Ollie had the menu planned a month ahead of time and spent the weeks in between fretting over it. Dealey finished writing his paper for the occasion on the Friday beforehand, knowing that during the next several days he would be spending much of his time at functions planned for the Dallas visit of President Charles W. Eliot of Harvard University. These duties began on Saturday morning, two days before the Critic Club meeting. He was chairman of the reception committee, and he had to see that the city dignitaries got together at the depot at the right time. At his insistence, they were all to wear top hats and formal dress, because President Eliot was the most distinguished university president in America. But President Eliot did not anticipate the honor with which he would be received in Dallas, and on that Saturday morning he casually descended from the train wearing the baggy tweed suit in which he had been traveling for days.

All day Monday, the twenty-third, the preparations for the Critic Club dinner were in progress at 157 Maple Avenue. Boswell, the chauffeur, and Merrity, the yard boy, were recruited for housework. The windows were washed, silver polished, furniture dusted, floors cleaned, and extra leaves put in the dining table.

Promptly at 6:30 that evening, Ollie seated the 14 gentlemen around the oval-shaped table, and Boswell and Merrity, in stiff white coats, began serving the soup. There were nine Critic Club members and five special guests. Dealey had increased the number of special guests by one when he realized that he was about to have 13 persons for dinner. He never admitted to being superstitious, but he avoided meetings with exactly 13 persons present.

Dinner-table conversation took various interesting turns. Dr. Wilson and Captain Wooten got involved in an argument over which was the more indispensable to the successful completion of the Panama Canal—modern engineering or medical science. To change the subject, Dealey complimented Judge Lewis on his faithful work with the United Charities of Dallas. The judge in turn called Dealey "the father of the United Charities." Dealey said he would like to introduce the real originator of the United Charities of Dallas, and he pointed to Ollie, who was busily supervising the untrained waiters. While she blushed, he told how shortly before Christmas in 1895 she had gotten the school children of Dallas to donate food and clothing for the poor. This was the beginning of the United Charities in Dallas, an idea she had brought from Lexington, Missouri, where she grew up.

The conversation turned to President Eliot's visit to Dallas, and Dealey told them that President Eliot had told him he belonged to a club in Boston very much like their own Critic Club. It was called the Saturday Club. It was organized in the 1850's, and the early members had included Henry Wadsworth Longfellow, James Russell Lowell, Ralph Waldo Emerson, and John Greenleaf Whittier.

After the dinner was finished the gentlemen went into the parlor, and Dealey passed out cigars. He was anxiously wondering how the group would react to his paper. He began:

I desire to make a few suggestions with reference to civic responsibility. Like a good many other towns or cities, Dallas has developed in a haphazard sort of way, the absence of a purpose or plan in the minds of its founders being clearly seen. To correct such conditions, many cities are developing the City Plan. These are prepared by experts. After proper study of local conditions, a map is made showing various improvements, which, when the plan is adopted, should be worked out as rapidly as circumstances and money may permit, so that when the purpose is finally carried out, the city so treated becomes more attractive to the eye, healthier, and generally a better place to live in.

Glancing up, he noted that most of the men were puffing thoughtfully on their cigars. After delineating the broad outlines, he developed what he considered to be the more urgent aspects pertaining to the Dallas situation.

With a territory within our city limits sufficient to satisfy a population of a million, there are several sections of Dallas where the poor families are huddled together on 25-foot lots. They live in miserable hovels, two, three or four rooms each, poorly arranged, poorly ventilated, but very successfully constructed to emphasize the cold of the winter and the heat of the summer. This entire section is unattractive. The streets unclean and unimproved, no sidewalks worth the name. Tin cans and dirt are everywhere in evidence. Look into the houses and it will be found that the desolation on the outside is an index to the interior. Poverty, untidiness, and filth abound, the bathtub a mile away . . . Out of this environment, it can easily be seen, naturally arise the spirit of unrest, of discontentment, of immorality and criminality, and the frightful expense produced by these results must finally be paid by some one else. Who?

After the guests had departed, Ollie asked how the paper had gone over.

"Good," Dealey said. "They didn't agree on what was most important, but they all agreed that Dallas needs a city plan."

CHAPTER SIXTEEN

1909-1911

THE ALAMO REPLICA, "A DIVINE INSPI-
RATION." A "SIMPLE DINNER" FOR PRES-
IDENT TAFT. THE CAMPAIGN FOR A CITY
PLAN . . . J. HORACE McFARLAND MAKES
A SPEECH . . . GEORGE E. KESSLER HIRED.
DEALEY'S CAMPAIGN FORMULA WORKS
AGAIN TO GET THE UNION STATION.

THE GROUP OF CITY-PLAN ENTHUSIASTS WAS DEVELOPING
nicely, but more "converts" were needed, and a meeting of the
National Conference on City Planning in Washington, D.C. in
May, 1909, provided another good opportunity for Dealey to
cultivate a larger following. He instructed Otto Praeger, the
Washington correspondent of the *News*, to write a series of articles reporting fully on the talks at the conference. After the series
was printed, he clipped out 50 sets of the articles and sent them
to 50 local citizens.

"Put these clippings in your pocket," he wrote each one personally, "and read them at your leisure—on cars or at home. . . .
After you have read them, will you kindly return them to me
under cover of the accompanying envelope?"

The purpose in asking for the return of the clippings, he told
later, was to make sure they were read. A man will usually read
an article before he has to return it.

Looking ahead to the fall, it appeared that the campaign would
have to wait until after the State Fair was over. This big annual

event always monopolized public interest through the month of October. Also, he had an extra stake himself in the forthcoming Fair. The *News* was going to finance the building of a replica of the Alamo on the State Fair grounds. The idea had come to him one evening when he and Mr. Lombardi were attending the previous Fair. Mr. Lombardi said it was a "divine inspiration." Shortly afterward he sent an architect to San Antonio to take the measurements of the Alamo and to draw the plans for a half-size replica. The architect estimated it would cost 5000 dollars.

"The great mass of people of North Texas never have the opportunity to see the Alamo," he wrote the Park Board in July, explaining his idea and asking permission to erect the structure. "But they can see and study this exact replica of the original, and thus will be created or augmented in the minds of the younger generation a patriotic feeling and pride for the noble band which fought and died for the freedom which we now enjoy."

The official opening of the Alamo Replica was on October 16. True to form, he made the preparations thorough and complete, including a special "Alamo Edition" of the *News,* a wooden platform for the ceremony, a band to play, a flag to raise, and everything else that was needed. After a few words by the mayor, Dealey delivered a patriotic speech in the best tradition, with a stirring account of the Battle of the Alamo and these lines from Alvin E. Farr's poem, "The Alamo":

> Our heroes only caught a glimpse
>   Of glories yet to be;
> The sun that sank in death to them
>   Was dawn of liberty!
> And rarest flowers of love and peace
>   Their fragrant beauties shed,
> And Texas owes her happy homes
>   To her devoted dead.

Some weeks prior to the completion of the Alamo Replica project, Dealey had himself saddled with another time-consuming task. Mayor Hay asked him to be the chairman for the banquet honoring the president of the United States, William Howard Taft, on the occasion of his visit to Dallas. Taft was coming to Texas to have an international conference at El Paso with the president of Mexico.

A presidential banquet involved no end of details. Even the menu was a major problem. Dealey proposed "a simple dinner," reasoning that the president would have his fill of rich food at the international conference and would appreciate a change, possibly "a plate of corned beef and cabbage." The menu committee thought at first he was joking. Finally they compromised. On the printed program the menu was entitled "A Simple Dinner," but it listed the following:

Salted Almonds
Canapé à la Russe
Strained Gumbo

Celery   *Olives*

Apollinaris

Fresh Crab Meat à la Newburg
Broiled Sirloin Steak
Saratoga Chips   *Green Peas*
Lettuce and Tomato Salad
Fancy Ice Cream
Assorted Cake
Neufchatel Cheese
Coffee
Fruit
Cigars

There were to be no alcoholic beverages, only Apollinaris, "the Queen of Table Waters." This proposal astounded some members of the banquet committee, but Dealey prevailed. Public banquets should stop being a place for men to get "liquored up," he said, and now was a good time to set the example.

For the printed program, Dealey conceived a cover piece that symbolized the proud history of Texas . . . something he thought up while working on his speech for the Alamo Replica opening.

Fastened in a cluster to the cover by an embossed gold seal were six miniature golden flagstaffs flying perfect little flags made of fine silk—the six flags of Texas—for the six sovereign nations that had ruled over the land: France, Spain, Mexico, the Republic of Texas, the Confederacy, and the United States of America.

October 23 came. The president arrived in Dallas, and the banquet got under way. Seated at Table Number 4, Dealey was about to settle down to eat when he noticed at one of the far tables that a man was putting a hip flask beside his plate. He had heard rumors of a revolt against the "ice-water banquet." He walked over to the man, whom he knew well, and bent over his shoulder.

"If you don't put the flask away, Mr.——," he said quietly but firmly, "I shall have to ask you to leave the banquet."

The man nodded, closed his flask, and put it away. No other flasks were seen during the evening.

Prohibition was nine years away yet, but the precedent for "ice-water banquets" was established in Dallas with the Taft dinner . . . another mark in the Dealey image impressed on the city.

For days the planet Venus had been visible in the daytime, but oddly, in Dallas it went virtually unnoticed until suddenly at about 3 o'clock in the afternoon on December 31 a mass enthusiasm swept the city, and by the thousands people stood in their yards and in the streets pointing and craning their necks and gazing toward the southwest at the pale white star high in the sky. A good sign for 1910, many said.

Dealey had never seen such a lively, contagious spirit in the people. The time was ripe to open the big push for the city plan. He intended to have the editorial council discuss the campaign at its Monday afternoon meeting on January 17, but just before noon that day Arthur Geen dropped dead at his desk, and that took the heart out of the staff. Mr. Geen was the bookkeeper, and one of the 1885-ers. Only seven of the men who were present at the start of the Dallas *Morning News* were left now. Dealey had a special liking for Mr. Geen, because like himself, Geen had immigrated to America from England when he was a boy. They had understood one another perfectly, and each had the interests of the *News* uppermost in his heart. "One by one," noted the editorial tribute to Geen, "the worthy exemplars of the old-time devotion and fidelity to duty are passing away and the kind man who just passed belonged to this class."

On January 24 the discussion of the city-plan drive was held at the editorial council meeting, with Finty, Sterett, Hooper, McMurray, Toomey, Doran, Clark, Lombardi, and Dealey participating. Each of them contributed ideas, and certain phases of the campaign were outlined in detail. Beginning the next day, Finty should start a series of comprehensive articles, recapitulating all that had been said before at various times which was pertinent to a city plan for Dallas. The articles should emphasize that a city plan would enhance all forms of civic improvement. Clark and Sterett should prepare a series of editorials to accompany the articles. To follow up Finty's series, the *News* would reprint each day for about three weeks one complete article from either *The American City,* or *Town Development,* or from a special issue of *The Survey* devoted to city planning. Dealey instructed K. K. Hooper to gather together all the literature he could find on city planning and to keep up with it. He should become the staff's city-plan expert. Toomey and Doran would handle the news aspects as the campaign developed.

The Chamber of Commerce was asked to assume the public leadership, and a committee was appointed to report on "the procedure for getting into action." Called the "Committee of Five," it included Rhodes S. Baker, Alex Sanger, J. B. Wilson, Henry D. Lindsley, and Dealey. The choice of men couldn't be better, Dealey felt. Each man was his close friend, and committee work was his strength.

The Committee of Five was ready to report the next day. For "getting into action"—(1) stage a public lecture by a national authority on city planning; (2) appoint a Plenary Committee, embracing all interests and organizations concerned with city planning; and (3) hire competent engineers to draft the city plan. The procedure seemed simple, but its execution would require months of work.

City-plan publicity in the *News* issued forth at the rate of three and four columns a day, and on some days more than a page. All angles were developed. A high school essay contest was started, cartoons printed, and leading citizens quoted by the scores. The pastor of the East Dallas Christian Church delivered a sermon on city planning, taking his text from Revelations 21:2, which told of John's vision of the holy city. The *News* carried the sermon in full, and other preachers were quick to follow suit with sermons in similar vein.

On February 9, a three-column picture of an attractive downtown scene in Buffalo, New York, was run on an inside page under the caption of "An Example of Civic Attractiveness." Dealey had collected a two months' supply of pictures showing all types of civic attractiveness—residences, parks, public buildings, bridges, etc.—and he instructed the managing editor to run one each day and to get new pictures as long as they were having good effect. The series became legendary. It was continued daily under the same caption until June 4, 1918, a run of eight years, three months, and 26 days. No other newspaper ever presented in picture display as thorough a survey of the city beautification to be found in the United States and foreign countries.

The national authority on city planning invited to make the public lecture in Dallas was J. Horace McFarland, national president of the American Civic Association and widely known for his pamphlet, *The Awakening of Harrisburg.*

McFarland was a wiry little man. His large walrus mustache, extra-high stiff collar, long-tailed coat, and Yankee accent added measurably to the authoritativeness of his remarks. But above all, his stereopticon impressed the audience. When he flashed a series of Dallas scenes on the screen, there were exclamations and much twitter in the auditorium.

"I wish I could say these scenes are tolerable," he said, "but they are not. If Dallas hopes to be a big city, you must get rid of such conditions." Showing a picture of the Elks Arch on Main Street, which had been there since the Elks national convention in 1908, he exclaimed imperatively, "That arch will have to go!"

"No!" someone in the audience protested, in a half-suppressed voice, and everyone laughed heartily.

After the lecture was over the meeting went into a business session, and the president of the Chamber of Commerce named 38 men to the Plenary Committee on City Planning. This action carried out the Committee of Five's second and third recommendations, and this night's work closed the first phase of the campaign.

The next phase would be to induce the city council to hire competent engineers to prepare the city plan. In view of the public pressure which had been built up, the city council was easily persuaded to vote the funds necessary, and immediately Dealey wrote to George E. Kessler, urging him to come to Dallas as soon as possible. Kessler had a national reputation for city planning, and Dealey had known him since his work on the State Fair of Texas in 1904.

"The feeling is right," he wrote to him, "and you are the man for the job."

For more than two months Kessler was delayed, and it taxed Dealey's resourcefulness to maintain the high pitch of interest in city planning. To make it more difficult, there seemed to be a flood of exciting news: The daring aviator, Steve Brodie, brought his flying machine to Dallas and used the State Fair grounds for a landing field, until he crashed there. . . . In March, while a Negro was being tried in a Dallas courtroom for rape, a mob tied a rope around the Negro's neck, yanked him through the second-story window, dragged him to the corner of Main and Akard, and hanged him to the Elks Arch. . . . Preparations for the 1910 Glidden Tour—Cincinnati to Dallas to Chicago—absorbed automobile enthusiasts. . . . John D. Rockefeller made the nation gasp by establishing a 500,000,000-dollar trust fund for worthy public causes. . . . About the middle of May, Halley's Comet appeared, sweeping its tail of glowing gases alarmingly close to the earth.

But not for a single issue did the exciting news push city-plan publicity out of the columns of the *News*.

Kessler arrived in Dallas on May 21. He was a round-faced, heavy-set man of German descent. His manner was pleasing and polished, and he was utterly sincere in everything he said. Before meeting with the city council, he requested three days to tour and inspect the city. With this background, he said, his recommendations would be more definite, and, he hoped, more convincing. A touring car, chauffeur, and change of hosts for each morning and afternoon were provided. In the selection of the hosts, Dealey took a hand and made certain that each member of the city council and the Park Board had a chance to get personally acquainted with the eminent city-plan engineer. Kessler was his man, and he intended to see that he got the job.

After the city council's first conference with Kessler, on May 24, it was decided to hold another meeting before taking action. Dealey had private assurances that Kessler's hiring was a foregone conclusion, but he kept thinking that some insurmountable obstacle would pop up the next day. But none did, and on May 26 the *News* headlined the triumph on the front page, a position seldom rated by local news in that era:

KESSLER CHOSEN
TO PREPARE
CITY PLAN

Dealey felt prouder of this accomplishment than any other he could recall. A city plan for Dallas was at last in sight. He pledged Kessler every cooperation that the *News* could offer, and as soon as the plan was ready, the *News* would publish it complete with maps in daily installments.

On the day Kessler was to depart for his home in Kansas City, Dealey wanted to see him off at the depot, and he was anxious to have his sons meet him before he left town. Ted was at an impressionable age, having just been graduated from the Terrill School for Boys, and he was going through the uncertain process of picking a college to attend and deciding on a career to follow. Walter had just arrived back home from his second year at the University of Texas in Austin.

An hour before train time, Dealey drove the big four-door Cadillac, recently purchased second hand, by their house on Maple Avenue to pick up the boys. On the way to town, Walter, who was in the front seat, noticed that his father was using the hand feed altogether and avoiding putting his foot on the new-type foot accelerator. Giving Ted a wink, Walter slipped his foot unnoticed on to the foot accelerator. As his father slowed down for a cross street, Walter pushed down on the gas. The car speeded up and shot across the intersection.

"Hey, something's gone wrong!" Dealey shouted. "Something's gone wrong!"

He yanked the hand feed up, but the car raced ahead. Desperately he turned off the ignition key and struggled with both the foot and hand brakes.

By the time the car stopped, Walter and Ted were laughing so hard they rolled in the seats. Getting the car started once more, Dealey drove on slowly and warily to the appointment at the train station. He was still proud to introduce his two sons to Mr. Kessler, but the incident sort of took the edge off.

In October the City Plan for Dallas was about half finished, and Kessler met with the city council and the City Plan League to get approval on certain vitally important recommendations before completing the project. He read his report to the group, and, nearing the end, he stopped and looked up.

"Now I come to what I regard as the most important recommendation of all," he said, "namely, the establishment of a belt railway around the city of Dallas, a union depot, joint freight yards, and following this, the absolute elimination of railway tracks on Pacific Avenue."

The idea of a union depot and joint freight yards was no surprise, having been talked of before in Dallas, and the proposal of a belt railway around the city was plausible enough, but the gentlemen were thunderstruck at the thought of removing the tracks from Pacific Avenue. The tracks had been there since 1873, and they were largely responsible for the very location of the business district. The many spurs and rail sidings from the T. & P. tracks to wholesale houses and factories along Pacific Avenue were as old as most of the men present.

There was an exchange of glances, and remarks were passed.

"It can't do any harm," someone spoke up. "Go ahead and put it in the report."

Immediately following the meeting, a reporter asked Kessler how he meant to force the railroads to abandon the tracks on Pacific Avenue.

"I don't mean to force the removal of their tracks," Kessler said, "but instead to offer the railroads a substitute so attractive they can't resist it."

This remark, Dealey felt, typified both the strength and the weakness of Kessler. The plans he conceived were so attractive and so promising in every way to a city that they were almost irresistible. But plans never sold themselves. Progress never came easily. It wasn't human nature. No matter how good the plans, you still had to worry and work and plead and coax and stir up people to get progress. This was a hard piece of reality, and he put the thought into a paper which he was preparing to read before the American Civic Association at its convention in Washington, D.C., in December.

"The Kessler plan will be the beginning of the real crusade," he wrote. "The working out of the ideal must be realized day by day, month by month, year by year."

Before the end of the year Kessler submitted partial plans for solving the railroad problems of Dallas, and the *News* publicized them, but it was a Dallas wholesale shipper, Albert F. Foute, who sparked the frontal attack on the railroad problem.

Visiting Dealey at his office early in December, Foute told him how distressing local freight service had become.

"Why, I've known a car of canned goods to stay in the yards three weeks while the railroad argued about it," he said, "and shipments out of St. Louis get to many places in Texas before ours do."

Dealey began to see how to put over a campaign to get the joint freight yards and a union depot. Could Foute get a group of shippers together and provide factual stories which would describe the chaos? Dealey put K. K. Hooper to work exclusively on the assignment. Stay with the job, he told him, until the railroads do something along the lines of Kessler's plan.

On Christmas Day the big guns of the *News* opened up on the railroad problem. Would people read a long four-column article such as this on Christmas Day? The *News* believed they would. It was the one day in the year when even the busiest man sat around the house wondering what to do with himself.

The campaign followed the old tried-and-proven formula: First, a series of comprehensive articles. Accompany these with pictures and maps showing what other cities have done. Fire a round of editorials. Print columns and columns of quotes from leading businessmen. Climax the movement with a mass citizens' meeting.

On the morning of February 8 there were more private railroad cars parked on sidings in Dallas than had ever been there before at one time. Some of the railroads sent two and three high executives for the conference with the shippers and city officials of Dallas.

At Dealey's insistence, Kessler arrived from Kansas City that same morning in time to be a "surprise" speaker at the opening session. This was his chance to convince the railroads that his plan offered "a substitute so attractive they can't resist it."

Following this meeting, the railway and local groups held separate meetings to choose representatives for further negotiations that afternoon. On Dealey's nomination, Alex Sanger, A. P. Foute, Louis Lipsitz, and Royal A. Ferris were chosen to represent the local group, and they were dubbed "the biggest little committee in the history of Dallas." Each man was small in stature, but the results they accomplished were big.

"A union passenger station will be erected as soon as possible," the spokesman for the railroads announced at the end of the day. The agreement included joint freight terminal facilities too.

Again, however, it was a case of "only the beginning." Three years would pass before the railroads completed their plans, estimates, and compromises. The "biggest little committee" would meet 263 times to carry out its work. The construction of the freight yards and union depot would take another three years. It would be October of 1916 before the project was completed. But on February 8, 1911, the test case had succeeded. The City Plan for Dallas could be "sold."

CHAPTER SEVENTEEN

1911-1913

**PROGRESSIVENESS ON THE MARCH. A
BUILDING FOR THE FUTURE. "HAIL TO
SOUTHERN METHODIST UNIVERSITY."**

There was a young man from the country, who, on perceiving
for the first time an arc light in the city street, exclaimed: "Whare
is the oil in that thare thing?" But he is no more to be pitied than
the city youth who, visiting in the country and observing honey on
the breakfast table, remarked: "Oh, I see you keep a bee."

DEALEY WAS MAKING SPEECHES, AND THIS STORY ABOUT THE
country boy and the city boy set his audiences chuckling. But his
humor had a point. City people should look on farmers as their
equal. "Let's get rid of superciliousness," he reproved. With unusual ardor, he was championing the cause of the farming class
in the spring of 1911. It was not a new interest, but a new em-
phasis. It was in part a response to DeWitt McMurray's good
editorship of *The Semi-Weekly Farm News.* McMurray was adding something new to the *News'* long-standing espousal of diversified farming. *Intensification* was the new way. Dealey encouraged
McMurray in the program and backed it up with cash prizes for
the best farmer-written articles on intensification. But there was
something the farmer needed more than diversification or intensification, Dealey believed. The farmer deserved a better "shake,"
a better way of life. There was too great a disparity between the
good life in the city and the hard, underpaid life on the farm.

At McMurray's urging, Dealey was moved to write a paper on the "square deal" for the farmer. He entitled it "Social Relations of Rural and Urban People," and the *News* ran it over his by-line, one of the few he ever got into his own newspaper.[1]

The "square deal" was simply being considerate of one another and mutually helpful. It was the law of compensation. Dealey often spoke of the "inevitable law of compensation." By his interpretation it was a combination of Christ's Golden Rule and the proverb about casting bread upon the waters.

"The dense population of the city," he said, "creates a concentration of wealth, power, and influence, and these, in turn place a serious responsibility on those having this power and influence to see that equal opportunities for advancement are accorded their rural cousins."

In Texas the concentration of wealth and power to the city had taken place after Dealey had settled in the state. When he arrived in 1870, Galveston, with its 14,000 citizens, was the largest Texas city by far, and Dallas had scarcely more than 2000. Since then he had watched the great migration . . . by railroad and wagon train from the states to the East . . . by boat from Southern and Central Europe. He saw the people spread from the Gulf to the Red River and speed the breaking up of the plantation and the fencing in of the range land. The state's population surged to almost 4,000,000, and the cities grew like mushrooms, several claiming 100,000 people. Wealth and power gravitated to the cities, leaving the farming class crying for attention.

Dealey urged certain practical aids that cities should provide the farmer: (1) Build "Farmer's Headquarters," centrally located, which the farmer and his family could make their resort . . . provided with washing and toilet facilities, reading and writing rooms, stationery, etc., all free of charge. (2) Provide aids to marketing of the farm products so that the farmer would get a larger share of the profits. (3) Build good farm-to-market roads. (4) Above all, improve their educational facilities.

Progressiveness was in the ascendancy in the United States. In government it was personified in Woodrow Wilson; in industry, Henry Ford; in a state, Wisconsin. Dealey sent Tom

Finty, Jr., to Wisconsin to study the remarkable system of cooperation there between the state legislature and state university in
working out progressive legislation. He hoped Finty's report
would lead Texas to follow a similar path to greater things. He
had the *News* carry several chapters of the new book on reform
in state governments by his brother, James Q. Dealey, who now
ranked as professor of political and social science at Brown University. He hired a new writer on the *News* and sent him on a
trip around the state studying housing conditions. The writer was
George Waverley Briggs and he was to become Dealey's lifelong
friend and confidant. In charging Briggs with his first assignment,
Dealey told him he believed poor housing was more to blame for
social strife, disease, and crime than any other single cause. Take
three months on the study and search for ways to a solution.
Texas is a young state yet. Perhaps there are ways for our cities
to avoid the slum conditions of New York, Philadelphia, and
other large Eastern cities. From November 19 to December 17,
1911, the *News* carried an article a day on "The Housing Problem in Texas," and then compiled the series into a booklet and
distributed it widely.

There were times when Dealey got a perspective on his job that
made him humble at the thought of attempting it. No man could
be all the things a newspaper publisher should be. How could anyone maintain a scholar's alertness to all the progress in human
affairs and give leadership in all the important social and civic
movements? But that was only part of the job. At the same time
he must cope with the unending problems of a newspaper as a
manufacturing plant. In 1911 the burden was very heavy. While
working with the editors on reforms in agriculture, state government, city planning, and housing, he was equally engrossed in the
problems of a new type dress, a new press, and building expansion.
These "factory" problems were never simple. The dilemma in
1911 was whether to get the new press first or enlarge the building. Logically, expansion should come first, but with circulation
up to 45,000 daily and 70,000 Sunday, the demands on the old
press had reached the breaking point. The final decision was up
to Dealey, and he decided for the press.

It arrived in the fall—a three-deck sextuple Hoe with color attachment, capable of printing 72,000 twelve-page papers in an hour. To a newspaperman it was a beauty. Dealey and Tom Rinehart, the pressroom foreman who had run off the first issue of the Dallas *Morning News* on the little Bullock press in 1885, watched the trial runs of the big Hoe with much satisfaction. The roaring noise made a kind of music to them. During most of their lives the clatter of the flatbeds and the whirr and rumble of the heavy rotaries had meant "all is well." They liked the clean smell of fresh newsprint and the nose-clinging lampblack smell of the pressroom.

In the plant expansion plans there was one big all-important "if." Would "the two ladies" approve the cost of a new building? Mrs. Nettie E. Belo was still president of the company and majority stockholder. The approval also of Mrs. Jeannette Belo Peabody must be forthcoming, as Mrs. Belo was deferring more and more to her daughter in major business decisions. Neither Dealey nor Mr. Lombardi relished the thought of proposing a new building and suggesting a cut in the quarterly dividends to finance it. The details of plant expansion—costs . . . future profits . . . keeping abreast of progress . . . preparing for a great future— these were difficult to explain to someone not concerned with the daily operations, particularly women.

In March Mr. Lombardi made a special trip East to lay the case for the new building before the ladies. En route back he wrote Dealey from Washington: "I got Mrs. P.'s consent to all our plans and suggestions, as I wired you (except for the brick) but not without considerable persuasion. She preferred to have us borrow the money . . . but finally agreed to cut dividends."

During the next few months Mr. Lombardi's persuasion had to be employed several times to allay the ladies' fears regarding their financial sacrifices. On June 28 he wrote Dealey from his summer home in Berkeley, California:

> It would seem that the picture of the [future] new building in the edition of May 21 has frightened Mrs. Belo by its magnificence. . . . I have received . . . letters from the folks in Italy which indicate

that they are growing very nervous about the extent of the building and improvements we are making. . . . They do not wish to buy any more stock. . . . Now this reflects Mrs. Belo's attitude who is always very conservative. . . . Mrs. Peabody however says she will stand by me in all I presented to her on my trip to Cambridge.

Dealey replied to Mr. Lombardi:

. . . We realize, of course, that before we get through we will be spending a good deal of money, but yet it will not be throwing it into the gutter by any means; it will be strictly assets. . . . The building we are going to put up will, in my opinion, last us for fifty years. We are certainly building for the future. . . . As you know, the experience of almost every concern in Dallas is that they did not have vision enough, and therefore, their buildings have soon proved inadequate. That was the case with us. . . . But now we are building in quite a different manner.

At the end of July, Dealey was able to write Mr. Lombardi that construction on the new building would begin within three weeks. Most of the letter, however, was devoted to describing the election reporting bureau which "the makers of the *News*" had perfected.

"The *News* yesterday morning," he wrote, "accounted for more votes than has ever before been reported by any newspaper on a Texas election on the morning following." Finty and Toomey were due much of the credit for organizing the far-flung communication system that reached out to practically every county in the state. It captured the public fancy, but it had brought some headaches. Beginning early Sunday morning the telephones at the *News* were so swamped with long-distance calls from people wanting "inside information" that no one at the office could make an outside call. Sunday night the editors were disturbed at their homes at all hours and got hardly any sleep.

Late in August the excavation for the basement of the new building got started. Dealey held a conference with the contractors to make sure they were taking precautions against any possible cave-in or collapse of the present *News* building, which was alongside. A near-tragedy had occurred when the basement of the present building was dug in 1900. At that time the original

News building had collapsed. All that remained standing was the north wall; there was a clock on the wall that continued to tick away and keep good time. It happened on a Sunday morning, and Charles M. Seay was the only man in the building. He jumped to safety just as the floor was giving way. Bill Sterett always said it was lucky the man was Seay, because he was the most religious man in the organization, and the Lord took care of him.

The new building incorporated the most modern ideas in newspaper plant construction. It housed nothing but the mechanical departments, and was completely cut off from the old building, where the news-editorial and business departments remained. In this manner the noise and vibration of the presses were confined, a plan which Dealey and Architect Greene had discovered in the Kansas City *Star* building when they were touring newspaper plants in the spring of 1912.

The old Grand Windsor Hotel had once stood where the new building was located. The press room was approximately where the dining room had been, and Dealey enjoyed telling that in 1883 he had slept in a room on the fourth floor of the Grand Windsor, which was about in the same spot where the new job printing room was now.

Elsewhere in Dallas there was another building project in which Dealey had a special interest. This was Dallas Hall, the first of the buildings for Southern Methodist University. Since February, 1911, when the Methodist Conference approved a university for Dallas, the *News* had given every support in raising the 300,000-dollar building endowment. Although free cash was hard for him to find at this time, Dealey pledged 500 dollars of his personal funds. The cornerstone ceremony was set for November 28, 1912. The campus was six miles from downtown Dallas, but a special train and a caravan of automobiles brought a crowd estimated at several thousand. The elite of Dallas was present.

From the speakers' stand, it looked like a field of black derbies, colored here and there by a wide, round-brimmed lady's hat. There were five speakers ahead of Dealey, and he wondered if the crowd would still be listening by the time he spoke. But it could have been worse—there were six more speakers to follow him. At length, President Robert S. Hyer was saying complimentary things about the Dallas *Morning News* . . . "rendering signal service in crystallizing the sentiment of the people to support the establishment of this university."

It was his turn. For a moment he wished he could throw away his notes and express the expansive feelings teeming in his head . . . about the wonderful progress sweeping ahead in America . . . this university in Dallas was a tiny part of the great progressive movement . . . the decade ahead would be history's greatest. But it would take a William Jennings Bryan to put his feelings into words. He did not dare attempt it. Instead, he stuck to the remarks he had prepared and practiced.

"I trust the conductors of this university," he said, "believe that education is not so much the communication of knowledge as the establishment of principles and the regulation of the heart . . . Hoping that its achievements may equal its possibilities, I say, Hail to Southern Methodist University."

CHAPTER EIGHTEEN

1913-1915

THE DALLAS *JOURNAL* IS STARTED.
DEALEY HELPS GET THE FEDERAL RE-
SERVE BANK FOR DALLAS. A VISIT WITH
TED AT HARVARD. SUDDENLY GRAND-
PARENTS. THE WORLD BURSTS INTO
WAR.

"THE THERMOMETER HERE," J. J. TAYLOR WROTE IN THE "STATE
Press" column of the *News* the last week of August, 1913,
"climbed a yard or two above the nail on which it hangs and did
trapeze stunts on the sunbeams, but the weather has not been to
say real hot . . . not what would be called extremely warm."
Dealey worked to catch up on correspondence so he could "duck
out," as he put it, for a little relief, from his hay fever as well as
the heat. He turned out letters by the dozens.

A letter to Alex Sanger, chairman of the Shippers Union Station Committee: I have been unofficially informed that there is
some kind of project being considered for the closing of practically all of the streets west of Houston Street to the river, in
consequence of the Union Station Development. . . . I shall oppose very strenuously anything that prevents proper and convenient ingress and egress now and in the future from Commerce,
Main, and Elm Streets to the western environs of Dallas. . . . In
the years to come there is going to be a wonderful development of
industries west of the river. . . .

A letter to The Roycrofters, East Aurora, New York: On June 27, 1904, I remitted to you the sum of $100, accepting your proposition addressed to Life Members of the American Academy of Immortals Only. . . . Now it occurs to me that my name must have been left off of this list of "Immortals," because it doesn't seem to me that I have received the books you promised . . . none the last seven years. . . .

A letter to M. N. Baker, vice-president of the Dallas Park Board: Please note the enclosed clipping from the *News* of yesterday. This is the Woodchuck Hollow matter I have written to you about, beginning about three years ago, and about which we have had conferences since. I hope you will write a personal letter to Mayor Holland . . . urging consummation of this very desirable movement to make a park of the Cole estate. . . . (Copies to all members of the Park Board.)

To Mrs. Jeannette B. Peabody: Thank you for the kind words about the new building . . . the future will prove the wisdom of our investment, as I told you at your mother's funeral in Winston-Salem. . . . With Mr. Lombardi as the new President . . . the *News* will move steadily forward. . . . Thank you for the new hay fever remedy . . .

To C. Lombardi, Berkeley, California: The Prohibitionists are at it again, trying to start a newspaper in Dallas and steal Finty away as editor . . .

To J. D. Lorentz, New York: Your consoling thoughts upon my Mother's death are appreciated . . .

To Mr. George E. Kessler, Kansas City: There is going to be a real effort to get the Union Station located about the spot indicated on the enclosed map of Dallas . . . Of course the change will involve the carrying out, in general, of all your recommendations, such as, the removal of the river and raising and developing the lands now called the "bottoms." . . .

By the end of the week the work was shored up, the tailor had finished his new suit, the dentist had filled the cavity in his left molar, the circulation department had been instructed where to send his copy of the *News* for the next three weeks, and he was ready to duck out.

On Monday the vacationers—Dealey, Ollie, and Maidie—were chauffeured to the train station by Walter in the family Cadillac. Walter was remaining in Dallas, and Dealey experienced that peculiar pride that a father feels the first time he goes off and leaves his business in charge of his son. Of course no large responsibilities were actually left in Walter's charge, but it made a year now that Walter had worked at the *News,* and under the tutelage of kind Mr. Benners, the business manager whom Dealey had schooled in the ways of newspaper-making, Walter was already handling the load of an experienced man. Dealey was extremely proud of both his sons. Ted was finishing his bachelor's degree at the University of Texas this year and would do graduate study at Harvard the next year.

While away from the demanding details of the daily operation, he tried to get a broad view of the year past and a sight on the year ahead. He had been thinking of an afternoon newspaper. Only one paper a day out of a newspaper plant left the machinery and the building idle a large part of each day. He felt Dallas needed a more aggressive afternoon paper, and if the *News* did not fill the need, it was an invitation to some outsider. Also, the "bulldog editions" of the morning papers out of Fort Worth and Houston were hurting the *News'* state circulation. They were predating papers, as early as 5:00 P.M., and catching the early evening trains. An afternoon paper was the answer to their tactics. Advertising revenue also was a big factor in the picture.

By the time the vacation was over, the decisions were clear. They would start the afternoon paper as soon as possible, and call it the *Journal.* There were many wheels to set in motion . . . equipment to buy, paper contracts to make, advertising rates to set, a complete organization to staff, union contracts to negotiate, new work schedules for the day shift and the night shift . . . no end to details.

On March 29, two days before the first issue of the *Journal* was to appear, the typographical union voted to strike. Dealey appealed to the International Typographical Union headquarters in Indianapolis, Indiana, explaining the main grievance. The typographical force for the *Journal* was largely made up of men who had worked for the *News* on a night wage scale, and they were striking against the lower day scale. The union headquarters wired the local union representative to call off the strike. But the local man pocketed the telegram without telling anyone about it.

On Wednesday morning, April 1, it looked like no paper that day. But as the "eleventh hour" approached, the local representative lost his courage and told the force to go ahead with the work.

The tension subsided, and Dealey eased up a bit with the remark that in one respect the newspaper business never changed— "It is always one damned thing after another." It was 3:10 P.M. when Mayor W. M. Holland pulled the lever and the presses started to roll. The big sign overhead in the pressroom read: "The Baby Is Born. It's a Real Man."

For its first issue the *Journal* almost got the perfect beat, but not quite, missing it by one day. They had the big news but could not break it. The story began its development three months earlier immediately upon passage of the Federal Reserve Bank Act on Christmas Eve, 1913. On Christmas morning the *News* summed up the case for Dallas as the logical site for the regional bank which was to be established in the Southwest.

Each large city in the nation began using every resource and political entree it commanded to get a regional bank. On February 14 Dealey got a helpful tip from Otto Praeger, a former correspondent of the *News* who had just recently been appointed Postmaster of Washington, D.C. Postmaster General A. S. Burleson was coming to Texas. The postmaster general was the man with the influence to swing the case for Dallas. Immediately Dealey arranged for J. Howard Ardrey, spokesman for the Dallas interests seeking the bank, and Tom Finty of the *News* to meet Burleson in St. Louis.

Ardrey and Finty were to ride back on the train with the postmaster general, making the most of the opportunity. So that they could communicate between Dallas, Washington, and St. Louis without giving away secrets, Dealey devised a telegraphic code— President Wilson was *Allah,* Burleson was *Mercury,* Colonel House was *Tacitus,* Secretary of the Treasury McAdoo was

Croesus, Dallas was *Delightful,* Houston was *Handicap,* Fort Worth was *Floral,* and so on.

Ardrey related the happenings in St. Louis in an account given many years later:

> An amusing but almost fatal slip-up nearly occurred in St. Louis. Tom Finty and I had to change hotels, and left word to have messages forwarded. During the day we received a message from Otto Praeger in Washington, saying Burleson was leaving for St. Louis. By the date on the message, we knew Burleson could not arrive in St. Louis until the next day. We planned to spend the evening going to the theater. Finty, though, for some reason went down to the Union Station and happened to be there when the Baltimore & Ohio from Washington arrived. He was much surprised to run into the Postmaster General on the platform. He at once rushed to the phone and told me to grab the bags and get to the station in time to accompany Mr. Burleson to Texas. This I did. We later learned the reason for our miscalculation in Mr. Burleson's arrival. In forwarding the message to our second hotel, the first hotel moved the date up one day. On the Pullman, Mr. Burleson modestly enough was riding in a lower berth, but Tom and I engaged a drawing room where we could talk in greater privacy. There I gave Mr. Burleson the story I had given to Col. House, McAdoo, and Houston [Secretary of Agriculture, a member of the committee to select the banks]. When the train conference broke up, I am convinced we had sold him on the idea." *

Back in Dallas, Ardrey, Dealey, and Finty continued working all possible angles. The rivalry from Houston and Fort Worth varied from hot to cold, and Colonel House was suspected of helping Houston because of a brother he had in the banking business there. On March 24, Praeger wired Dealey from Washington:

> DELIGHTFUL IN NO DANGER OF FLORAL BUT HANDICAP
> THREATENING. WIRE MERCURY DATA SHOWING DELIGHTFUL
> MORE DESIRABLE THAN HANDICAP. THINK TACITUS MAKING
> TROUBLE BUT MERCURY IS DEPENDING ON ALLAH.

---

* In a letter to G. B. Dealey dated June 30, 1932, Mr. Ardrey stated: "Looking at the matter in retrospect, I consider the most decisive incident of the whole effort was the opportunity afforded by the . . . long and uninterrupted interview with the Hon. A. S. Burleson . . ."

Late the night of March 31, Praeger wired Dealey:

THIS IS THE LINE-UP: SAN FRANCISCO, ST. PAUL, KANSAS CITY, ST.
LOUIS, CHICAGO, CINCINNATI, DALLAS, ATLANTA, RICHMOND,
PHILADELPHIA, NEW YORK, BOSTON. DON'T CHIRP UNTIL YOU
GET THE SIGNAL.

Dallas had won! Those in the know at the *News* building were
jubilant, but they could not "chirp till they got the signal." The
Journal would put out its first issue the next afternoon. They
hoped for a break on the story all the next morning. The waiting
was excruciating. But the signal did not come until the next day—
just in time to catch the last make-over of the *Journal's* front page
on its second day of publication.

The bank remained one of Dealey's interests, and he continued
to work at helping the Federal Reserve System get established. In
June he was in Washington, D.C., en route elsewhere, and called
on his friend Cato Sells, the Commissioner of Indian Affairs. Mr.
Sells suggested they go visit President Wilson, but Dealey said he
had nothing to see the president about. Sells said the president was
not unaware of the stanch support the *News* had given him for
several years, and he felt the president would like to meet the man
who was most responsible for it. As they arrived at the White
House, a cabinet meeting was breaking up and Dealey met several
of the cabinet members, and was then ushered in to meet the
president. Dealey congratulated the president on the success of his
efforts for the Federal Reserve Banking System and offered the
opinion that in order for the regional bank in Dallas to succeed
from the start, a man with prestige in banking circles should be
appointed as the first Federal Reserve Agent. President Wilson
said the suggestion was an excellent one and that he would not
forget it. No names were mentioned, but later E. O. Tenison, a
competent and respected banker of Dallas, was named the Federal
Reserve Agent, and W. F. McCaleb, a banking expert, was named
Deputy Federal Reserve Agent.

After leaving Washington, Dealey went on to Providence,
Rhode Island, to visit with James Q. at Brown University, and to

make plans with him for their trip to Europe that fall. He was
looking forward especially to visiting England. It would be 44
years since they had left there. Ollie and Maidie and Ted would
go along too.

The last stop on his trip East was Cambridge, Massachusetts,
where he had business about the paper to discuss with Mrs. Peabody, and where also he would visit with Ted, who was attending
Harvard. The first evening he and Ted went together to call on
the Peabodys. Ted had been to dinner at the Peabodys' house before, and he told his father that unlike people in Texas, Dr. and
Mrs. Peabody both dressed formally for dinner every evening.
Dealey tried to picture in his mind what Dr. Peabody would look
like, because, oddly, in all the years since Jeannette Belo had married the Harvard professor, they had never met. At the Peabodys'
house the door was opened by an extremely dignified man dressed
in what appeared to Dealey to be formal evening clothes. He
grasped the man's hand and shook it vigorously.

"Dr. Peabody, I have looked forward to meeting you for many
years," he said enthusiastically. "This is a real pleasure."

"But, sir," was the restrained reply, "I am the butler."

It was a disquieting beginning for the evening. On the way back
to the hotel, in return for a promise not to tell about the hand-
shaking with the butler, Ted got an okay on the "100-dollar over-
coat with the fur collar" that he had been refused previously.

Nothing can be more lifeless than a hot, cloudless July Sunday
in Texas. After midmorning even the birds take cover, and only
the locusts with their incessant drone seem to thrive. Sunday,
July 26, 1914, was just such a day in Dallas, but election returns
from the Democratic primary kept things interesting. "Farmer
Jim" Ferguson, the Bell County banker, appeared to be the
people's choice for governor of Texas. There was not much else
in the news. Austria was still sending diplomatic notes to Servia
demanding punishment of the culprits responsible for the assassi-
nation of Archduke Ferdinand at Sarajevo.

Before getting away to church, Dealey inspected the maple trees
in front of the house and told Boswell, the handy man and

chauffeur, to whitewash the trunks on Monday. The trees had surely grown since they planted them. The trunks were a foot or more in diameter. How could they grow so fast? Was it fast? Since they were planted, the children had grown up, three were married and had their own homes, and two had babies. Life was like that—suddenly you were grandparents. That afternoon Walter and his wife were coming over, and later that evening they expected a visit from Annie and her husband, Dr. Rice R. Jackson, with their small son, Henry Allen. Fannie and her husband, Dr. Henry B. Decherd, usually dropped in on Sunday. Fannie's daughter, Ruth, was the newest grandbaby. It would be a regular family reunion because Ted and Maidie both were home from college on vacation.

That same hot July Sunday, several thousand miles away in Vienna, C. Lombardi, on a tour of Europe with his wife and relatives, wrote a letter:

> Hotel de France
> Wien I. Schoffenring 3
> July 26, 1914

Dear Mr. Dealey:

I had noticed myself that the London Times had become a narrow partisan newspaper, like all of Lord Northcliffe's publications. This reminds me that the press is much more partisan, and bitterly partisan, in England, France, and Italy than now in America. Our best papers in America are broader, more tolerant, and more enterprising than most of the leading European papers.

. . . . This is one of the finest cities I have seen . . . An incredible amount of space is devoted to parks, gardens and boulevards and playgrounds. Even the electric lampposts are surrounded with fresh flowers in iron baskets at about half their height. It would do your heart good, you who are so enthusiastic about civic beauty and civic attractiveness, to see this city, and I hope you will visit it when you take your European trip . . .

Just at present we are witnessing exciting times here, Austria and Servia being on the verge of war. By the time you get this it will have been decided whether it is to be or not to be . . . On the announcement last evening that Servia had rejected Austria's terms, a great popular manifestation spread over the streets, squares, and boulevards singing patriotic songs. It was kept up so late we could not sleep till after one o'clock.

Cordially,
C. Lombardi

That was July 26, 1914 . . . a peaceful day in most of the world. One week later practically the whole of Europe was raging at war . . . not just Servia and Austria but Germany and the Austro-Hungarian Empire against Russia, France, Belgium, and England. The shock was complete. The swiftness with which it came was incredible. One week before, the threat of a general war was hardly a topic of conversation in America. Then, suddenly, war was a horrifying reality. German soldiers were already marching through Belgium and France.

One thing was certain—no trip to Europe for the Dealeys until it was over. He had no real fear that America would get involved in the fighting, but a long European war could mean disaster to American business. Cotton prices had already plummeted. The whole thing was going to hit advertising hard. He hoped the Lombardis were all right. No word from them since the fighting began.*

Business grew worse quickly, and Mrs. Peabody expressed alarm at the dwindling profits.

"With such a magnificent plant," she wrote on November 24, "the whole cost of production is necessarily much greater than ever before in the history of the business . . . but I trust you will cut down the force and salaries and all unnecessary expenses as much as possible. . . ."

Had the *News* expanded at the wrong time? Dealey pondered the question, but he got reassurance when he looked at the picture of David Crockett hanging on the wall of his office. Years ago he had put Crockett's picture in every office in the building, to remind

---

* The Lombardis managed to get to Switzerland a few hours before the borders were closed, and from there to America.

every employee of his famous motto, "Be sure you're right, then
go ahead."

That was the best any man could do. Sometimes it turned out
you were wrong. But in the long run you came out ahead. He
remembered distinctly that Governor O. M. Roberts had said
Texas newspapermen had Crockett's "goaheaditiveness." He remembered it because the governor had said it to the Missouri
Press Association delegation in 1882 when they were touring
Texas, and that was when he met Ollie.

CHAPTER NINETEEN

1915-1918

JOURNALISM WEEK AT THE UNIVERSITY
OF MISSOURI. THE *NEWS* DEVELOPS A
STYLE BOOK. A CLASH WITH JIM FERGU-
SON. THE UNION STATION DEDICATED.
THE UNITED STATES DECLARES WAR.
TOOMEY DIES.

DEALEY WAS A HANDSOME MAN AT 56. HIS HAIR AND MUSTACHE
were gray, but he was agile and vigorous. He held himself erect
and kept his weight down, and his shortness in height was not
noticeable. His good health, he liked to tell, was due to three
things: early-morning calisthenics, moderate eating, and eight
glasses of water a day. He still rode horseback before breakfast,
but the automobiles on Maple Avenue and other streets in the
neighborhood were getting numerous and they made Old Pet, his
horse, skittish, and he was thinking of quitting the ride. He
dressed with meticulous care, always in good style, and never
ostentatiously. In the office, year in and year out, hot weather or
cold, he wore a black alpaca coat, a practice dating back before
1900. In jewelry, he was constant to a plain gold tie pin and a
large gold Masonic ring bearing the 33rd-Degree emblem,[1] and
of course the indispensable heavy gold watch chain, which swung
smartly up from the lower left pocket of his vest to the second-
from-top buttonhole.

At 56, Dealey had spent 41 years with the *News* . . . eight years more than John F. Lubben, the next man in point of service, and only five of the 1885-ers were still "keeping at it." Of the hundreds in the organization there was scarcely a man Dealey had not hired personally. The building, the machinery, the equipment —every item had passed his approval. Only the broad policies of the paper predated him. Ownership of the paper rested principally with two ladies; and Mr. Lombardi was the president; but Dealey was the *News*.

In the spring of 1915 the war in Europe was no longer in the spectacular phase of movement that had brought the Germans to the gates of Paris. It had settled into endless trenches and was locked in a deadly stalemate. In America business was erratic, a few industries seriously hurt, but others boomed and prospered. Americans had become inured to the horror on the other side of the ocean, and life continued pretty much the same as always.

That spring Dealey went about life as usual. He gave much time to recouping the depleted treasury of the local United Charities. He entertained the Critic Club and read a paper entitled "Do We Need Legal Aid Societies?" For a month before the city election in April, he quietly pulled political strings in behalf of Henry D. Lindsley for mayor. As May approached, his main thoughts were given to the forthcoming Journalism Week at the University of Missouri, where he was to make the opening address, at the invitation of Dean Walter Williams of the famous pioneer School of Journalism.

At the University of Missouri, Dealey renewed his friendship with Dean Williams. He brought greetings to the dean from Harry D. Guy, the young man whom the dean had recommended to the *News* out of the 1913 graduating class . . . Harry was in the advertising department and doing well. Dean Williams showed Dealey through Switzler Hall, where journalism was taught. Dealey said he would have ideas to take back to his friend Dean Will H. Mayes of the new School of Journalism at the University of Texas. The Texas school was still in its first year, and had 35 students. This movement to establish schools of journalism was a fine thing. Too long in coming.

On Monday evening, May 3, at the University Auditorium

there was a good crowd of students and visiting journalists.
Dealey's address was the main event. He warmed the audience
with a few impromptu remarks, and before commencing to read
his address, he told a story about a young preacher's first sermon
in a church in Scotland.

"What did you think of my sermon?" the preacher asked the
sexton.

"Well," said the sexton, "since ye asked, I simply ha'e this to
say: First, ye read it; second, ye didna read it well; and third, it
was na worth reading."

The joke was one Dealey had in a tiny blue notebook in which
he scribbled stories good for speeches, and he kept the book in his
desk drawer. It contained about 30 jokes at that time, and not
many more were ever added. Over the years he told the same
stories so often they became known as "Mr. Dealey's stories."

At the outset of his paper, he surprised some of the audience by
declaring: "Revenue is more necessary and important than policy
to a newspaper."

Looking up, he said he knew Dean Williams hadn't wanted him
to say that.

"But," he quickly explained, "I do not wish to be understood
as lacking in a sense of responsibility to the public and to my own
conscience; but I do wish definitely to be understood as being alive
to the practical side of the business . . . for without the practical
foundation of financial success there can be no superstructure of
general welfare." Earnestly he proceeded to give his listeners a
summation of the business wisdom he had acquired in 41 years.

Now let us consider the question of newspaper policy. Practically
speaking, policy and revenue are on a parity. For a newspaper, to
be permanently successful, must live a life of rectitude and must
approximate the high ideals, intellectual and moral, set for it by
the thinking minds of the public. There is a popular idea abroad
that a newspaper should give the people what they want. . . . This
I do not believe to be true in its entirety. Generally the readers
should be given what they want so long as what they want is good
for them. But a newspaper always has a moral responsibility . . .
to help its readers to higher standards.

Let us liken the newspaper to a magnet and the people to a bed of iron filings. If we hold the magnet far above the filings and move it about, it will have no effect on them. Place it directly upon the filings and it will gather up only a small part of them. If, however, we hold it just above these atoms, not too high or too close, and move it about, we can control the movement of any and all the metal and pull it along. This is true with the newspaper and the people. The one should be adjusted to the other, not so near or not so far as to lose effectiveness.

Approaching the end of the address, he departed from the written text to say that he was coming to what he considered to be the crux of the whole issue between revenue and policy, and he knew Dean Williams would concur with him.

It is possible for a newspaper *unconsciously* to grow immoral. That is, by consulting self-interest before consulting moral interest. . . . It is sometimes exceedingly hard to see evil in a method or a practice that puts money into our pockets. If, for example, a quack doctor who thrives on vice and ignorance wants to spend a thousand dollars for newspaper space, it is easy for the publisher to say . . . he is not a guardian of the public health. . . . But a continuation of such a policy will mean eventual death to the newspaper. The public is too intelligent to stand for it. . . . There are enough honest people to support all the newspapers the public needs, and—sweet thought—honest people are not slow to recognize an honest newspaper.

Back from Missouri, Dealey promptly set in motion one idea he had picked up. In a characteristic memorandum—"so short, so polite, and so full of signification," as one member of the staff described Dealey's interoffice memos—he directed Managing Editor Toomey to compile a book of "Rules and Suggestions for Editors." As a starter, he submitted a file on the subject which he had been collecting for about ten years. One memo, dated 1907, suggested that the *News* headline writers study the New York *Sun* as a model. A 1912 memo to Toomey asked: "Would it be practical to omit the names of poison taken by suicides from news items? It seems to be a general opinion that these items influence others to resort to the same means of taking their lives . . . We have talked about this several times.—GBD." Another note to Toomey, undated: "To speak of 'Jew' girls or 'Jew' stories is very objectionable."

With regard to the spelling of proper names, Dealey had a mania. Not many things could rile him, but to see a misspelled name in the *News* sent his blood pressure up. He never let one pass. Invariably he circled it and sent it to the editor responsible. Occasionally he asked for a personal explanation. "Well, the damage has been done," he would say, ending the interview. "Let's try to take steps that will avoid it in the future, and be sure to correct the file copies so the error won't perpetuate itself." In the *Rules* book he underlined:

> *Browne is not Brown and Chase is not Chace. A reporter who is inaccurate is even less valuable than one who cannot write the English language.*

As for his own name, "G.B." was not "Geo. B." and woe unto the editor who let it get into the *News* as "Geo. B." The aversion to "Geo. B." developed about 1912, and he took the pains to change certain earlier records, such as the minutes of the Critic Club, which went back to 1908.

Despite the sinking of the SS *Lusitania* and other war-provoking acts by Germany, the United States clung to neutrality. Dealey's sympathies were wholly with the Allies. He believed the right was on their side, and naturally he had a deep faith and pride in the English character. But as long as the final reckoning could be put off for the United States, he believed it best. The *News'* policy would be to follow the president.

In the meantime there was work to be done. There was social legislation to foster, city-planning articles to write, and talks to make, and Ted to start on a newspaper career . . . a shortage of newsprint to worry with, a new pastor to help select for his church, a Masonic lodge to charter in Highland Park, and Kessler to bring back to Dallas . . . a new home to build, the Sydney Smith Memorial to dedicate, and a magnificent Union Station to open.

In 1915 there was a chance to get a state law providing for county parks and Dealey personally directed the publicity which the *News* put behind it. The law passed, and Governor James E. Ferguson signed the bill, and Dealey hoped that some of the unkind rumors about "Farmer Jim" were untrue, because he and the governor saw eye to eye on a number of things. Under Ferguson the Robertson Insurance Law was repealed, the compulsory school law passed, and the governor was trying to improve the lot of tenant farmers. Dealey had advocated these measures before the governor ever did.

But, unhappily, the governor did some things that people did not approve of, and he could not stand criticism. After the *News* made pointed inquiries about the Eastham Prison Farm matter and accused the governor of "lobbying with the regents of the University of Texas to bring about the election of a man of his choice to the presidency," Ferguson picked a quarrel with the *News'* Austin correspondent, William M. (Tudey) Thornton, an excitable, explosive man, about five feet tall.

"The Governor jumped to his feet," Thornton wrote, in reporting the incident, "and ordered me from his office never to return, since I had called him a 'politician.' "

"Don't take the outburst too seriously," Dealey replied. He would ask the Galveston paper to send a man to the Eastham farm to get the facts "in order that we may be prepared to defend ourselves in case the Governor should attack us publicly."

Open conflict between the governor and the *News* did not develop immediately, but in his second term the governor sought to close the doors of the University of Texas by vetoing its appropriation. The *News* rose to the university's defense and, together with the university ex-students, figured large in Ferguson's impeachment.

City planning became a live issue again. The brave start in 1910 and 1911 had accomplished some wonders, but the impetus was lost before the end of 1911, and the broad scope of the plan was hardly touched. That Kessler was not retained after the end of his first year was a great disappointment to Dealey. During 1913 Kessler served the Dallas Park Board, thanks to Dealey's effort

in getting the Park Board members to visit Kansas City to see
what remarkable accomplishments Kessler had wrought in that
city. But again a year later the city officials let Kessler's contract
lapse, and to Dealey it seemed as if ten years' effort was slipping
through his fingers. Then in 1915 Henry D. Lindsley ran for
mayor, and he was one of the faithful who had stood shoulder to
shoulder in civic improvement work from the beginning. In April
when Lindsley was elected, Dealey wrote to Kessler, "Hooray!"
Now they could pick up with city planning again.

Steadily that year and the next, Dealey promoted and worked
to build a better Dallas and to spread the idea of city planning
throughout Texas—a talk to the Texas Town and City Planning
Association convention in Dallas . . . an article for *Texas Munici-
palities* on "The Well-planned City" . . . an invitation to the nation's
leading housing authority—John Ihlder of New York—to address
the annual chamber of commerce banquet . . . a paper for the
Critic Club on "Is It Desirable to Limit the Size of a City?" . . .
and for each employee of the *News* and *Journal* a two-hour auto
ride around Dallas in the company car "to see the improvements
so manifest in all sections of the city . . . and to know Dallas. The
car will leave at 4:30 P.M. each day, taking first the force in the
stereotype foundry and the composing room. . . ." Nothing too
big or too small to build a better city. Just keep at it.

The climax—in many ways and for many people as well as for
Dealey and his city planning—came on October 14, 1916. It was
the opening of their Thirty-First Annual State Fair—"the biggest
and best"—and it was a double-header dedication day for the
6,000,000-dollar Union Station and for the inspiring Sydney
Smith Memorial at the entrance to the State Fair grounds. One
was a monument to material progress, the other a shrine to the
arts, to the æsthetic aspirations of the city.

It was a day of triumph—a day of waving pennants and stream-
ing ribbons, the swishing of neatly starched dresses, the tread of
thousands of men on parade, the squawks of balloons, the blare of
bands, the great morning gathering at the magnificent Union Station, a day of smiles and sunshine, the cries of a thousand vendors,
the yells and songs of college students . . . "Pretty Baby," "There's

a Long, Long Trail," "Alexander's Ragtime Band," . . . a day of solemn words of prayer and the polished points of oratory, the glitter of epaulets on the governor's staff, the fluttering of the Stars and Stripes. It was a day dedicated to progress and to beauty and to the joy of living.

It was a day of triumph for Dealey. He was master of ceremonies at the opening of the Union Station, "by unanimous choice of the committee on arrangements." There would have been no Union Station had it not been for Dealey. The splendor of the dedication equaled the magnificence of the building. Governor James E. Ferguson, accompanied by his official staff members in full-dress uniform, made the main address, the most eloquent of his career, people said. One hundred and twenty visiting railway officials participated. The "biggest little committee" in the history of Dallas was thanked for meeting 263 times to clear the way for the great project. The speeches went on for two hours . . . and Dealey ended with a plea that Dallas continue to follow Kessler's city plan and beautify the surroundings by creating a plaza directly in front of the station, and by building handsome buildings on the three remaining sides of the plaza so that the 2,000,000 people who annually would pass through the doors of the station would say, "Behold, here is a beautiful city."

As if one triumph was not enough, in the afternoon Dealey presided at the unveiling of the Sydney Smith Memorial, the massive fountain and bronze statuary created to grace the entrance to the State Fair grounds. The art and the four years of work on the monument were Miss Clyde Chandler's, the sculptress, but the means and the determination that Dallas should have this altar to beauty were Dealey's.

All the while the war in Europe went implacably on, and the inevitable entry of the United States moved closer. Germany's unrestricted submarine warfare brought an end to diplomatic relations. Then came the perfidious German plot with Mexico and the evil scheme to separate Texas from the United States. On April 6 President Wilson declared war.

In the first outburst of patriotic excitement, the nation could

not realize what war meant. Parades. Gallant speeches. But no
realities. Even men like Dealey, serious and far-seeing, were not
yet aware of the consequences, and were inclined to whistle in
the dark.

> I do not see how the war is going to seriously affect business in
> this country [Dealey wrote to Mrs. Peabody one month after war
> was declared]. . . . It is our intention to endeavor to persuade the
> people to go along doing business as usual but to economize by
> cutting out wastes. The serious outlook, so far as we are concerned,
> is the paper situation. . . . What the future will bring forth, no
> man knows. However, I am still an optimist, and, speaking gen-
> erally, I think the people of the earth will realize more blessings as
> a result of the war than the awful consequences they are now ex-
> periencing.

About 20 years later Dealey came across the foregoing letter,
circled the last sentence, and scribbled across the top: "Bum prophecy. GBD."

But the realities of war came fast to the United States after
April, 1917. German submarines created havoc with Allied ship-
ping and threatened disaster. Food rationing . . . cable censorship
. . . defense-bond drives . . . passenger-train curtailment . . . Red
Cross training . . . community prayer . . . army camps. The war
touched everything. Congress passed the Conscription Bill. Ten
million men, 21 to 30, registered for the draft, and the war was on
a personal basis. The drawing came on Friday, July 20. Like any
other father, Dealey searched the long listing of numbers in the
columns of the *News*. Walter was far down on the list, but Ted
was up for the first call. Ted appeared before the draft board on
August 8. On two counts, as a husband and father and as an essen-
tial newspaper employee, he was deferred for an indefinite period.

In the midst of this distressing period Dealey and Ollie had to
make a move from the big house on Maple Avenue. Months before
the United States entered the war, they had laid their plans for
a new house—something small and in the new Highland Park residential area—and the sale of the old place was negotiated. Instead
of building, almost an impossibility during wartime, they bought
a new brick house recently completed at 3657 Maplewood Avenue.

When it came time to move, Dealey was inwardly sad. He knew they would get settled down in the new place and probably like it fine, but there were some memories and meanings that went with the old home, and nobody could pack them up and take them away. In 1901 when they moved in, they had a house full of children, and Maidie was only five years old. In the intervening years, all five children had grown up, and it had been a happy family and countless memorable things had happened there. Now the children were all married, even Maidie. Somehow this big lovable old two-story house, with the shady maple trees in front and the yellow plum trees in back, seemed to Dealey to be attached to all his good fortunes. The day of the move, after the last piece of furniture was out and the door was locked, Ollie noticed the ice card was still in the window, and Dealey went back inside to get it. In that last lonesome look around the bare rooms, he could not avoid thinking that something good was coming to an end.

In hundreds of ways, the war increased the burdens on large newspapers. Sixty-three members of the *News* and *Journal* organization went into the armed services. For those on the staff who had to carry on the job, it became a peculiarly exhausting kind of work, especially for the men in key positions . . . constantly stretching the work day, taking up the slack when no substitutes could be found for the vacancies, developing an insatiable curiosity for the latest bulletins from the telegraph room, alternately elated over good news and depressed at the bad news, continually enervated and fatigued. Dealey's stamina held out, but not so for others in the organization—sickness hit Toomey, Finty, Doran, Benners, Clark, Scott, and Hunt—all key men. A vacation or a stay in the hospital sufficed to restore all but Toomey. His old liver ailment was aggravated. Dealey sent him to Mayo's, and later to the Ozarks for a complete rest. Toomey was his favorite. Over the years he had pushed this likable Irishman all the way from mailing room boy to managing editor. Toomey was a man of many talents—an accomplished reporter, an editor with a rare good sense of judgment, a skilled artist, and a writer of plays. Dealey could not forget the time Toomey went to New York in 1909 on his vacation to sell a musical comedy which he and the *News* poet, Harry Lee Marriner, had written together.

"Playwriting is a fascinating and beautiful study," Toomey wrote back to Dealey, "but play-selling is disagreeable and disgusting. The ignorance and conceit of the average producer is appalling."

Toomey died October 13, 1918. There was a thought from a letter that Colonel Belo had written Dealey at the close of the Spanish-American War which very fittingly could be applied to Toomey: "Many men have become heroes in the Army and Navy, but there are also heroes in civil life."

In the summer of 1918 the Western Front was ablaze as the war entered its fifth year. The Germans came desperately close to crushing the Allies at the Marne. Then the tide turned. On November 7 a United Press bulletin flashed the end of the war. Across America enterprising newspapers went to press, and in Dallas the *Journal* put out an "Extra." Dallas closed up. The town went wild. It was the false armistice.

The next day Dealey asked to see the man who ordered the "Extra." He was Harry C. Withers, an up-and-coming young editor. A few days earlier Dealey had notified him he would be made managing editor of the *Journal* on November 14. How had Withers made such a colossal mistake? Withers explained. The UP bulletin had given no qualifications. How could a man know?

"Even so," Withers added, "I haven't slept since. I'd almost as soon be pushing up the daisies."

"Don't worry," Dealey said. "If you hadn't done what you did, I would have felt like firing you."

In truth, of course, it was the end of the war, except for the formalities on November 11.

The long night was over.

CHAPTER TWENTY

1919-1924

A FEAST AND A BONUS FOR THE EMPLOY-
EES. DEALEY BECOMES PRESIDENT OF
THE *NEWS*. "LL.D." GETTING THE TRACKS
OFF PACIFIC AVENUE. WAVES OF TROU-
BLES. THE *NEWS* FIGHTS THE KU KLUX
KLAN. PARTING WITH THE GALVESTON
NEWS.

FOLLOWING THE WAR, MANKIND HELD ON TO THE ILLUSION OF "the good world" for a brief period. But in less than a year the worries and quarrels returned. Around the globe statesmen worried about Bolsheviks and Russia. France worried about Germany. Britain worried about the Irish. The United States worried about the League of Nations. Texas' Governor Hobby worried about Mexico. Congress worried about national ownership of railroads. Capital worried about labor. Southern farmers worried about low cotton prices. Housewives worried about the high cost of living . . . and milk was 12 cents a quart!

In contrast, it was a period when things seemed to be sailing along smoothly for Dealey, and the *News* experienced unusual prosperity.

A great wave of business development and progress is upon us [Dealey wrote a friend], due partly to the resumption of certain work stopped during the war, and partly to the discovery of fabulous wealth in oil. A well-posted man remarked to me only

yesterday that there are more people visiting the American Exchange National Bank in Dallas every day than there are people
visiting any one bank in New York City. I don't doubt it.

Now was the time, he told the Board of Directors at the mid-
year meeting, for the *News* to start the group-insurance program
for the employees. He had been plugging away unsuccessfully for
employee insurance since the annual stockholders' meeting in December of 1916. In 1917 he had proposed a pension-fund program,
and the following year, an employee welfare fund. But each year
the board had voted to wait. This time, however, the board passed
the paid-up employee insurance program.

It was occasion for a *News-Journal* "family party." A banquet
committee was appointed, but Dealey kept a check on details.

"My experience with banquets," he wrote in a memo to the
banquet chairman, Harry Withers, the *Journal's* managing editor,
"is that when people get up to talk they are handicapped and
bothered by the noise of waiters clearing off the tables. Have it
understood on this occasion that as soon as we are through eating,
the hotel waiters will get out of the room. We won't be late, and
they will have all the time they want to clear the tables after we
have departed. And the men who are thus clearing the tables can
say in the language of the poet:

> 'I feel like one
> Who treads alone
> Some banquet-hall deserted,
> Whose lights are fled,
> Whose garlands dead,
> And all but he departed.' "

Three hundred and fifty *News-Journal* employees together with
their families filled the hotel dining hall the night of October 1,
and they were in good spirits because word leaked out that "the
Boss" would announce a bonus for each employee, equal to one-
and-a-third weeks' wages. Dealey had the main talk, and he began
with a story which he confessed to be somewhat old—about the
doctor who told the man with dyspepsia to go ahead and eat the

sauerkraut and wieners and drink some beer, and if it killed him, he would assume the responsibility. He said he found it too expensive to tell a new story any more because there were so many employees in the building that by the time everybody had stopped to tell it to the next man, it had cost the *News* 200 or 300 dollars' worth of time.

After explaining the new employee insurance program and announcing the bonus, he concluded: "This is the dawn of a new day in the relations between the owners of this concern and those who are making it successful . . . and it is the beginning of some other things that we are going to do."

In 1919 language like this was seldom heard by the employees of large businesses, whether in Dallas or elsewhere in the country. The whole question of the working man's lot deeply concerned Dealey, however, and he was entering into several projects to make life better and easier for the man who earned weekly wages. One was a housing project initiated by members of the Critic Club "to build adequate, comfortable, and sanitary homes for working men on a basis within their limited ability to pay." Another project was to get a Morris Plan bank in Dallas, designed to serve the man of small means . . . day laborers . . . weekly wage-earners.

C. Lombardi died June 23, 1919.

"Mr. Lombardi's death," Dealey wrote to Mrs. Jeannette Peabody in July, "has so occupied my mind that I have had little time to consider anything else . . . I have not yet formulated the reorganization of the editorial department."

To replace Mr. Lombardi was not going to be easy. This self-educated man, who used a French encyclopedia and who always carried a small-sized book in his coat pocket to improve idle moments while riding on streetcars or waiting on appointments, had carved his own niche in the organization. Primarily he had represented "the two ladies"—Mrs. Peabody and Mrs. Alfred Belo, Jr., the principal owners—and he had done so with complete satisfaction, while at the same time he had kept the best interests of the newspapers as public servants uppermost. He had contributed materially to the business management, and he had maintained a broad scope of interests that the editors admired.

A new president of A. H. Belo & Co. had to be elected. Twice before Dealey had refused the office, but this time when "the two ladies" asked him to assume the title, he accepted. His election to the office was made official January 27, 1920, at the annual stockholders' meeting. To mark the date and the meeting with a sign of accomplishment, he put through his plan to increase the capital stock of the corporation from 300,000 to 1,500,000 dollars. For many years each share of stock with a par value of 100 dollars had had a market value of 500 dollars, if a share could be found for sale. Only once in the last eight years had annual dividends dropped below 20 dollars a share, and during the last two years dividends had been 40 dollars a share. In January, 1917, Mrs. Peabody had asked whether it was really wise for her to buy shares at 500 dollars a share.

"If the tangible and intangible assets of the concern are today worth one cent," Dealey replied, "they are worth $3,000,000. Several years ago I estimated the shares to be worth $1000 apiece."

Upon his election to the presidency the letters of congratulations to Dealey poured in, and trade journals and newspapers gave him a "good press." He had the letters and clippings bound together in a handsome black leather binding with gold lettering. In the book, placed between a letter from Charles L. Sanger, head of the largest mercantile business in Dallas, and a letter from J. Horace McFarland, long-time president of the American Civic Association, was a note on a half sheet of newsprint copy-paper, written in pencil:

My dear Mr. Dealey,

I am glad endeed to no that you are become to be our president which I no everybody will be proud of in the building. May God bless you and may you live a sunny life. Present herewith fifty cents.

Will Williams,

Day Fireman

Will Williams was a Negro, and he worked in the basement, but he and "the Boss" were personal friends.

To proffer their congratulations to Dealey *en masse,* the employees of the *News* and *Journal* held a surprise party in the mailing room. The secret was kept perfectly, and on the afternoon of the party Dealey was asked "to come see how a piece of equipment in the mailing room had got broken." As he came through the mailing room door several hundred people started applauding and cheering. It was a brief affair . . . a few short speeches, a new silver service to replace the one recently stolen from the Dealey home, a beautiful bronze vase, and a green leather-bound book of handwritten tributes from every employee in the building.

The next day Dealey wrote Mrs. Peabody about the party: "I wish you could have been present. It just proves that a conspiracy can go on in the building for a whole month and I not know a thing about it . . . The meeting was wonderful and absolutely paralyzed me for a few minutes. The book . . . was worth forty-six years of work."

The future looked bright. There was much to be thankful for, much to be proud of, and much to look forward to. Honors followed one after another. He was named honorary vice-president of the National Housing Association for 1920-21 . . . appointed to the Board of Governors of the American City Planning Institute for 1920-21 . . . elected first vice-president of the Southwest Political Science Association at its organization on the University of Texas campus in April, 1920. But the honor of which he was proudest was bestowed upon him in June, 1921, by Southern Methodist University. President H. A. Boaz conferred the LL.D. degree and acclaimed him "the foremost citizen of Dallas."

A few days after the academic ceremony was over, two of the older heads on the *News* staff left this note on Dealey's desk: "Dr. G. B. Dealey—The old doctors cordially welcome the young doctor into the fraternity of the illustrious.—(signed) Dr. Knott and Dr. Taylor." The "old doctors" were Cartoonist John Knott and Columnist J. J. Taylor, both of whom had received the D. Litt. from Baylor University the previous year.

The years immediately following the war saw Dealey moving ahead with his city planning work. His latest scheme, the Dallas Property Owners' Association, organized in March, 1919, was succeeding nicely in its second year of operation. His real feat was in persuading the Association to engage George Kessler as its city-plan consultant. If there was one thing Dealey was ashamed of Dallas for, it was the niggardly way the city had dealt with George Kessler. Other cities paid him handsomely and spent millions of dollars upon his recommendations. But Dallas had begrudged him the few thousand it had paid him.

What would happen if the *News* should ever let up in its fight for a planned city? By doggedly keeping at it, year after year, the *News* and a small band of stalwarts among the businessmen had gotten some monumental accomplishments: the Union Station, the double-track belt railroad around the city, the Turtle Creek development, and several other key provisions of Kessler's plan. These achievements were enough to set the lines of development of the city for all time to come. But much of the Kessler Plan was still untouched.

After the war the most important objective to accomplish in the city plan was the removal of the tracks on Pacific Avenue. It was this proposal which in 1910 had stunned members of the city council and the chamber of commerce. But someone had laughed and remarked, "It can't do any harm," and the rash proposal became a part of the original city plan.

Until 1916 nothing was done about it. Then, under Henry D. Lindsley's administration as mayor, the city council and the *News* teamed up and campaigned for the removal of the tracks. A year of effort and wrangling finally brought one tangible concession from the Texas and Pacific Railway. If Dallas would provide, free of cost, a new right-of-way and a new industrial district, the T. & P. would remove the tracks.

Could Dallas produce? The offer was made in December, 1916.

During four years, although slowed down by a war, dragged through two new city administrations, through hundreds of meetings of various committees, through legal injunctions and court trials, through more than a thousand articles and editorials in the

News, the "impossible" was accomplished. A fund of 750,000 dollars was raised, the property for the new right-of-way was purchased, the railroads were compensated, the business firms which lost rail sidings were placated, and the removal of the tracks was begun on June 30, 1921.

A "spike-pulling ceremony" was staged at the intersection of Pacific, Masten, St. Paul, and Live Oak Streets, and the twelve men who contributed the most to the success of the project were each asked to pull a spike and to talk briefly. In introducing Dealey, the master of ceremonies said the idea of removing the tracks from Pacific Avenue actually went farther back than the Kessler Plan, and was first proposed by G. B. Dealey in 1909 at a meeting at his home, the reference being to the meeting of the Critic Club at which Dealey had presented his paper on a city plan for Dallas.

The sun was blazing hot, and Dealey shed his white linen coat and quipped that the weather was at least "good for cotton."

"It has been said," he commented, "that if the average young man at the age of twenty-one could foresee all the troubles of his life, the prospect would be unbearable and he would succumb. But, as a seawall turns back the waves of the ocean, he overcomes one before the other reaches him. So if these gentlemen had realized the enormous task ahead of them, it is quite likely that none would have had the boldness to tackle the job."

Dealey's philosophical observation that day had the compassionate ring of a man whose own troubles were piling up. For a time after the war life had gone along smoothly. Even newsprint had given no cause for worry. But for the past year the waves of trouble had been rolling in.

One worry which he could not get out of his mind had started with a strange letter from Mrs. Alfred Belo, Jr. Mrs. Belo wrote, in April of 1920, that a man in New York City had made an offer to buy the *News*. To get to the bottom of the matter Dealey hurried off a letter to Mrs. Peabody in Massachusetts. Mrs. Peabody replied she did not think there was the slightest cause for anxiety. "Even if Mrs. Belo sold her stock, she could not sell the *News*, as you and I have the controlling interest." But despite Mrs. Peabody's assurances, Dealey could not help worrying. If "the two

ladies" should ever combine and agree to sell, his own few shares
would be meaningless. All that he had worked for, and all that the
News stood for could go by the board in an instant.

Trouble and worries came from unexpected sources.

The oil boom was on in North Texas and the oil-stock pro-
moters were flooding the newspapers with their advertising. When
it proved impossible for the *News* to sift the honest propositions
from the dishonest, Dealey closed the columns of the Belo papers
to all oil-promotion advertising. Since Spindletop, back in 1901,
he had watched the oil booms come and go, and always a lot of
innocent people got swindled. The *News* would no longer be a
party to it. The loss in revenue to the *News* was estimated at
500,000 dollars, and it was hard to take. But what hurt worse was
that people did not seem to appreciate it, and some outspokenly
accused the *News* of "blocking progress" . . . "killing business"
. . . and "besmirching the good name of Texas." The *News* held
firm, however, and it was vindicated when the federal authorities
stepped in and sent a number of oil-promotion swindlers to prison.
Then the readers sang a different tune. The *News* was the paper
with "foresight" . . . "courage" . . . "the watchdog of the people."

The *News* could have used that half-million dollars, because
business was taking a turn for the worse, and circulation was
down. Since the high point of the war days, the *News* had dropped
7000 in circulation by 1921, down to 61,000 daily and 93,000 Sunday, the *Journal* had lost more than 25 per cent of its circulation,
from 48,000 to 34,000.

There were still more waves of trouble.

The Dallas Property Owners' Association was losing its popularity, and city planning was getting the old run-around. The man
selected to take Mr. Lombardi's place quit suddenly after two
years of grooming for the job. Finty was overworked and complained that if he tried to keep up the lick indefinitely he feared he
would come to an abrupt halt. Three carloads of newsprint were
ruined by water and 30 carloads were tied up by a longshoreman's
strike. For months there was nothing to do but curtail the size
of the *News* and *Journal* and large quantities of advertising had
to be turned away.

But the worst was yet to come.

Dallas was still a "Saturday town," and on the warm evening of May 21, 1921, the crowds "downtown" were bustling and noisy. Precisely at 9 o'clock the lights on Main and Elm Streets went out. From the doorway of the old Majestic Theater on Main Street a white-clad figure emerged carrying the American flag. Behind him came a second masked figure carrying a burning cross. One by one they emerged until 789 hooded men were marching along Main Street in single file, ten paces apart. Not a word was spoken by the marchers, and an awesome hush came over the crowds on the sidewalks. The cars and trucks ceased their honking and stopped along the route of the parade. As the procession wended its way down Main Street and back up Elm, the fiery crosses cast an eerie light on the banners which read: "The Invisible Empire," "White Supremacy," "Pure Womanhood," "All Native Born," "For Our Daughters," "Grafters Go," "Gamblers Go," "Degenerates Go," "Right Will Prevail," and other slogans.

It was the Ku Klux Klan.

For a newspaper to challenge the Klan was not to be considered lightly. The cost could be extreme. The retaliation could be brutal. But every tradition, every principle the *News* stood for was diametrically opposed to the intolerance and the mob spirit of the Klan. The next day the *News* editorialized:

> **The spectacle of eight hundred masked and white-gowned men parading the streets . . . was a slander on Dallas . . .**
>
> **White supremacy is not imperiled. Vice is not rampant. The constituted agencies of government are still regnant. And if freedom is endangered, it is by the redivivus of mob spirit in the disguising garb of the Ku Klux Klan.**

The fight was on. Three weeks later the Klan horsewhipped its first Dallas victim, an ex-soldier accused of annoying his former wife. No trial, no hearing . . . just stripped down and whipped . . . and told to leave town. "Cowardly, brutal, and lawless," the *News* accused. Systematically it reported every known violence of the Klan anywhere in the nation and encouraged every legal effort to drive out the Klan. It pointed out specifically how the Klan violated the Constitution and the laws of Texas and of the United States. At every opportunity it interviewed respected men in high office and quoted their condemnation of the Klan.

But the Klan spread like an epidemic. Quickly it was in control of city and county governments over much of Texas, and equally powerful in other states. In Dallas thousands belonged to the Klan, and many more thousands were sympathetic. With cunning it struck back at the *News*. First, its members stopped their subscriptions to the paper. Then, Klansmen stopped advertising in the *News* and boycotted the firms that continued to advertise in it.

Giving no quarter, the *News* ran the syndicated serial exposé of the Klan originated by the New York *World,* and it used all of its resources to help organize the Dallas County Citizens League to oppose the Klan. M. M. Crane, the eminent attorney of Texas, headed the league, and the *News* put William G. Sterett and other staff writers at the league's disposal to help prepare pamphlets and other publicity against the Klan. But the battle was far from won.

The 1922 elections revealed the fearsome strength of the Klan. In Dallas every elective office, with the exception of the School Board, went to a Klansman. In the state campaigns the election of Klansman Earle B. Mayfield to the United States Senate proved its state-wide power.

The thing that was gradually doing the most harm to the *News* was the Klan's insidious rumor that the *News* was a Catholic organ and that Dealey and the editors were Catholics. Because of the rumor, subscription cancellations ran into many hundreds, and the frightening thing to Dealey and the responsible men of the paper was the constant threat that the effect of the rumor would snowball. Fighting the Klan was like fighting an invisible foe. "The Invisible Empire" was a diabolically appropriate name. No one at the *News* could tell where the rumor would take effect next. Earnestly each of the hundreds of inquiries and accusations was answered with a personal letter by Dealey or by one of his sons or by a ranking editor.

"The *News* is neither owned nor controlled by members of the Catholic Church," they explained, giving the church affiliation of each editor and principal stockholder, "but the *News* does believe in religious tolerance for all sects."

For more than a year they were uncertain whether or not to come out boldly with a series of full-page declarations about the matter. If it was the wrong thing to do, as several of the executives held, it could be ruinous. Yet not to do so might be equally as bad.

In the meantime, advertising was off appreciably, and circulation continued downward, being 3000 less at the end of 1922 than before the fight with the Klan began. The cash surplus of 200,000 dollars had been wiped out entirely. In order to declare the usual 8 per cent dividend so that Mrs. Peabody and Mrs. Belo would not suffer any loss of expected income, it was necessary to convert to a cash value more than a 100,000 dollars' worth of the company's Dallas real estate.

Mrs. Jeannette Peabody was sufficiently alarmed to make a special trip from Massachusetts to Dallas in January, 1923, to discuss "the deteriorating situation." The *News* was far from being broke, but it was hurting seriously for money, and of course there was the ominous prospect that the Klan actually might gain absolute political and economic control of Texas and in time make good on its repeated threat "to bankrupt the *News*."

The solution was not going to be simple because the problem was complex. It was more than the fight with the Ku Klux Klan. The basic problem, without doubt, was the nation-wide business depression, beginning late in 1920 and lasting into 1922. The depression, in fact, had provided a favorable climate for the growth of the Klan, and in the midst of the depression the *News* had suffered the accidental loss of much newsprint and consequent loss of advertising revenue.

Upon Mrs. Peabody's arrival in Dallas, a series of conferences were held in which the management and the editorial council participated. While these discussions were under way, an unexpected offer to buy the Galveston *News* came from W. L. Moody, Jr., well-known businessman and financier of Galveston.

Sell the Galveston *News?*

To think of it seemed almost sacrilegious. The *News* was born in Galveston. The "Old Lady by the Sea" was the mother of the brood.

Was the money actually needed that badly?

In a way, yes; and in a way, no.

There was no chance for a stock dividend the first quarter of 1923, and little likelihood of dividends for some time, certainly not until the business situation changed for the better.

It might be wise to sell the Galveston *News*. The Galveston paper had not really made a profit for A. H. Belo & Co. since 1910. On the books it showed a few thousand dollars' profit each year, but only because the Dallas papers absorbed the majority of the joint expenses. The chief obstacle in the way of a profitable operation of the Galveston *News* was the original commitment to make the Galveston paper and the Dallas paper partial duplicates of one another. When the Dallas *Morning News* was established, Dallas was smaller than Galveston. Now Dallas was four times larger. The type and size of newspaper demanded by a city of 200,000 was too costly for a city of 45,000. Something would have to be done to break the original idea of duplicate papers. Would it not be better to make a complete break?

On March 22, 1923, the sale of the Galveston *Daily News* to W. L. Moody, Jr., was consummated in Galveston. "Surely it was a sad day," Dealey wrote of the event. "Well do I remember the day in 1874 when I started to work for the Galveston *News* as its office boy. Some of the happiest days of my life have been spent in her service. And the signing of the contract of sale was something akin to the cutting of my heartstrings." [1]

Following the announcement of the sale, the Klan boasted openly that the Dallas *Morning News* had its back to the wall and it too would soon be sold or bankrupt. But the Klan was crowing too soon; in fact its power was already dissipating. The constant pressure by the various forces against it had begun to take effect. But no one knew for sure how strong it actually was.

During the remainder of 1923 and the first part of 1924, the fight between the *News* and the Klan was quiescent. The final and deciding battle came during the race for the governorship of Texas in the summer of 1924. The two gubernatorial candidates who emerged in the runoff of the Democratic primary drew the lines sharply. Judge Felix D. Robertson was the acknowledged Klan candidate. Mrs. Miriam A. Ferguson, wife of the erstwhile impeached governor, James E. Ferguson, attracted the support of the anti-Klan elements.

The situation threw the *News* into a dilemma. It was ready to fight Robertson and the Klan. But how could it honestly support the wife of the man whom it had helped impeach from the governor's office?

It was Ted Dealey who was most responsible for causing the *News* to face up to the situation and make a decision. Ted had covered the campaign as a roving correspondent, and he had a clear grasp of the basic issues involved and a personal acquaintanceship with most of the candidates.

Tonight the runoff campaign in the governor's race will open [he wrote to his father in a memorandum dated August 5, 1924]. I would like to make the following suggestion:

That from now on until August 23rd, we make a vigorous attack on the Klan and all Klan candidates, editorially and in any other legitimate way.

For several years we got out against the Klan and fought it . . . The persons who were alienated will always continue to hate us as long as they feel the way they do about the Klan. We will not hurt ourselves now by taking up the fight against the Klan once more. All the hurt that could come to us has already been felt.

But we will help ourselves by such a positive attitude, commercially and morally. The tide now seems to be swinging against the Klan . . . Now is the time for us to REAP THE FRUITS of the seeds we planted two or three years ago.

It is the duty of the *News* to take a positive stand in this campaign. The traditions of the paper demand it. We have never maintained a neutral attitude in emergencies when it behooves everyone to see that the sheep are separated from the goats.

Mrs. Ferguson . . . will undoubtedly make Texas a good gov-

ernor. Felix Robertson is an avowed Klansman. . . . Now is the
time to wop him where it will do the most good.

The editorial council was not unanimous in its opinion, but Dealey and the majority decided with Ted, and the *News* launched
its attack against Robertson and the Klan the next day.

On August 23 Mrs. Ferguson was elected governor of Texas.
Robertson and the Ku Klux Klan had lost, and the spirit of the
Klan was broken. Almost as rapidly and mysteriously as it had
arisen the Klan died out in Texas.

In a paper written in 1930, "A Newspaperman's Retrospect of
Fifty Years," Dealey stated: "Perhaps the most courageous thing
the *News* ever did was to fight the Ku Klux Klan."

CHAPTER TWENTY-ONE

1921-1924

MAKING THE *NEWS* NOTED. WFAA GOES
ON THE AIR. DEALEY SPARKS A PROMO-
TION SERIES. REVIVES THE *ALMANAC*.
RECALLS THE "BIG SIX" AT A *NEWS* FAM-
ILY GATHERING.

DURING THE "HARD-TIMES YEARS" FROM 1921 TO 1924, DEALEY
and the editors did much soul-searching over what they interpreted
to be the *News'* lost prestige. Ironically none of them seemed to
realize that the strong stand for honest advertising, the courageous
fight against the Klan, and the innovations and improvements
of that period would garner some of the highest laurels in the
News' long history. Because advertising and circulation were
down, they kept wondering if the paper was "slipping." Their
self-recriminations probably hit bottom in the summer of 1922.
"Toward the close of our conversation in the lunch room," Finty
wrote in a memorandum to Dealey on July 24, 1922, "you suggested the employment of a 'big man,' saying that the *News* ought
to do things that would make it noted and cause it to be considered
an authority. You mentioned Dr. J—— of the University of
Texas as a type. With the general view I am in agreement; but I
do not believe the Dr. J—— type would solve our difficulty. . . ."

If Dealey could have looked into the future, even a few years,
he would have known that they were doing things that would
"make the *News* noted" and that they already had certain young

men who would soon "cause the *News* to be considered an authority" . . . authority, that is, in new areas, because the paper had lost
no authority previously acquired.

They were tinkering with one venture which had them all fascinated, but also puzzled as to its ultimate value. It was their wireless sending station, with its broadcasting studio curtained off in a
corner of the *News* library and the transmitter in a little frame
shack on the roof of the building. In 1922 Dealey could not see
clearly how it was going to pay for itself. Walter, his elder son,
was the main one who had persuaded him that this radio thing
had potentialities which could be of use to a newspaper. Walter
was the assistant general manager of the newspaper now, having
received the title in 1920. In his nine years with the organization
he had matured into an able executive, and Dealey often referred
to him as "my right bower and chief assistant."

Walter had caught the radio "bug" early. When the Detroit
Daily News put in a radio telephone transmitter in August of
1920, Walter had said it was a good thing for a newspaper and
the *News* ought to have one. The Westinghouse station, KDKA,
in Pittsburgh, had created a sensation with its initial broadcast of
the Harding-Cox election on November 2, 1920. By 1921 the idea
of using radio for news events was catching on. WJY in Jersey
City, New Jersey, broadcast the Dempsey-Carpentier fight in
July, and later that year a play-by-play account of a National
League baseball game in Pittsburgh was broadcast while the game
was in progress. Scattered receiving sets in Texas were picking up
these distant broadcasts, and on November 27, 1921, the *News*
editorialized: "Jefferson, Texas, enjoyed last Sunday a sermon delivered in Philadelphia, Pennsylvania. A wireless telephone [and
sound amplifier] installed at a cost of less than $200 made it
possible. . . . Events of this kind are big with possibilities."

That same week in November, 1921, Walter and the chief
engineer of the *News* telephoned to one of the local wireless "experts," a Mr. R. M. Lane, asking that he pay them a visit. They
went on top of the *News* building. Was the smokestack good
enough to hold up a wireless antenna? How much would a sending transmitter cost? The wind was biting cold, so they left the

roof and went to the executive offices on the first floor to discuss
the matter. There Dealey joined the conversation and handed
out cigars. "How long do you think this radio fad will last?" he
wanted to know.

It was three against one, and Walter, the chief engineer, and
Mr. Lane soon had Dealey convinced that radio was more than a
fad. "Within six months the whole nation will be radio mad," Mr.
Lane said.

"If we put in a sending station now, Papa," Walter said, "it will
be comparable to what the Galveston *News* did when it decided to
establish a branch paper in Dallas. Back then the idea was to 'ship
the *News* by wire.' The time has come 'to ship the *News* by wireless.' "

"All right," Dealey said, "if the *News* is going into this thing,
we ought to give the people of the Southwest the best station possible."

Six months later WFAA was testing its 100-watt signal
strength from a 124-foot-long antenna that stretched from a
tower on the roof of the *News* building to a tower on top of the
Dallas County Bank Building (now the Texas Bank and Trust
Company Building). On Sunday June 26, 1922, WFAA went on
the air with two hours and ten minutes of programing:

        2:00 to 2:40 P.M.—Music. Bible talk.
        6:00 to 7:00 P.M.—Baseball scores (Major and Texas Leagues.)
                           Music. News bulletins.
        9:30 to 10:00 P.M.—Health talk. News bulletins. Baseball scores.
                           Bedtime tale.

Dozens of telephone calls and telegrams came in during the
broadcast, and the next day letters and postal cards poured in.
A Denison listener expressed the general enthusiasm when he
said: "You came in so loud, it nearly knocked my earphones off.
Sure enjoyed 'The Sunshine of Your Smile.' "

Dealey took no part in the first broadcast except to join the
spectators in the library who were watching the proceedings. It
reminded him, he told the group around him, of the first long-
distance telephone call made from Dallas. It was July, 1895, and

they had quite a show for it in the parlor at the Grand Windsor Hotel. Mayor Frank Holland of Dallas talked to Mayor Fly in Galveston. The delight of the crowd was Mayor Holland's retort when the Galveston mayor said something boastful about the deep water over the bar at Galveston Island. "Say, Fly," Mayor Holland said, "schooners have been passing over the Dallas bar every day for years."

The new radio station at the *News* was an exciting and wondrous experiment, but it grew more expensive by the week . . . new equipment . . . more hours on the air . . . more space in the building . . . more employees, two, then three, then six. Was it worth the cost? No one seemed to attach much importance to the first commercially sponsored broadcast in the United States, which took place in August of 1922 in New York City, for which WEAF received 100 dollars for ten minutes. Dealey was resigned to supporting the enterprise as an expense of the newspaper, and in a brief talk over WFAA on the occasion of the station's increase in power to 500 watts, October 30, 1922, he said:

> I am glad to say a few words on the general subject of the relation of the radio to a newspaper. . . . Why should we get into the radio game? What do we get out of it? The answer is simple. The chief asset of any institution is the good will of the public. From the beginning we recognized that the radio was not only a remarkable scientific discovery, but it also presented an opportunity for public service that would be recognized and appreciated by everyone. If we obtain the good will of our listeners we are content. We are more than content; we are immensely pleased. This station belongs to the great American public of the Southwest.

WFAA was one of the first 80 broadcasting stations in the United States, and among the first 30 licensed. By mid-1922 the *News* was carrying a daily radio feature and its Sunday radio page was one of the best in the nation. Dealey, Walter, the announcer in the little studio in the corner of the Library, the engineer in the shack on the roof, the radio editor, and others in the organization were doing things "to make the *News* noted." They were not the "Dr. J—— of the University of Texas" type, but they were "causing the *News* to be considered an authority." Besides that, within a few years, this "radio game," as Dealey called it, would be one of the most profitable businesses in the country.

While the enterprise in radio was getting under way, other efforts to regain the "lost prestige" were being generated. In February, 1922, Dealey instructed all editors and department heads to submit ideas for a series of page articles on the achievements of the *News*. Deftly, he delineated the objective:

> Very generally my idea is to bring out that Dallas cannot live on itself. Its sustenance must come from the outside. And in order to continue to build it up, it must be advertised on the outside. The character of the paper which the *News* puts out and the outside circulation of the *News* have been very important factors in causing Dallas to grow from 20,000 when the *News* was established in 1885, to 200,000 in 1922.
>
> The *News* during all these years has brought favorable attention to Dallas, and has convinced people that it is a desirable place to do business. . . . The paper has been the means of adding tremendously to the population of Dallas, particularly because families in other places have realized from the advertising which the *News* has given that Dallas is a good place to bring up and educate their children, and they have moved to Dallas.
>
> So far as the business of Dallas is concerned, both retail and wholesale, Dallas is not a city of 200,000 confined to its corporate limits, but for trading purposes it extends to Garland, Greenville, Waxahachie, Sherman and a hundred other towns within a radius of seventy-five miles. In other words, it is a "city of a million inhabitants," and within this charmed circle of potential business, the *News* always has, and today dominates in quantity and quality of circulation. It is the paper of the million.—GBD.

As the man to take the "symposium of ideas" from the editors and department heads and turn them into copy for the campaign, Dealey selected the newest member of the editorial staff, Lynn W. Landrum, a man with a forceful pen. Earlier in the winter, Landrum had suffered an attack of pneumonia, and Dealey had taken him some extra blankets and visited with him. He liked this outspoken and God-fearing young man who had made a name for himself in West Texas as a "country editor" before coming to the *News*. By the end of May the series of page articles had been com-

pleted and published. "If the job did nothing else," Landrum
wrote to Dealey, "it gave me an insight into the *News* and its
accomplishments. I wish we could get the people to see it too."
Landrum was not the "Dr. J—— type," but he would become one
of the editors who would "make the *News* noted."

In former years among the achievements of the *News* which
had caused it to be considered an authority was the publication
of the *Texas Almanac and State Industrial Guide.* The last edition had appeared in 1914. Its discontinuance was not because
Dealey had ceased to believe in the value of the publication. It was
due mainly to the effects of the war, and, following the end of the
war, no member of the staff who was competent to do the job
could be spared for the work. In 1904 Dealey had been chiefly
responsible for the revival of the *Almanac,* after a lapse of 30
years. He looked on it not primarily as a money-making venture
but as one of the public services which the *News* could render the
whole state of Texas. The dissemination of the basic information
it contained served to educate Texans and to tell the rest of the
world about Texas. By keeping at it, this led to more commerce,
better agriculture, and new industries for Texas. Of course it re-
dounded to the credit of the *News* to perform this service, and
eventually a more prosperous state led to a more prosperous newspaper.

During the troublesome times around 1922, Dealey thought
repeatedly of reviving the *Almanac.* But whom could he assign to
do the job? Curiously, the source of much of his trouble, the Ku
Klux Klan, was indirectly responsible for producing the man to
revive the *Almanac.* It happened in this manner. In 1922 the back-
ers of the Texas Chamber of Commerce got at loggerheads over
the Klan issue. As a result, financial support was withdrawn and
the organization folded. Stuart McGregor was one of the staff
members left unemployed. A year earlier he had called at the *News*
to obtain permission for the Texas Chamber of Commerce to
publish the *Texas Almanac.* Dealey had emphatically refused, saying that the *News* intended to revive the publication as soon as one
of the editors could find the time. Remembering Dealey's comment, McGregor visited Dealey and asked for the job of getting

the *Almanac* out for the *News*. He was hired. After working two years under the direction of Tom Finty, Jr., who had edited the last several issues, McGregor became the individual who revived the publication and put it on a permanent basis. The appearance of the 1925 edition of the *Texas Almanac and State Industrial Guide* helped to produce the kind of prestige that the *News* needed "to be considered an authority."

Leadership was what Dealey wanted. The *News* must be the best in the Southwest in whatever it did. Steadily he moved to acquire this leadership in more directions—a new type of Sunday Magazine Section, a metropolitan-type Sunday Book Review Page, and a regular Agriculture Department in the daily paper.

He set Ted, his younger son, to editing an eight-page Sunday Magazine Section. Since 1915 Ted had received training in various departments of the paper, but mainly he had worked at reporting and had made a name for himself with his noteworthy field assignments and his astute coverage of Texas political campaigns. He had a strong literary bent, and soon in the Sunday Magazine Section he was turning out one of the most significant periodicals of historical and literary material in Texas.

Despite Tom Finty's lack of enthusiasm for having the "professor type" on the staff, Dealey put Dr. John H. McGinnis, professor of English at Southern Methodist University, in charge of the paper's new department called "Reviews of Books and Literary Shop Talk." It occupied a full page each Sunday. Having done book reviews for the *News* intermittently since 1916, Dr. McGinnis knew what appealed to the public, and he knew the field of literature. He had a way of getting notable literary figures to do signed reviews, and the scope of his page earned the admiration of the literary circles in the Southwest. Quickly his Book Page compared favorably with those of the best newspapers in New York, Boston, Kansas City, and other metropolitan centers.

A regular Agriculture Department for the daily issue of the *News* was a new tack in 1923. Since the days of Colonel Lowe, an ardent supporter of diversified farming, the *News* had been a leader in progressive ideas for agriculture, but it had concentrated such material mainly in *The Semi-Weekly Farm News*. In days gone by this was the principal medium for reaching the farmers. Times had changed, however. The automobile had come. Rural Free Delivery had been started. Now a large portion of the farmers took the daily newspaper. Also, the number of "city farmers" was increasing, and they read the daily paper. The auto-mobile made it convenient for the wealthy land-owner to live in the city and drive out in the morning to his farm to supervise and oversee the work and then return to the city at night. Absen-tee investors in farm land were on the increase too. To meet changing conditions, Dealey started a regular Agriculture Depart-ment in the Dallas *Morning News* and made Victor H. Schoffel-mayer the new Agriculture Editor, shifting him from *The Semi-Weekly Farm News,* where he had begun as an assistant in 1917.

Schoffelmayer was a man with ideas and a flair for promotion, and his "More Cotton on Fewer Acres" contest soon attracted nation-wide attention. The *News* offered a 1000-dollar grand prize to the Texas farmer who could grow the most cotton on an unirrigated five-acre plot. At the banquet honoring the first winner, John W. McFarlane, held in Palestine, Anderson County, Texas, Dealey made a speech in which he said:

> Twenty-odd years ago the average crop of Anderson County was one-half bale to the acre. This year the *News* has stirred one man in Anderson County to use his "think tank and elbow grease" and he has demonstrated that even under adverse conditions two bales per acre can be produced . . . So, let the slogan be, "Wake Up, Texas," and let us encourage McFarlaneism.

The contest was held each year for four consecutive years and the idea caught on and other organizations added money to the prize fund until thousands of dollars were being given to the farmers for better methods for raising cotton. The contest did more to dramatize the idea of scientific farming and crop diversi-fication to the farmers of Texas than anything else the paper had ever done.

The *News'* prestige was on the rise. The defeat of the Ku Klux Klan in August of 1924 was a good sign. There were personal

honors for Dealey . . . vice-president of the Associated Press, an
LL.D. degree conferred by Austin College at Sherman . . . appointment to the Pan American Congress of Journalists. He was
asked to run for the governorship of Texas by Judge E. J. Man-
tooth, an influential citizen of East Texas. To the Judge, Dealey
replied:

> I take it that you are bestowing this compliment on the head of
> the *News,* in recognition of the record of the *News* . . . I wish to
> acknowledge the compliment very sincerely. But the idea you con-
> vey does not appeal to me in the slightest. As the head of the *News*
> I think I have a position that in the long run can accomplish more
> and do more for the people of Texas [than the governor can].

Not all the honors went to Dealey, however, as Ted Dealey
was offered an appointment to the Board of Regents of the University of Texas. Ted declined on the grounds that there was a
rule of the *News* "which forbids its editorial employees to accept
political appointment." When certain staff members hinted that it
might be proper to make an exception in Ted's case, Dealey circulated a pink memorandum to the staff. No one in the building
could use pink paper in interoffice communication except Dealey,
and it signified a matter of high importance. He wrote:

> . . . apparently the reasons for the rule have not been understood
> generally. The rule is that all persons employed in the editorial,
> news and business departments shall refrain from active partisan
> politics.
>   On last Friday night, after Ted's declination had been received
> in Austin, Dr. Splawn, president of the University, called me on
> long distance phone and for 15 minutes argued for my waiving our
> rule in this instance, saying some very complimentary things con-
> cerning Ted's fitness for the position and the need of his service.
> I explained to him why it would not be proper for me to do so.
>   The reasons for this rule were set forth as early as 1893 in the
> editorial columns of the *News* . . . quoting a letter written by Col.
> Belo, who explained that although the *News* had advocated the
> election of Grover Cleveland as President of the United States, he
> would not give letters of recommendation to persons seeking ap-

pointments at the hands of President Cleveland, nor would he himself accept an appointment, because "as a journal maturely committed alike by profession and practice to independence and frankness in the discussion of public men and public affairs, the *News* might have occasion to criticize the incoming administration with reference to some feature or incident of its policy."

... Let all of us beware of entangling alliances.

GBD

The object lesson to prove the wisdom of the rule came a year later. In the next state election the *News* broke with Mrs. Ferguson's administration and actively supported the candidacy of Dan Moody for governor. The "entangling alliance" would have been embarrassing.

The *esprit d'corps* of the organization was high. Toward the end of the summer of 1924 a spontaneous movement developed among the staff members to hold a dinner for Dealey in honor of his fiftieth anniversary with the institution. It was staged on October 12, 1924, and the employees presented him with a solid gold watch "which was a duplicate of the timepiece presented that year to General Pershing on his retirement as General of the Armies of the United States."

In response to the tributes, Dealey said: "By some strange reversal of the rightful order of things, it is the custom among us to receive greetings and felicitations upon attaining a birthday. Rather ought the child to honor his parents on the anniversary of that day of sacrifice . . . With that in mind, I want to tell you something about the big men of the *News* of the earlier days; I want to talk particularly about those whom I term the 'Big Six.' I refer to Willard Richardson, whose term of service was from 1844 to 1875 . . . Colonel A. H. Belo . . . John J. Hand . . . D. C. Jenkins . . . R. G. Lowe . . . T. W. Dealey . . ."

"These men laid the foundation for the *News* of today," he said, "and are entitled to the larger part of the credit for what has been accomplished."

He concluded with a quotation from Robert Burns:

The bridegroom may forget the bride,
His wedded wife was made yest'een;
The monarch may forget the crown
That on his head an hour has been;
The mother may forget her child,
Who smiles sae sweetly on her knee,
But I'll remember thee, Glencairn,
And all that thou hast done for me.*

The employees' esteem for Dealey was sincere. He led them triumphantly through good times and bad. He set the pace that produced the Southwest's best newspaper, and they were proud to be a part of it. He knew them all. He praised their achievements, and called their mistakes, and helped them in their troubles. No deserving employee had ever come to him with a personal problem and gone away without being helped. No employee had ever been sick for long without getting a letter or gift or personal visit from Dealey. It was an office rule that sick reports, even for one day's absence, went immediately to his desk. He made it his business to take care of the employees. In return, they worked hard, and they loved "the Boss."

---

* Last stanza of "The Lament for James, Earl of Glencairn."

CHAPTER TWENTY-TWO

1924-1926

MRS. PEABODY SUGGESTS A TRUST FOR
THE *NEWS*. GREAT EXPECTATIONS.
BRIGGS' "WEMMICK" OPINION. LONG NE-
GOTIATIONS. DEALEY AND ASSOCIATES
ACQUIRE THE *NEWS*.

HABITUALLY DEALEY CONDUCTED HIS CORRESPONDENCE WITH
the old-time letter writer's patience that had largely disappeared
with the stage coach and sailing vessel. Whether a reply was days,
weeks, or months in coming, he remained imperturbable, and
nothing but the direst emergency could move him to use the long-
distance telephone . . . a painful extravagance. "A 2-cent stamp,"
he would say, "can do anything a phone call can do." But if there
was ever a time when he counted the days while waiting for an
answer, it was the last week of March, 1924. Two weeks earlier
he had written a letter to Mrs. Peabody, timing it to reach her
home in Cambridge, Massachusetts, on the twentieth, the date she
expected to be back home from a trip to Bermuda. The subject of
the letter, following up a proposal which had originated with
Mrs. Peabody, had become the ambition of his life.

The immediate events leading up to the letter began more than
a year earlier, during the crucial period which the *News* experienced at the end of 1922 and the beginning of 1923. On January
17, 1923, Mrs. Peabody had arrived in Dallas to hold conferences

with Dealey about the situation. Following the conferences, she wrote to him while still in Dallas:

January 24, 1923

My dear Mr. Dealey:

As our conversations are not recorded, I want to set down in writing for your file one or two points. . . .

I wish to assure you of my profound admiration for your work during the whole association with the *News* and especially for the last twenty years. . . .

It would be far more satisfactory to you to be the owner of A. H. Belo Co., as are the managers of all the other Texas newspapers. I realize that it is irksome to you to have to make statements to us. If the world were to end with you and me, I should never ask for another statement, never ask for a detail of the business, but I feel the property is a trust from my father, through me, to my children . . .

In asking Mr. Lombardi, Sr., Cornelius Lombardi, and now Ennis Cargill to come into the business, I have not intended to signify any doubt of your management ever. My one thought always has been to strengthen your organization. Perhaps I have been officious in making these suggestions, but as I have expressed to you so many times, I have always thought that if any time you were taken, the *News* would be in the position it was when Mr. Lowe, Mr. T. W. Dealey, and Alfred went, and there would be no George Dealey . . .

I have no desire, as I wrote you, to go into the detail of the management; it would be presumptuous in me to do so. My one thought is to express to you my gratitude for holding the property together and my profound belief that we should have sold out long ago had you not wished to continue to manage the property. As a sacred trust from my father, that would have been disastrous.

In regard to Peggy, she does not wish to learn the business. Her one desire is to have a position for three months, just a minor position, with whatever salary anyone else would get. I think Mr. Doran or Mr. Finty could give her assignments . . . I suggest she be allowed to write up Paderewski, hand her copy in, and if it is not satisfactory, turn it out.

On the whole, the letter was gratifying. One point, however, gave Dealey some worry. Near the end, Mrs. Peabody said:

". . . my profound belief that we should have sold out long ago had you not wished to continue to manage the property."

Suppose he was out of the picture. Would the two ladies sell under those circumstances? Would they sell to someone wholly new to the organization? If so, it could drastically affect the management and be disastrous to the spirit of the institution.

But in thinking this, possibly he was borrowing trouble. In the same letter Mrs. Peabody spoke of the property as a "trust from my father, through me, to my children." It was planned that her daughter, Peggy, would spend three months working at the *News,* and the indications were that Peggy would be the one who would keep the *News* in the hands of the heirs of Colonel Belo, although it was known that neither she nor any of the children of Mrs. Peabody or of Mrs. Alfred Belo had shown a real interest in a newspaper career.

The next event was a tragedy. Peggy, who had always been frail and sickly, fell ill in February of 1923, and it was discovered that she was suffering with tuberculosis. After seven months of desperate illness, she died in September of 1923.

About a month after Peggy's death, on October 24, Mrs. Peabody wrote to Dealey from her home in Cambridge, Massachusetts:

My dear Mr. Dealey:

I do not feel at all well. I am very nervous and feel the strain now as I did not feel it during the long pull. I miss Peggy more and more. . . .

As I told you and Walter when I was in Dallas, Mrs. Belo and I had never thought of disposing of the property. Since Peggy's death, however, I have been thinking of the shortness of life and wondering what would become of the *News* when you and I were gone. The property will go life interest to Mrs. Belo, then be divided into five parts, controlled by five people as different as human beings can be, and in complete ignorance of the workings of the *News.* Mr. Cargill and I discussed very casually, as we never had time for serious conference, the forming of some kind of a trust fund; also selling some stock to citizens of Dallas, letting in the community, as was the case when the paper came to Dallas. Mrs.

Belo is in Dallas now. Mr. Cargill should be coming back from
Mexico. I wish you would call them together and talk things over.

Just what Mrs. Peabody meant by a "trust fund," Dealey did
not know exactly, but the direction of her thinking was quite
clear. It pointed toward his fondest hope, which he had never
openly expressed, that some arrangement might be made possible
whereby he and other key men of the *News* might acquire sufficient ownership in the property to assure the continuity of the
management and to perpetuate the spirit of the institution.

He must see Mrs. Belo and Mr. Cargill immediately, as suggested by Mrs. Peabody.

Before Dealey could talk with Mrs. Belo, he took the dengue
fever, and by the time he was well, Mrs. Belo had departed for
New York. However, he was able to confer with Mr. Cargill, who
confirmed that Mrs. Peabody had communicated with him and
clarified certain feelings which she had in the matter. In sub-
stance, she wanted to confide the *News* and its reputation and
responsibilities to Dealey and the few other men of his selection
who had given long service in the management of the property.
She could see no one outside the organization whom she deemed
worthy and able to perpetuate the trust that had come into her
hands. She hoped some workable and financially satisfactory arrangement could be found whereby the controlling ownership
could be transferred.

Financially satisfactory?

There was the mountainous obstacle. The more Dealey thought
of it, the more insurmountable it seemed. But it *had* to be over-
come.

He needed advice from some financial expert who would understand all the implications of the problem—the importance to the
News, to the employees, to the community . . . the risks and consequences . . . his own lack of money or resources for the purchase . . . yet his determination to do it. He turned to his good
friend and fellow member of the Critic Club, George Waverley
Briggs.

Briggs, a black-haired, dignified individual with a remarkable

fluency of speech, had been vice-president and trust officer of the
City National Bank since 1920. But prior to that he was an employee of the *News,* and he was the man whom Dealey picked in
1911 to travel over the state and do a series of articles on "The
Housing Problem in Texas." Briggs had remained on the Dallas
paper two years and then served as editor and managing editor
of the Galveston *News* until joining the American Red Cross in
1918 as assistant manager for the Southwestern division. The
following two years he served as State Commissioner of Insurance and Banking, and in 1920 he moved to Dallas to organize
the Trust Department of the City National Bank. Dealey and
Briggs, after the latter's return to Dallas, became close friends,
and Dealey sponsored Briggs' membership into the Critic Club.
Although Dealey was nearly 30 years the older, their ideals in life
were cut of the same cloth. Wherever Dealey had pioneered in
charitable enterprises and in cultural and civic developments,
Briggs had followed.

After thinking out his position as carefully as he could, Dealey
telephoned to Briggs early one morning. As a special favor, would
Briggs call at his office at the *News?* Ordinarily he would visit
him at the bank, but there was a special reason. He would explain.

At 4:30 P.M. that same day, Briggs arrived at Dealey's office.
He noticed the desk was cleared of work, and the secretary was
instructed not to disturb them as long as they were in conference.

After seating Briggs comfortably and providing him with a
cigar, two little attentions bestowed with the aplomb of 25 years
of practice, Dealey settled back in his chair and after a thoughtful
pause he asked, "You do read Dickens, don't you?"

"Yes." Briggs was very curious by now.

"Do you remember the book, *Great Expectations?*"

"Yes."

"Do you remember Mr. Wemmick? How he sometimes had two
different opinions on important matters? One was his office
opinion, and the other was his opinion at home, and the latter was
always his full and complete opinion. Do you recall the instance
when Mr. Pip called on Mr. Wemmick at the latter's office to consult him for his opinion . . .

" 'And that,' said Mr. Pip, 'is your deliberate opinion, Mr. Wemmick?'

" 'That,' Mr. Wemmick returned, 'is my deliberate opinion in this office.'

" 'Ah,' said Mr. Pip, pressing him, for he thought he saw a loop-hole here, 'but would that be your opinion at Walworth?' [Walworth was Mr. Wemmick's homeplace.]

" 'Mr. Pip,' Mr. Wemmick replied, 'Walworth is one place and this office is another. . . . My Walworth sentiments must be taken at Walworth; none but my official sentiments can be taken in this office.' " [1]

Briggs nodded. He remembered Mr. Wemmick.

Dealey fixed his eyes on Briggs and said, smiling but serious, "I am going to ask you an important question, and I would like to have your 'Wemmick opinion at home,' which is your inner-most personal opinion and not necessarily your opinion as a banker."

Briggs promised his "Wemmick opinion at home."

Recapitulating certain high points in the history of the *News,* Dealey explained in particular how death had intervened several times since the passing of Colonel Belo to change the normal course of events in determining what might be called "the guard-ianship of the *News."* Again in the recent death of Mrs. Pea-body's daughter, Peggy, death had taken the only grandchild of Colonel Belo who had shown any interest in carrying on the news-paper traditions of the family.

"So it is," he said, "that Mrs. Peabody has become concerned about the destinies of the *News.* Please understand that she orig-inated the idea that I and others in the management of the *News* acquire the controlling ownership. No details have been discussed, but of course Mrs. Peabody and Mrs. Belo would want adequate compensation, and I would never want to suggest any reduction in the price below its actual value."

"Now for the question," Dealey said. He reminded Briggs to bear in mind that he was not a rich man. He owned a home, a few shares of bank stocks, about 70 acres of Trinity bottom land which had never been developed as he once expected, and 355 shares in

A. H. Belo & Co., which had a stock issue of 15,000 shares. Probably his personal net worth was 80,000 dollars. But this was far short of the 2 or 3,000,000 dollars that the *News* was worth.

"If these ladies should reach the final conclusion to sell," Dealey said, "do you think such an enormous sum of money could be made available without encumbering myself and all my family and the other chosen *News* employees with ruinous debts? That is the question on which I want your 'Wemmick opinion at home.' "

Briggs said immediately that his Wemmick opinion could be summed up in one word : "Certainly."

Dealey asked how he could be so certain.

Because of what he knew about the past earnings of the *News,* Briggs stated. He owned five shares of stock in the *News,* and he knew the handsome dividends it had always paid.

"Put it this way," Briggs said; "the paper itself is in position to finance the purchase."

"What do you mean?"

The procedure was not uncommon, Briggs explained. It was simply a matter of pledging the business to pay the original owners the real value of the property over a given number of years.

"Will you give me a memorandum outlining this plan?" Dealey asked.

The conference ended with Briggs agreeing to do so. Outside the office, night had come to the streets, but day was still in the sky. Boswell, the Dealey family chauffeur, was waiting at the Commerce Street door to take the two men home. As they drove away, the western horizon across the river had a warm glow . . . a sort of golden crown. Dealey asked Boswell if he thought the rich-colored sunset might be a good sign. The old Negro had a canny way of sensing "the Boss' " mood, and he knew the signs were in "the Boss," not in the sky, but he philosophized at length on the evening sky, and concluded that he " 'lowed as how it was a good sign."

Within two weeks Briggs had worked out what he called "the approach to the problem." In preparing it, he had obtained certain information about the finances of the *News* and had been authorized to bring into consultation his two superiors at the bank, Mr. R. H. Stewart and Mr. J. A. Pondrom, who were old and trusted friends of Dealey's.

The plan was premised on three factors which the bankers considered extraordinary—or at least uncommon—in the domain of trade. They were: (1) a willing seller and a willing buyer; (2) the readiness of the purchaser to maintain the income of the sellers over a long period of time approximately at the dollar level to which they had become accustomed for many years; and (3) the purpose of the sellers to moderate the terms of the sale to facilitate its fulfillment by the man who had played an important part in creating the values that were to be passed—and to whom, above all men of their acquaintance, they desired to entrust the destinies of the *News*.

The transfer of ownership would be accomplished through the organization of a new corporation designed to take over the present corporation. It would compensate the present owners mainly with securities such as bonds and preferred stock, bearing fixed rates of interest, and thereby assure them an annual income that would not be subject to the ups and downs of the newspaper business.

It was with this plan in mind that Dealey wrote to Mrs. Peabody in March of 1924, and asked for a personal conference to discuss the matter. The dream of a lifetime was sealed in his letter. A prompt reply would be most opportune, because he would be leaving Dallas on April 17 for New York City, where he planned to attend the annual meeting of the Board of Directors of the Associated Press. He was second vice-president of the AP. After the AP meeting, he hoped to go on to Cambridge, Massachusetts, and have the conference with Mrs. Peabody.

The reply arrived April 1:

My dear Mr. Dealey,

I shall be very glad to see you and Mr. Cargill on April 24 and I hope you will plan to stay a day or two with me. I can put you both up and make you comfortable, and should like to hear all about the business. I think Mrs. Belo had better come over also and join the conference, as you will probably not have very much time to see her in New York. . . .

Excellent! He was over the first hurdle.

In New York Dealey attended the AP meetings, the climax of which was a banquet honoring President Calvin Coolidge on April 22. Dealey sat at the head table, which included Adolph Ochs of the New York *Times,* Victor Lawson of the Chicago *Daily News,* E. Lansing Ray of the St. Louis *Globe-Democrat,* Paul Patterson of the Baltimore *Sun,* W. H. Cowles of the Spokane *Spokesman-Review,* Melville E. Stone and Kent Cooper of the Associated Press, and other notables of the Fourth Estate.

After the AP meetings were over, Dealey met with Mrs. Belo and Mr. Cargill, the latter having come to New York from Houston, and they made the short trip to Cambridge together. On two successive afternoons the business conferences were held at Mrs. Peabody's home, and each day promptly at 4 o'clock the butler served tea to the group. In the morning Mrs. Peabody took the guests to see some of Boston's famous historical landmarks— Copp's Hill with the old North Church where the lantern was hung in the steeple as a signal to Paul Revere, the Old State House, Faneuil Hall, and other places. At Dealey's special request they visited the second-floor dining room of the Parker House where the famous Saturday Club of Boston was accustomed to meet when Emerson and Lowell and Longfellow were members. This would be something to tell the Critic Club about.

Cordiality prevailed throughout the business talks, and Mrs. Peabody and Mrs. Belo expressed agreement with the general plan which Dealey outlined. But before making any commitments or indicating any terms, the two ladies wished to consult with a financial adviser and with their children. On that point the talks ended.

Upon his return to Dallas, Dealey asked Briggs to assist in putting the plan into concrete details and guiding it through the legal labyrinth. For this task Briggs recommended an attorney whose knowledge of corporation law and corporate structure he valued above that of all other lawyers known to him—Eugene P. Locke of the firm of Locke & Locke in Dallas. Locke accepted. He was a keen-eyed man who was acquainted with the background of the *News,* and, like Briggs, his personal interest in assisting Dealey to acquire controlling ownership of the *News* transcended the mere business considerations.

It was four months after Dealey's trip to Cambridge that he had the first indication from Mrs. Peabody that she was still pursuing the matter of the change in ownership. In a letter dated August 31, 1924, she wrote succinctly: ". . . Mr. Cargill will tell you my views on the selling proposition. Mrs. Belo's being in Europe will delay matters for some time, I think."

Mr. Cargill reported that the ladies were interested first in a complete evaluation of the property. The evaluation should be done by a committee of experts acceptable to both parties. Mr. Owen D. Young, chairman of the board of the General Electric Company, and a personal friend of Mrs. Peabody and Mrs. Belo, would serve as their financial adviser. The law firm of Baker, Botts, Parker & Garwood of Houston, which had been the Houston representative of the *News* since before 1900, would act for the Belo family in drawing up the contracts and legal papers.

Progress was being made, and Dealey was pleased. He wanted to tell Mrs. Peabody so. He wanted to tell her he appreciated what she had done already, but it would be presumptuous to write as if the transfer of ownership were taken for granted. Soon afterward, however, he found a way to say what he felt. On October 13, 1924, the day following the celebration in honor of his 50 years with the *News,* he wrote:

My dear Mrs. Peabody:

Well, the big day has come and gone. . . . I reluctantly consented to appear before a full gathering of the clans. And now that it is all over, I am enthused and delighted with the whole affair. It was, indeed, the big epoch of my life. . . .

Some of my thoughts of you and yours, I tried to express publicly in my remarks.

In this brief note I want to acknowledge your splendid letter that I opened in the presence of Ennis Cargill on the morning of the 12th and to thank you from the bottom of my heart. . . .

"But I'll remember thee, Glencairn,
"For all that thou hast done for me."

Most sincerely and cordially yours,

G. B. Dealey

The preparation for the transfer of ownership dragged on. Invariably it took four or five months between each major step. During these months of delay Dealey sometimes wondered if the financial risk would be too great an undertaking for a man of his age. At 66, most men looked to retirement. Yet he was making the greatest commitment he had ever made. Probably he would live long enough to see the payment of the obligations assured. Physically, he felt he was equal to another 10 or 15 years of active life. But no matter how long he lived, there were his two sons, Walter and Ted, to shoulder much of the burden. The other men in the management who would share in the ownership—John F. Lubben, Tom Finty, Jr., and E. B. Doran [2]—were all younger men than himself, and together with Walter and Ted they could see the venture through to a successful conclusion.

In the summer of 1925, three newspaper experts came from New York to Dallas for a few days to aid in the determination of the value of the property. They were Don C. Seitz, formerly of the New York *World* and later with the *Outlook,* Sam P. Weston, a newspaper engineer, and James W. Brown, publisher of *Editor & Publisher.* Their visit was kept so secret that even the reporters on the *News* did not know the distinguished newspapermen were in town. After weeks of study and adjustments in estimates, the final evaluation agreed upon by all parties concerned was 2,725,000 dollars.

Now it was up to Eugene P. Locke, representing the management, and Ralph B. Feagin of Baker, Botts, Parker & Garwood, representing the Belo heirs, to fashion the final and specific plan of reorganization.

The number of shares of common stock in A. H. Belo & Co. outstanding was 15,000. The Belo heirs held jointly 10,177 shares, or slightly more than two thirds of the total stock. Dealey owned

396 shares, having acquired 41 shares in recent months. In all, there were 92 persons owning stock. Of these, 70-odd were scattered small holders, owning an average of 50 shares each, and in practically every case they were heirs or legatees of holders of the original issue.

The Belo heirs and the management controlled sufficient stock to vote any plan acceptable to themselves, and they could have proceeded in the reorganization without regard for the numerous scattered small holders. But Dealey insisted that the interests of the scattered small holders be given full consideration, and on November 27, 1925, at Dealey's request, Locke wrote to Feagin proposing changes in the first draft of the plan:

> ... It is probable that many, if not most, of the scattered small holders will prefer cash or, if willing to take securities, they probably will not wish in return for their individual small holdings [an arbitrary amount of] three kinds of securities. ...
>
> The preservation of the good will of these numerous stockholders is important. ...
>
> I feel sure that if our clients can put before these scattered small holders the purpose of the reorganization and can offer to them their choice of several proposals, either bonds or preferred stock or cash, or any combination of these, the stockholders will feel that the proposals are fair and advantageous. ...

It meant more delay. But Dealey wanted every stockholder voluntarily to accept the proposed reorganization and transfer of ownership. He wanted a unanimous vote of confidence.

Very little progress was made in December, but Dealey was cheered by a Christmas letter from Mrs. Peabody. She wrote:

My dear Mr. Dealey,

> The most generous box of pecans arrived safely and will be a great pleasure to us all, as we sit before the fire and eat them. I hope you will have a happy Christmas with all your loved ones around you. I think you have chosen the road to happiness by your manner of life. It has been arduous but has its rewards in the name you have made for yourself in serving your city, your state and your country, and in the splendid family you have raised to carry

on your ideals. Walter is a worthy successor to an illustrious father. May you both live and prosper long, is my Christmas and New Year's wish.

Sincerely,

Jeannette B. Peabody

By February 10 the lawyers were finished with the legal papers. The contract was a legal masterpiece.

The key to the reorganization plan was the implicit trust placed in the Reorganization Agent, and Dealey was the Reorganization Agent. In the experience of the lawyers, the power entrusted to Dealey, a minor stockholder in the old company, was unprecedented. But they had never before encountered a situation in which everyone concerned agreed that a minor stockholder deserved to own controlling interest in the business, and, furthermore, wanted him to have it.

The reorganization plan was a document of many pages, but boiled down to its essentials, it rested on these three points:

1. The new corporation would issue the following preferred stock and securities:

Bonds, 6 1/2%, 20 years	$1,000,000
Preferred Stock, 7% cumulative	1,100,000
Demand & Short Term Notes, secured by Government bonds	625,000
TOTAL	$2,725,000

2. Each share of stock in the old company would be worth $181.66-2/3 in stocks and securities of the new company. Unless otherwise requested, the substitution would be accomplished on the following basis:

Bonds	$ 66.66-2/3
Preferred Stock	73.33-1/3
Notes	41.66-2/3
	$181.66-2/3

3. Common stock in the new corporation would be issued under the following authorization:

Common stock of such classes and number of shares, and of such par value, or without par value, as the Reorganization Agent shall determine, to be issued only to such persons (irrespective of present ownership of stock in the company) and for only such consideration as the Reorganization Agent may determine.

Number 3 was the provision which would enable Dealey, the Reorganization Agent, to acquire controlling interest in the new company without the need of a large amount of cash. Also, it gave him a free hand in picking the men in the management who would share in the ownership.

By March 9, 1926, all of the Belo heirs had signed the contract and had entrusted their shares of stock in the old company to the Depositary. Most of the scattered small holders quickly adopted the articles of reorganization, but two held out. They were sisters, and on May 27 Dealey wrote to them:

> The property of the *News* is a heritage that was handed down from Mr. Richardson to Colonel Belo *et al.;* and from them to those who are now in control. It is a property of great value and importance to Texas because of its past history of achievement and because of its record in endeavoring at all times, as far as memory goes back, to assist in every possible manner in the material, mental and spiritual development of the State and its people. All of us, therefore, who are in active control have regarded the institution as a trust, and, so regarding it, and desiring to throw every possible safeguard around it to the end that it may continue its record of service and usefulness, have determined upon the reorganization that is now in progress.
>
> .... The only two instruments remaining to be signed are those which you and your sister ... have in your possession.

Following this personal appeal, the two sisters signed, and the vote of confidence in Dealey was unanimous.

The many loose ends were finally brought together on July 15, 1926. The Library of the *News* was used in order to accommodate all the individuals vitally interested in the final signing of contracts and transfer of stock. There were the lawyers, the bankers, the financial advisers, the special representatives of the Belo family, and the members of the *News* management principally concerned.

Through several steps A. H. Belo & Co. transferred its assets to A. H. Belo Corporation, the stockholders elected a board of directors, and the new board its officers—G. B. Dealey, president, holding 52% of the voting stock; Walter A. Dealey, vice-president; John F. Lubben, secretary-treasurer; and Directors Tom Finty, Jr., E. B. Doran, Edward M. (Ted) Dealey, and Ennis Cargill.

The transactions prolonged the meeting into the late afternoon.

"Before we adjourn," John Lubben spoke up, "I would like to hear a few remarks from the president of our new corporation."

"I think he has worked hard enough on this reorganization and ought to be let off without making a speech," Walter Dealey observed.

With a little wave of his hand, Dealey indicated he would like to make a few remarks.

"I don't know how many of you can appreciate it," he said, "but my mind today goes back fifty-two years. . . ." He paused a moment to control his emotion, and then spoke feelingly of his association with the hundreds of men who had built the institution, and the trust that was now reposed in the men "around this table."

Each man in the room was called on in turn for remarks, and the cigar smoke grew thick, everyone abundantly supplied from Dealey's inexhaustible box of El Productos.

"I think 'The Big Six' are looking down on us with approval today," he mused, after all had spoken. "Well, if there isn't anything more, I am going to call on Mr. Cargill to ask the blessing of God on our work. He is an official of the Episcopal Church."

All rose and stood with bowed heads while Mr. Cargill prayed. The meeting then adjourned.

CHAPTER TWENTY-THREE

Winslow Park

SEPTEMBER USUALLY FOUND DEALEY AT HIS FAVORITE VACATION haunt in the Ozark Mountains. Since 1914 he and Ollie had spent a part of each summer at the Winslow Park Club near Winslow, Arkansas. The club was a private mountain resort, and the Dealeys owned two cottages. One cottage was named "Sleepy Hollow" . . . as Dealey described it, "a wonderful place to turn over and sleep another hour." The other cottage was named "Chinquapin" for the giant chinquapin trees surrounding it. The shade on the mountain was so deep that one could almost move it with his hand, and the air was cool and pure. Many years earlier, when Colonel Belo was alive and spent his summers in Maine or in the Adirondacks of New York, Dealey had resolved that some day he would have a summer retreat . . . and be able to write back to his friends about the "good life," as Colonel Belo had done . . . "Can you imagine my sitting by a logwood fire whilst writing this?" the colonel had said in a letter written to Dealey in August of 1892, and Dealey had thought of it every hot August since then.

With other families who had discovered the summertime delights of Winslow, Dealey and Ollie joined in organizing the Winslow Park Club. The club's 400 acres were located on the crest of the nearest mountain overlooking the town. When completed, the grounds had 40-odd cottages, an imposing mountain lodge built of native stone, a roadway, running water, electric lights, a sewer system, and a nine-hole golf course.

The club's "Rules and Regulations" unmistakably bore the

Dealey impress. "Persons developing bad colds and coughs should stay on their own premises," read Rule Number 7. In the first draft the rule had specified "children" only. But Dealey had changed it to "persons," noting that it did not make sense to him to confine the children if adults were allowed to spread the dreaded germs around.

Usually in July and not later than the first of August, Ollie and one or more daughters or daughters-in-law, together with their children, took up residence at Winslow Park. Dealey would follow the first part of September. Although he spent less time at Winslow than many of the other club members, while he was there he liked to play the role of unofficial host to the mountain, greeting guests and new arrivals, arranging the programs for "Family Night" on Wednesdays, making the announcements at dinnertime in the big dining hall at the lodge, and generally seeing that all were enjoying themselves. Once on some particular occasion a party was going on at the lodge, and as usual he was making the rounds, talking with the various groups, when he discovered a rather shy young lady standing alone near the entrance. He promptly took her by the arm, squired her over to the refreshments table, and helped her to lemonade and cake.

"Now, we'll introduce you to some of these folks," he said.

"But I'm Eva, the washwoman," she said. "I came for a wash bundle."

"Well, you just stay and be our guest tonight," he said.

Finding just the right group to introduce her to, he soon made her forget that she had come for a wash bundle.

At "Family Night" on Wednesdays, he never failed to have the program include several cornet solos by Mrs. John F. Butler of Austin, Texas. The Butler cottage was next to the Dealey cottage, and Mrs. Butler could play the old songs that appealed to Dealey: "My Old Kentucky Home," "Drink to Me Only With Thine Eyes," "Killarney," and others. On Sundays he assisted with the Sunday school for the children and always had them sing "Onward Christian Soldiers" and "The Church in the Wild Wood."

The few weeks of relaxation at Winslow had to serve him for

the next 12 months, because he never took off from work at any other time of the year. He caught up on his sleep, took long drives through the mountains, and sat by the hour on the spacious front porch of his cottage, talking with neighbors and absorbing the restfulness and beauty of the landscape. His delight in the evening was to sit on the "hurricane deck" of the lodge exchanging reminiscences, watching the 9 o'clock passenger train with its lighted windows wind through the valley below like a giant glow-worm, listening to the echoes of the whistle as the train diminished into the distance, and smoking good cigars until the ash grew long and drifted off on the mountain breeze.

A picnic supper on the golf links in which the whole colony participated could always be counted on for September 18, which was Dealey's birthday. The watermelons were brought in a day early and put in tubs of ice by Old Ben, the kindly handy man who "came" with the mountain. At the picnic Dealey usually found some newcomers to tell that the first thing he ate after arriving in America was watermelon . . . and that then he knew he was going to like America. When it was about time for the picnic to break up, Mrs. Butler and one or two others would slip off into the darkness and walk to the other end of the golf links. There she would play on the cornet. Back at the picnic, the group would gather around the fire and listen quietly to "Believe Me If All Those Endearing Young Charms," then "Carry Me Back to Old Virginny," followed by "All Through the Night." As the far-away, clear notes of the cornet began "Auld Lang Syne," the group would join in singing, and when the song ended, the picnic was over.

CHAPTER TWENTY-FOUR

1927-1930

LIVE OAKS FOR S.M.U. DEALEY KEEPS AT
CITY PLANNING. ADOLPH OCHS PAYS A
COMPLIMENT. HONORS COME TO DEALEY.
ANOTHER DRIVE FOR CHARITY. THE
TWENTY-YEARS-AFTER DINNER.

"WE RECEIVED THE LONG CARDBOARD TUBE, BUT THERE WAS
nothing inside except air," Dealey wrote to Bremer W. Pond,
noted landscape architect of Boston, Massachusetts, who was
drawing the master plan for the 133-acre campus of Southern
Methodist University. "Perhaps you intended to send some cool
New England air to help us out during this warm spell." The
time was July 6, 1925.

Luckily, before the empty tube was thrown away, the drawings
for the campus were found wrapped around the outside of the
tube, and beautification proceeded at the S.M.U. campus. Dealey
was chairman of the campus landscape committee and, as usual,
whatever he touched assumed order and plan.

The spindly little oaks and pecans that were planted the first
year flourished, and by the fall of 1927 the *quercus virginiana* had
borne fruit, and Bishop C. C. Selecman, the university's president,
telephoned to Dealey to "come out and see the acorns."

Like the young live oaks, many projects and plans of Dealey's
were bearing fruit in 1927 and 1928. It was the harvest time of
an abundant life. He had a good inner feeling, and it reflected
itself in his healthy look, his firm step, and the sure way he dis-

patched business details. His fair skin had a fine, clean texture
and hardly showed a wrinkle except around the eyes. Only his
white hair and white mustache revealed that he was almost "three-
score and ten."

In the fall of 1927 Dealey was preparing for the National
Conference on City Planning to be held in Dallas the following
spring. He was the general chairman of the conference, and the
meeting offered a pleasant climax to the 20 years he had devoted
to city-plan work. Eight months ahead of time he sent a memo to
his key executives on the paper:

> *Messrs. Doran, Finty, E. M. Dealey, Lubben, W. A. Dealey—*
>
> At an early convenient date I would like to present to you gentle-
> men a suggestion I have with reference to preparing to make the
> most of the City Planning Conference that is to convene in Dallas
> next spring. A half hour will do.
> How would it do for us to meet at lunch in Room 15 on the date
> agreed to? We can talk about it while we are eating. —GBD

Short memos and brief conferences . . . "suggestions" rather
than orders . . . that was Dealey. Always considerate; but sooner
or later every employee learned that GBD's "suggestions" on pink
memo paper were to be acknowledged promptly and executed ac-
cordingly. To fail to do so would bring a quick summons to his
office.

In city planning, Dallas had accomplished much, but in 1927
the city was at the crossroads again. The Ulrickson Plan—a mod-
ernization of Kessler's City Plan for Dallas—would be up for
the public's vote in December of 1927. As with every crucial
city-plan issue since 1910, Dealey felt that the responsibility to see
the bond issue put over rested ultimately with the *News*. Other
men and organizations worked for the cause, and their efforts
were important and necessary, but nevertheless he believed that
only a newspaper could put the issues across to the public. His
zeal for city planning had caused George E. Kessler to declare
to a meeting of city planners in Kansas City in 1919: "G. B.
Dealey of Dallas, Texas, has done more for city planning than any

other individual in the United States." He and Kessler had understood one another as if they had been friends all their lives. Kessler's death, coming suddenly in 1923, had been a real shock and
a personal loss, and by a strange coincidence the telegram of Kessler's death was handed to him while he was addressing the Galveston Rotary Club on "City Planning."

The big question confronting Dallas in 1927 was whether or
not to levee the Trinity River. The cost would be tremendous, but
the city planners said Dallas could *not* afford to do otherwise.

The Trinity was Dallas' greatest handicap. Kessler had pointed
out the fact in 1910. "Within ten minutes' walking distance of
the highest valued lands in the city," Kessler wrote in the original
City Plan for Dallas, "is a great area having practically no more
than farm values, upon which a great [industrial] city will spring
up . . ." The area referred to was the Trinity lowlands, but before
any development could come about, Kessler advised, Dallas would
have to move the river channel to the west side of the valley, "and
confine it there by means of levees approximately twenty-five feet
high and 1200 feet apart."

It had been difficult to convince the people that the great levee
was the only practical way to control the river. From 1910 to
1927 many solutions were seriously proposed—even the idea of
creating a great lake between Dallas and Oak Cliff by damming
up the river. At different times five of the country's best hydraulic
engineers were consulted, including the famous General George
W. Goethals, chief engineer in the construction of the Panama
Canal, but they all confirmed that Kessler's plan was the best.
The job was to be a mammoth undertaking, estimated to require
the removal of a volume of earth equal in cubic content to one
twelfth of the earth moved in digging the Panama Canal, but
there was no other satisfactory way to control the floods of the
Trinity and reclaim the bottom lands.

The Trinity Levee project was only a part of the Ulrickson
Plan for Dallas—possibly a one-fourth part in cost—but it was
the keystone. The Ulrickson Plan called for a 40,000,000-dollar
program of city, county, and private improvements. It was the
climax of four years of intensive voluntary city-planning work.

Dealey's role in the undertaking had started at the beginning, with his appointment to the "25-Year Committee," a body of 25 leading businessmen assigned by the chamber of commerce to study the needs of Dallas for the next 25 years. Like Pallas Athene, the 25-Year Committee had sprung forth full-grown and fully armed. From the first meeting, it understood the major problems of Dallas, and it was determined that Dallas should emulate St. Louis and outclass Houston. A St. Louis bond issue of 87,000,000 dollars was its inspiration, and the success of Houston's man-made ship channel was its envy.

From the 25-Year Committee to the City Planning Committee to the Ulrickson Plan [1] was a complicated four-year process, but finally Dallas had before it a new master blueprint.

As in every issue for tax-supported public improvements, opposition abounded. There were the "peanut politicians," as Dealey termed them—men who sought public favor by decrying the heavy tax. There was another group of men with vested interests who stood to lose something if a rival industrial area sprang up west of the business district. And there was still a third kind of opposition—the people who were saying, as the stranger in the crowd had said to Dealey in 1903 when the ill-fated park tax was up for vote, "I wonder what them guys are getting out of this?"

But in 1927 the "strangers in the crowd" were not so numerous. Over the last 20 years the people of Dallas had received a continuous education on the benefits of city planning and civic attractiveness. The *News* had kept "everlastingly at it." This education was the foundation for future progress, and on top of this foundation was built a superstructure of attendant efforts toward the same cause, including the work of the Chamber of Commerce, the City Plan Commission, the Kessler Plan Association, and in earlier years the Dallas Property Owners' Association, and, before that, the City Plan and Improvement League.

Twenty years of ground work was indispensable, but when the time came to put over the bond election for the Ulrickson Plan, there was need for a final publicity push. Again the old tried and proven formula was put to work—a flood of daily publicity of every type, coordinated with the personal appeals made by an army of workers contacting schools, churches, professional groups, and clubs of all types. As in the past, the *News* was the backbone of the campaign, but a new element was added—the radio. Talks explaining the Ulrickson Plan were given over WFAA, the radio station of the Dallas *Morning News,* and there was something new and dramatic in this approach to publicity. It was a powerful new medium of mass communication. Walter Dealey's fledgling of 1922 was about to take wing and soar beyond all expectations.

On December 15, despite extreme cold weather, the progressive-minded voters turned out in large numbers, and the multimillion-dollar city bond issue carried easily. The Ulrickson Plan was assured.[2]

At 4:30 o'clock on the afternoon of July 24, 1928, at the south end of the west levee site, about 1000 people watched a giant dragline excavating machine throw its five-cubic foot shovel forward and lift the first earth for building the Trinity Levee. The project was under way. Earlier in the day several hundred of the participants had lunched together under a tent near the site and celebrated with an afternoon of speech-making. Dealey was among the speakers.

"This is a red-letter day for Dallas," he said. "Strange as it may seem, in 1902, more than twenty-five years ago, I stood on the old Commerce Street bridge and looked down into the valley and became possessed of the idea that some day the flood situation would be corrected and the valley would be reclaimed . . . I am well aware that during all these years most people regarded the project as chimerical and a huge joke." After telling of the first two unsuccessful efforts to levee the Trinity River in which he had participated, the first being stopped because of the world war and the second failing for lack of funds, he said, "But Fate decreed that the efforts should become 'Trinitarian,' and the third effort was the charmed one, and we are here today to congratulate the men who are responsible. . . . Their motto has been 'Never say die.'"

At the Dallas Country Club on the evening of March 26, 1928, Dealey and Ollie were hosts to the members of the Critic Club and their wives. They were celebrating the twentieth anniversary of the Critic Club. The conversation at the table turned to a remarkable compliment which Adolph Ochs of the New York *Times* had paid to the *News* at a luncheon in Houston on March 9.

"It happened like this," Dealey related, being pressed to tell about it:

> I was unavoidably late, getting to the dining room twenty minutes after the works had started. I was being seated at one of the many tables when Mr. Jesse Jones came over from the head table and escorted me to a seat on Mr. Ochs' right. I had quite a conversation with Mr. Ochs during the luncheon and remarked to him that I had seen him first in 1893 at the American Newspaper Publishers' Association gathering at the World's Fair. He recalled that gathering and said that he had known Col. Belo longer than that.
>
> Then it was that Mr. Ochs was called on to speak, and he said that when he bought the *Times* in 1895, he was determined to keep its columns as free of the vulgar, the inane, and the sensational, as was humanly possible. He added:
>
> "I received my ideas and ideals for a clean, honest, high-class newspaper from . . . the Galveston *Daily News* and the Dallas *Morning News*. I had before me the beautiful example in those papers."

After dinner the group moved to the Dealey home on Alice Circle to continue the meeting. Dealey had prepared a paper to be read—"A Brief Historical Sketch of the Critic Club."

He cited several papers read to the club in the past 20 years which had led to important constructive civic undertakings. For special mention he singled out Dr. J. F. Kimball's paper on "The Nurture of Genius as an Element in Planning Cities," which led to Dr. Kimball's writing of *Our City—Dallas,* to be used as the civics textbook for all Dallas school children. He said a paper read by George Waverley Briggs in 1922 led the Critic Club to appoint a committee to bring about the establishment of a Community Trust Foundation for Dallas, and he believed the foundation would soon be realized.

In telling about his first paper for the Club, he said:

The big question was what to write about. Dr. O. S. Fowler, the phrenologist, told me more than forty years ago that I was born with a good-sized bump of order, indicating an inclination for putting and keeping everything in place, and I have always liked attractive surroundings. . . . So, naturally, for the paper my first thought was to write something along the lines of civic hygiene and city planning, and I did, and it had something to do with city planning in Dallas.

At no period during the lifetime of the Critic Club [Dealey concluded], could there have been named fifteen citizens who would have excelled the members of the Critic Club in all manner of civic leadership. It is hard to estimate the public good that has been at least indirectly accomplished by the coming together of such men and in the discussion of the problems of the day. To me, personally, the association with the members has been delightful and inspiring.

The club members responded with a poem of appreciation, and presented Dealey with a silver water set consisting of a carafe, two goblets, and a tray.

In this period of his life many honors came to Dealey. The Texas Newspaper Publishers Association conferred on him the title of "Dean of the Texas Press." The *American Magazine* carried a long story of his life, under the heading "42 Pictures of Davy Crockett Help Run The Dallas News." The Dallas Chamber of Commerce held a magnificent banquet in his honor, attended by 500 friends . . . and Dealey modestly disclaimed the encomiums and said it was impossible to tell how he felt . . . "but you should see my insides." *Editor & Publisher* featured him in its series of "Romances of American Journalism," singling out the key to his success as being in the words he spoke to the *News* employees at the surprise party for him on his election to the presidency of the company: "My attainment to my present place is not so much due to any perfection in me as to the fact that I stuck to the job. That is the advice that I would give to others. Always stick to the job." [3]

Not only was Dealey paid honors, but he was sought to bestow honors. In May, 1928, he was chosen as the American journalist to present a silver vase to Dean Walter Williams at ceremonies

commemorating the twentieth anniversary of the founding of the
University of Missouri School of Journalism. He and Dean
Williams were kindred spirits, and the dean had managed to bring
him back to the Missouri campus frequently. He had made addresses at three Missouri Journalism Weeks—in 1915, 1922, and
1924—and on November 9, 1925, acting as "the representative of
the journalists of America," he made the responding address on
the occasion of the dedication of a stone from St. Paul's Cathedral
in London for the new Journalism Building at Missouri. Sir
Esme Howard, British Ambassador to America, made the presentation address. The stone symbolized the bond of common heritage
and mutual friendship between the press of Great Britain and the
press of America. After the ceremonies were over, Dealey mentioned to Sir Esme that he was born in England, and immediately
a fast and lasting friendship was born.

While Dealey was at Missouri, he spoke to a combined banquet
meeting of Sigma Delta Chi and Alpha Delta Sigma, the journalism and advertising fraternities, and the students honored him by
singing a toast:

> A toast to Mr. Dealey,
> The Boss of the Dallas *News*.
> When he sends up his "G.B.D."
> They tremble in their shoes.
> 'Cause he's doctor of the morning sheet,
> Director of the squibs,
> And a very, very truthful man,
> He never, never fibs.
>
> Living first in England,
> And working to beat hell
> Have earned for him a damned good job
> Which he does manage well.
> And although it's not quite honest,
> It might as well be true,
> We're going to make of him, a son, a son
> A son of Old Mizzou.

CHORUS:

So he's a son, a son, a son, a son
A son of Old Mizzou.
A son-of-a-gun, a son, a son,
A son of Old Mizzou.
Here's health, here's wealth and all success
To George B. Dealey, who,
Is a son, a son, a son, a son
A son of Old Mizzou.

(Tune: "Son of Old Mizzou")

On Dealey's fifty-fourth anniversary with the *News*—October 12, 1928—there was no organized salute to "the Boss," but on that morning his desk had a stack of interoffice envelopes bearing personal good wishes from numerous employes. He saved them all, because a letter of appreciation was something he could not throw away. Among them was one from Ted:

GBD:

Allow me to congratulate you on your fifty-fourth birthday with The News. The usual greeting I get around town is that if I ever live to be as good a man as you are, I will be "stepping some." I agree with this sentiment heartily.

—Ted Dealey

Dealey confided to his faithful friend, Mr. W. H. Benners, the *News'* business manager, who was getting along in years himself, that if these honors and congratulations continued, some people might get the idea that he was about ready to retire, when the fact was he was just getting started. To prove it, he was going to try to get a group of men together and raise 1,000,000 dollars for a children's hospital, which ought to keep him occupied for five or ten years, considering how long jobs like that usually took.

Dealey's interest in the building of a children's hospital had come of his close work with two other charitable institutions administering to the medical needs of children. One was the Scottish Rite Hospital for Crippled Children. He had contributed substantially to the construction of its new building in 1921-22 and never failed to make a large annual contribution to its maintenance. He felt a deep compassion for the small children who came to the hospital with clubbed feet and other malformations, and to see and talk with a child whose trouble had been corrected gave him great pleasure.

The other institution was the Freeman Memorial Clinic in Dallas, a charitable organization begun in 1921 as the Presbyterian Clinic for babies and children. A short time later it was endowed by Mr. P. R. Freeman of Dallas[4] and the name was changed. Dealey served on the Board of Directors and acted as chairman of the executive committee. An executive of the clinic described his work as "the sustained effort that kept it going. His standing order with the superintendent was: 'When you find a deserving case that can't be taken care of in the regular way, call on me for the money, but let's not mention it to anyone else.' "

In April, 1928, following a meeting of the directors of the Freeman Memorial Clinic, four of the directors were talking together in the office of the superintendent. Dr. Jack F. Perkins, chief of the medical staff, was bewailing the need of a children's hospital in Dallas . . . a place to take over where the clinic left off. In the state of Texas there was no hospital exclusively for children . . . no place with specialists and equipment and accommodations especially designed for children.

"Well, you doctors talk about this all the time," Dealey said. "Why don't we stop talking and build a hospital? The *News* will do its part to raise the money."

"I'll start it off by giving the land for the hospital," Mr. P. R. Freeman said.

It was to be called the Texas Children's Hospital, and to get the drive for funds started, Dealey invited about 40 Dallas businessmen to a dinner at Stoneleigh Court near the hospital area. After the meal he told them Mr. Freeman had donated a piece of land for a children's hospital which would adjoin the children's clinic there on the hill overlooking Reverchon Park. On this hill, he said, there was a cluster of institutions devoted to human mercy —the Scottish Rite Hospital for Crippled Children, Hope Cot-

tage, the Bradford Memorial Hospital for Babies, the Parkland
Hospital, as well as the Freeman Memorial Clinic. The place was
once called Woodchuck Hill, and he told how he used to ride there
daily on horseback, years ago before the area was built up.

"I have long thought of this hill as 'the soul of Dallas,' " Dealey
said.

Dallas needed to look to its soul now more than ever. A great
industrial project was in progress in the Trinity Valley, and the
city was planning 25 years ahead for its physical and economic
growth. Was it not time to plan 25 years ahead for the growth of
its soul?

Before the drive could accomplish much, it would run into a
depression. Years later, when nearly everyone else had forgotten
the unfinished project, Dealey would revive it again and see it
completed 11 years after its inception.

Quite appropriately but purely by coincidence, on the afternoon
following the start of the drive for the Texas Children's Hospital,
the board of directors of the United Charities of Dallas, at its
regular monthly meeting, paid a special tribute to Dealey. He had
worked with the United Charities since its founding in 1898. The
meeting on October 25, 1928, marked his thirtieth year of service
and the twentieth anniversary of his presidency of the organization. Assuming its leadership in 1908, his first act was to persuade
important city leaders to serve as directors and to work on various
committees, a policy that led to immediate success. Its fame
spread, and it became the model of similar organizations in Texas
and elsewhere in the United States.

"Mr. Dealey seldom missed the monthly board meeting in all
these years," Miss Flora Saylor, the executive head who had
worked with the organization since its beginning, said.

The brilliant and prodigious Tom Finty, Jr., became fatally ill
in the early part of 1928. To watch his slow decline was painful
and sad to all who knew him and especially to Dealey, who had
worked closely with him since before 1900. The penetrating and
analytical mind that had written so copiously for a quarter of a
century had lost its light.

"My slavish devotion to public affairs has kept me from being with my family and friends as I would like to have been," Finty wrote from the sanitarium in October, addressing the letter jointly to Dealey, Stuart McGregor, and George Waverley Briggs. The sad thought clung in Dealey's mind. Newspaper work was like that. No writer on the *News* had ever driven himself harder than Finty. Dealey ranked him with D. C. Jenkins, Colonel R. G. Lowe, D. Prescott Toomey, and William G. Sterett. In some ways he was the greatest of them all. Finty died April 25, 1929.

In thinking of the men who were dead and gone, Dealey realized that two generations of *News* employees had passed on since he himself had joined the organization in 1874.

To fill the gap left by the passing of Finty and the retirement of Alonzo Wasson, Dealey asked his brother, Dr. James Q. Dealey, who had retired from the faculty of Brown University and joined the *News* editorial staff in 1928, to take the position of editor-in-chief. He was inordinately proud of the scholarly achievements of his younger brother—a Ph.D. degree, 11 books on sociology, government, and allied subjects, and distinguished lectureships at home and abroad. There were some men on the staff who questioned the wisdom of raising a man with only a year's experience in newspaper work to the highest editorship in the organization. But Dealey regarded his brother's availability as a stroke of good fortune, and he felt his bringing Dr. Dealey to the staff was a feather in his cap.

The new editor-in-chief was "to have a free hand, to control the editorial writing in all publications of the company, and to project the *News'* influence into new areas."

"Of course," Dealey added in the letter of appointment, October 1, 1929, "it will be understood that in giving you this authority the well-known policies and traditions of the *News* will be continued. Also that there will be no departure from these well-known policies or traditions without authority from me."

The year 1929 raced along, accelerated by the automobile, the airplane, and the radio. Times were prosperous, and boundless optimism pervaded the country. The little stock tumble on Wall

Street in March had merely served as a tonic to invigorate the market more.

On October 23, 1929, five "old cronies" in Dallas got together for what they called a "Twenty-Years-After Dinner." They carefully selected the room in the new Baker Hotel that most nearly corresponded with the location of the banquet hall in the Baker's predecessor, the old Oriental Hotel, where President William Howard Taft had been feted on October 23, 1909. The five men were Joseph L. Brown, Albert Linz, R. H. Stewart, Charles H. Platter, and Dealey, the committee which had been in charge of the famous Dallas banquet. They had previously invited Chief Justice Taft to return, promising him the equal of the 1909 affair, but the Supreme Court was in session and he had graciously declined.

The same "Simple Dinner" was served . . . with its Canapés à la Russe, Strained Gumbo, Fresh Crab Meat à la Newburg, Broiled Sirloin Steak . . . even the bottle of Apollinaris.

After the meal they exchanged memories and smoked cigars until the air was blue. Among the reminiscences, it was recalled that while Bishop Alexander C. Garrett made the welcoming address, President Taft cleared away the dishes from in front of him and made notes for his talk by writing on the tablecloth. The president's speech was magnificent, they all agreed, one of the greatest ever heard in Dallas.

Leaving the dining room, they were walking leisurely through the lobby when an acquaintance asked if they had heard the latest news. There was a panic on Wall Street.

"It's probably just a healthy reaction," one of the group commented.

Unhappily, it was no healthy reaction, but the beginning of at least six years of hard times in the United States, and a worldwide depression which helped alter the course of history.

CHAPTER TWENTY-FIVE

1930-1934

DEALEY KEEPS CHEERFUL DURING THE
DEPRESSION. THE TRINITY LEVEE FIGHT.
RECRUITING FOR THE GUILD OF FORMER
PIPE ORGAN PUMPERS. WALTER DEALEY
DIES.

ALL DAY SATURDAY DEALEY HAD THE USUAL STREAM OF CALLERS, Saturday of course bringing a run of out-of-town visitors, usually including one or two small-town newspaper publishers, who were most likely to call with their families. He had many good friends among the country editors over the state, and considered their friendship a part of the *News'* stock-in-trade. On this Saturday—it was February 1, 1930—the conversations invariably got around to the business outlook, and in a casual way Dealey was taking soundings on conditions in various parts of the state. Generally business was bad everywhere, but there were still some optimists in the country who refused to believe that the hard times would be long-lasting. Dealey and the *News* were trying bravely to whistle in the dark, but the signs were not encouraging.

His last group of visitors kept on talking, and the afternoon was running out. Finally Dealey told Miss Utley, his secretary, whom he valued on par with a good editor, to ask Mr. Lewis to come in. By a subtle inflection in his voice, which no one else could have interpreted, Miss Utley knew to tell H. Kay Lewis, a reporter, not to wear his coat. That meant he was expected to be a guide and immediately get the visitors out of the Boss' office and give them a tour of the building. Had he been summoned "with coat," he would first get a story from the visitors—with Dealey guiding the interview—and then escort the guests on a tour of the building. So courtly and diplomatically could Dealey and Lewis handle these maneuvers that visitors felt they had received the ultimate honor, and in fact it was the ultimate courtesy.

The last group having departed, Dealey asked Miss Utley to stay overtime a few minutes to take one last letter:

To Mr. Wm. M. Davis,
Composing Room.

Dear Mr. Davis:

I am pleased again to extend congratulations on your birth-day. . . .

How Dealey remembered all the birthdays and anniversaries and the "little things" of every type that he wrote about to hundreds and hundreds of people—both on the *News* staff and among outsiders—was a mystery even to his secretary. He seemed never to forget anything . . . he was a veritable animated tickler file.

Having taken the letter, Miss Utley asked if she was to enclose an order on E. M. Kahn & Co. A five-dollar credit slip on this nearby men's store always accompanied birthday greetings to the "old reliables" in the organization.

The reply was going to be "Yes," but Dealey paused before answering, and in the momentary reflection he hoped the general business decline would not go so far that he would have to stop these small favors which gave him much personal pleasure. It seemed that the older he got the more he enjoyed presenting gifts to people. He had never been rich, but all his life he had given to relatives, friends, and worthy causes, almost beyond his means. Perhaps that helped explain why he had stayed in debt the first 30 years of his married life.

The hard times worsened in February. In Dallas the United Charities extended relief to more and more unemployed families.

Commercial activity was slow, and advertising volume was down. If the business pulse of the state could be taken by the price of cotton, it was at a new low—15 cents a pound. On February 18, 1930, a run started on one of the largest banks in Fort Worth, a "Gibraltar" of stability. While the bank employees served coffee and cheese sandwiches to the long line of persons waiting to make withdrawals, the Federal Reserve Bank in Dallas rushed several million dollars by truck to the beleaguered bank. The run was beaten, but the news of it shook the stoutest hearts among Southwest bankers. Elsewhere conditions were the same. In Chicago, Illinois, the Cook County treasury was broke, and county employees drew rations from a relief agency. In the newspapers across the country, full-page advertisements told of the sad fate of "Job-a-Week George," who had halitosis . . . and the sales of Listerine jumped . . . it was "hot copy" that made the most of the uneasy situation. The hard times were nation-wide.

Dealey had shouldered the business responsibilities of the *News* through four national depressions, but never before had he faced one when the company's financial demands were so pressing as they were in this period. The commitment that weighed the heaviest on the *News* was the interest and dividend payment on its bonds and preferred stock issued at the time of the reorganization. To default for six months on the bond interest could result in the control of the property reverting to the Belo family, until the obligations were met. Even though such an eventuality might be temporary or the grace period extended, to Dealey it was unthinkable.

The first week of March Dealey was ill in bed with a fever. Business was still worse, the weather was gloomy, and his spirits were utterly low. While he was sick, he received a letter from Mr. Wm. M. Davis, the "old reliable" in the composing room to whom he had sent a birthday remembrance a month earlier:

> . . . I should like to mention a kindness you did me about ten years ago, Mr. Dealey. I had been ill for six weeks, unable to work. When I had recovered, you asked me to call at your office. I shall never forget that visit. . . . Well, before I left, I was in possession

of three weeks' pay, also a check to pay my life insurance premium which was past due, and you asked me to name the amount that Bob Cammack could take out of my pay each week to make it up. I said $10. You said, "Make it $5." Oh, it is such a vivid recollection to me! I wish to state right here that you made me a very happy man by your kindness, and I shall never forget your favor to me and my family. . . .

The letter of appreciation, hand-written on tablet paper, was better for Dealey than any medicine the doctor could prescribe.

"You really don't know," he wrote Mr. Davis, "how gratified I was to get your letter, and of the good effect that it had on me, showing such a fine appreciation of a very ordinary act."

He had prayed for guidance to meet the troubled situation, and Mr. Davis' letter was an answer. The *News* organization was full of men with good hearts, like Mr. Davis, and if worse came to worse, he knew he could count on them, and they would help one another meet the hard times together. It renewed his courage and firmed up his optimism, and he resolved to be cheerful and stay that way. After all, it was like the old Missouri publisher said: "I'm an old man and have had many troubles, but most of them never happened."

As the depression dragged on month after month, Dealey's cheerfulness became no small marvel to the employees and to others who were associated with him. The *News* had to economize in many ways, but Dealey held off cutting salaries, and no regular employee was let off in order to trim the payroll.

During the summer of 1930 as the state political campaign got under way, the decision was up to Dealey whether to send out the usual large number of correspondents to follow the candidates. The papers could save by relying more on the news services, it was pointed out.

The *News* should never spare money in covering important news, Dealey said. It would make the *News* just another newspaper. Put the same number of correspondents on the road.

The governor's race was a hot one, as those involving Jim Ferguson always were, and it produced one of the little office jokes that endured long after the incident was forgotten. In the middle of the campaign, the *News* threw its editorial support to Ross Sterling, a citizen of Houston, despite the fact that two Dallas men were among the candidates.

"A box-office proposition," quickly charged one of the Dallas candidates. "I have known the Dallas *News* for 45 years, and most of the employees are strongly back of me. It was strictly a box-office proposition with the owners to support Sterling."

Dealey sent the story to E. B. Doran, the *News* business manager, with the question: "What did the 'box office' get?"

"We hope to get a page ad some day this week," Doran replied. "The *Star-Telegram* got two pages!"

For a long time after that the favorite remark around the building was, "What did the box office get?"

As winter came on, the depression grew more serious. In November the *News* and *Journal* opened its classified columns free of charge to HELP WANTED ads. The unemployed were in real distress. "Remember that one day's work out of a week," the *News* urged, "may keep a family from going hungry." Cotton dropped to ten cents a pound. Unemployment in the nation was estimated at 4,000,000, and the government was spending a billion dollars on construction to provide work.

In December President Herbert Hoover outlined a special relief program to Congress.

"In the larger view," the president told Congress, "the major forces of the depression now lie outside of the United States . . . retarding [our own] recuperation." The depression had spread around the world.

The rumor that the *News* was about to be sold flourished during the depression, but it was a perennial piece of slander that Dealey had heard many times since Colonel Belo's death in 1901. Naturally the depression gave it new credence, and it took odd forms and not infrequently was furthered by innocent parties. It often had the paper on the verge of bankruptcy and selling out to a railroad or to a newspaper chain. In January, 1931, one of the rumors —reported in a letter from a friend in Waco—even named the alleged purchaser and gave the date the deal was made. Dealey circulated the letter to the executives with a wry comment:

> About two years ago, I was at a luncheon at the Adolphus and Nathan Adams [president of the First National Bank in Dallas] came to my chair and whispered to me, "Is the *News* for sale? I have an inquiry." My reply was "Yes, it can be bought for 5¢ a copy, on any street corner in Dallas."

In the midst of the depression, as if everyone's business and personal troubles were not enough, Dallas was beset with a public wrangle that stalled the completion of the Trinity Levee and reclamation project for several years, coming just at the time when the mammoth project was almost finished. The new river channel was dug, the great levees built, the Trinity diverted, and only a few openings in the levees were waiting for the storm sewers which the city of Dallas was obligated to construct as a part of its share in the project jointly undertaken by the county, the city, and the property owners in the Levee District. In time of rain the storm sewers were designed to contain the massive water runoff and carry it underneath the levees into the new river channel. If left uncontrolled, the runoff would continue to flood the Trinity lowlands. The storm sewers were the key to the reclamation of the 10,500 acres "upon which a great industrial city would spring," as George E. Kessler had said.

More than 10,000,000 dollars had been expended on the levee project. To complete the storm sewers would require less than half a million more. But the city officials were reneging on the city's obligations. It was almost unbelievable that so little could thwart so much. But the depression had complicated the situation, and half a million dollars had suddenly become a large sum of money.

The *News* kept hammering at the obstructions and prodding the city officials, but nothing happened. Along with others, Dealey joined the battle on a personal basis. He called personally on various city officials and the directors of the Chamber of Commerce.

First, I tried to impress them with the idea [he wrote in a memorandum] that in my opinion the work with all that is coming out thereof, constitutes the biggest and most important project ever before the people of Dallas since my coming here forty-five years ago.

Secondly, I told these gentlemen there were two great opportunities before Dallas—one was the possibility of getting a magnificent 500-acre airport, which would be but three-minutes drive from Union Station . . . and three times larger than Love Field . . . which is too small now and is getting smaller every day. The other opportunity was the chance to acquire the land between the levees for a park—4500 acres of park property . . . [Some day] this land will be in the heart of Dallas. . . . I suggested that in ten or twenty years the land between Dallas and Fort Worth would be solidly built up.

In the struggle over the completion of the levee and reclamation project, both sides were formidable, pitting politics, newspapers, and large vested interests against one another. Many of the ablest leaders of Dallas were involved, and bitter and irreconcilable enmities developed between men who were formerly close friends. Dealey lost friends, and most regrettable to him, the Critic Club was split into two factions, and for several years the atmosphere at its meetings was very cool.

As a part of a continuing whisper campaign, the opposition accused Dealey of a "selfish interest" in the completion of the levee. The attack was brought out in the open near the climax of the fight, when the Dallas *Dispatch* charged in a front-page editorial: "The tearful plea of the Dallas *Morning News* that the city immediately put $130,000 into sewers under land of the Industrial Properties corporation . . . is not wholly civic. There are property interests involved." [1]

What were the facts? Out of the 10,500 acres in the improvement district, the Dealey family owned 15½ acres, plus another ten acres between the levees. These tracts were the land Dealey had purchased between 1903 and 1906. No other official of the *News* owned land in the district. The amount of land involved was inconsequential, and Walter and Ted Dealey urged the sale of the land or the deeding of it to the city in order to prove they were not trying to get rich at the public's expense. But Dealey said the piece of property had nothing to do with the rightness of the *News'* stand in the controversy, and he intended to keep it.

The aggravating delays continued, and on April 25, 1931, Dealey sent a forceful appeal to Mr. Arthur L. Kramer, president of the Chamber of Commerce, in which he vividly painted the dire consequences of further delay:

> . . . Therefore, my earnest hope is that you will immediately appoint a strong committee of three to examine thoroughly into all phases of the undertaking; that the work of the committee be expedited and, assuming that the report will be favorable, that immediately following, every ounce of strength of the President and Directors of the Chamber be continually and actively exerted until the project is successfully consummated.

His suggestion was immediately put into effect, and the prompt and cogent report of the committee seemed to be the turning point in the fight. Support slowly consolidated on the side of the Levee District.

It would still take two more years of constant pressure, however, to beat the opposition, and several more years after that to finish the Levee District project, start the industrialization of the area, and weld Dallas and Oak Cliff together.

While the harassment of the levee fight was going on, the depression was getting worse. Finally Dealey had to give up his dream of weathering the depression without cutting salaries, and in January, 1932, a 10 per cent reduction was applied to the salaries of all noncontractual employees. In June the crisis was worse, and the *News* asked the Typographical Union to accept a temporary reduction in its wage scale until January of 1933.

The union refused to accept the request by a vote of 20 *For* and 42 *Against*.

"I was surprised and amazed," Dealey wrote to the foreman of the *News* composing room. "I have spent a week considering the refusal and wondering why." Possibly the vote did not represent the majority, he speculated. The union membership was 218, but only 62 had voted.

After mature thought, therefore, I have determined to write this letter to you, which if you see fit, you are at liberty to show to some of the men who have been with us longest and who know us best.

When a new contract with the Dallas Typographical Union was under consideration last year, I suggested a renewal of the wage scale previously existing. My reason for doing so was based on a then firm belief that a turn in the economic tide was shortly thereafter to take place. . . .

I was optimistic all right, but as a prognosticator of economic conditions I was a miserable failure. . . . Much to our regret [in January, 1932,] we were forced to reduce salaries in all other than the mechanical departments an average of 10 per cent and . . . in addition, reduce expenses in every other possible way. . . .

The *News* brought the Typographical Union into Texas. . . . This institution has given to the members of that Union every day of every year, fair, honest and liberal treatment in the wage scale and in every other respect. That this is true, I have personal knowledge during the past 58 years. Now is the time to show appreciation of that treatment.

Newspapers today are struggling under economic conditions much more serious than the world has ever before experienced.

I shall make no specific argument for relief. If, after careful thought, the need of it is not apparent to you gentlemen, further words are useless. . . . The responsibilities are mutual and cannot wisely be ignored by your membership.

Portions of the letter were read at a meeting of the union on Sunday, June 26, and the membership voted to accept the reduction.

The depression continued month after month. In the last half of 1932 the Red Cross distributed 1,000,000 pounds of flour to needy Dallas families. Union carpenters set a four-dollar-a-day wage scale for repair and remodeling work. By the end of the year cotton was selling for five cents a pound. The once-fat Sunday issues of the *News* of more than 100 pages were down to 40 pages, with a low percentage of advertising.

In all the gloom, however, a few bright spots could be found. The East Texas oil field was discovered. The boom was riotous, and "hot oil" ran freely, but it brought new wealth to Texas at a time when it was needed the most. Radio came of age, the national networks arrived, with a quantity of free entertainment surpassing anything the average American had ever imagined . . . such programs as Great Moments in History, Amos n'Andy, Guy Lombardo, Floyd Gibbons, Al Jolson, Jack Benny, Will Rogers, and Eddie Cantor, whose "Potatoes are cheaper, tomatoes are cheaper, now's the time to fall in love" became virtually the theme song of the depression days.

By 1933 advertising in the country's newspapers and magazines had dropped to about half of the volume enjoyed in 1929, but radio advertising had increased each year, being twice as much in 1932 as in 1929, and suffering only a slight drop in 1933.

Fortunately the *News* owned a radio station—thanks to the urging of Walter Dealey—and WFAA had become one of the prized clear-channel stations in the United States, with 50,000 watts of power, and affiliated with the National Broadcasting Company. The station made its first clear profit in 1933. The amount was only 27,000 dollars, but it helped A. H. Belo Corporation meet the interest and dividend payments on its bonds and preferred stock that year.

Holding faithfully to his resolution to be cheerful and stay in good spirits despite the hard times, Dealey also tried to spread some cheer. Learning of Chet Shafer's "Guild of Former Pipe Organ Pumpers" in December of '31, he immediately enrolled his membership, at five dollars, having pumped the organ at the Trinity Episcopal Church in Galveston in the early 1870's. Whenever he found a fellow pumper, he delighted in reporting the prospect to "Chet," the Grand Diapason. The correspondence bounced back and forth—

Dear Chet:

Prof. Robert Hopkins, School of Music, Baylor University, Waco, Texas, is a former pumper and is eligible for membership in the Guild. Line him up!

Sincerely yours,

G. B. Dealey, F.P.

Dear George:

Will sandbag Bob Hopkins. Good work.

Guild activities have been increasing tremendously. Just as soon as we can get the debt revision problem solved—and bore a hole in the top of Postmaster General Brown's car to take care of his silk hat—we'll probably have the annual meeting of the G.O.F.-P. O. P. Better drop in.

Always,

Chet
Grand Diapason

Dealey circulated the sprightly letters of the "Grand Diapason" among a dozen or so ardent guild admirers in the building. Among his notable recruits for the Dallas loft were John E. King, managing editor of the *News,* who once pumped an organ in the Panhandle of Texas, and P. R. Freeman, the benefactor of the Freeman Memorial Clinic for Children in Dallas.

As Mr. Freeman had once blown out the bellows in the Grace Episcopal Church at Memphis, Tennessee, Chet exalted him to "Chief Bellows Buster."

On January 1, 1933, the *News* editorialized:

> **The United States needs at its head a combination of the stubborness of Cleveland, the aggressive energy of Theodore Roosevelt, and the intellectuality and clear vision of Woodrow Wilson. . . . The *News* is of the opinion President-elect Roosevelt will prove to be a real leader.**

The people in America wanted to be led out of the long depression more than anything in the world, and they wanted to believe that Franklin D. Roosevelt's "New Deal" would reopen the idle factories, create new jobs, stop the bank failures, and rid the country of unemployment, bread lines, and soup kitchens. If Roosevelt should fail, many people feared that within a year or so the masses would turn to some extremist like Huey Long, the "Kingfish" from Louisiana, or to an American Mussolini or a Hitler.

In March, Roosevelt took office, and his first dramatic act was to close the banks. After a brief "holiday," they opened with new safeguards against failures—and insurance for depositors. Why hadn't someone done this before? This Roosevelt was a genius.

"Remarkable," the *News* called his program by the end of March. Cautiously it made certain reservations, and it opposed repeal of Prohibition, but it declared: "The nation is behind him, believing that through his measures as a whole the depression will pass from the United States."

Dealey was personally even more enthusiastic for Roosevelt than his editorial writers. On May 16, 1933, President Roosevelt cabled a dramatic appeal to the heads of 54 nations, asking the world to renounce aggression and abolish arms so they might "move together toward peace and prosperity." Dealey was much impressed and spontaneously sent a personal telegram to the president:

HEARTIEST CONGRATULATIONS ON YOUR CLARION CALL TO THE NATIONS OF THE EARTH. THE GREATEST OF YOUR GREAT ACTS AS PRESIDENT.

He sent the message "deferred rate," however.

By January, 1934, it appeared that the depression had turned the corner. To start the New Year off right, all salaries at the *News* were restored to their former level. Although the margin of upturn in business was still small and admittedly tenuous, Dealey had a feeling of thankfulness. Along with the nation, the *News* was emerging from its greatest financial trial.

But it seldom happens that all things are right at the same time. As the burden of the depression began to lift, he was oppressed with a worry that had been growing in recent months. Walter, his elder son, was ill. As vice-president of the company, Walter had shouldered a major load of the responsibilities through the hard times. Working ceaselessly, sometimes all night long, Walter had made himself sick with fatigue and worry. His health was seriously impaired. One day in the office he "blacked out" and had to ask his secretary what was going on. His doctor ordered a long rest. Upon his return to work, he appeared to have his old vitality back, but shortly thereafter he died suddenly and unexpectedly on January 30, 1934.

To Dealey the loss of his elder son struck at the roots of his life. He sought consolation in his religion. In his own words, he always "kept in daily touch with the Lord," and when tragedy came, he put his faith in God, and it helped him bear his grief.

He had looked to Walter to manage the papers, to see that the indebtedness was finally paid off, and, along with Ted who was training to head up the editorial side, to carry on the traditions of the *News*. Dealey was 75, and it was time he was turning over the helm to a younger man. But that would have to wait a while now. New plans would have to be made.

CHAPTER TWENTY-SIX

1935=1939

TEXAS FEELS ITS HISTORICAL IMPOR-
TANCE. DEALEY REJUVENATES THE
DALLAS HISTORICAL SOCIETY. MAKES
THE GOLDEN JUBILEE EDITION "A
STEM-WINDER." A FABLED BUILDING, A
LEGENDARY CHARACTER. DOUGLAS
CHANDOR PAINTS DEALEY'S PORTRAIT.

ALL TEXAS WAS FEELING ITS HISTORICAL IMPORTANCE. THE
Texas Centennial year—1936—was approaching. What other state
had more to celebrate? What other state had been a sovereign nation, born in the glory of battle? Remember the Alamo . . . Goliad
. . . San Jacinto. Remember Sam Houston . . . William B. Travis
. . . Mirabeau B. Lamar. Remember the Texas Rangers . . . the
Indian fighters . . . the cattle drives . . . the Chisholm Trail. Every
county and every town across Texas was opening the records, pro-
claiming its heroes, and marking its sacred ground. Hastily organized historical committees worked feverishly to ready the sights
for the millions of visitors expected from out of state. On the
Courthouse Square in Cameron, Milam County, Texas, up went a
fine bronze statue of Benjamin Rush Milam . . . a hardy man in
buckskin with a long rifle and powder horn . . . "Who will go
with old Ben Milam into San Antonio?" From El Paso to Texarkana, from Brownsville to Amarillo, monuments to patriots and
markers for historic moments.

There had been a third of a century to prepare, but people had
been dilatory. In 1902 James Stephen Hogg, the former gov-

ernor, had urged a great celebration "in keeping with Texas' inspiring history. . . ." There had been flurries of activity since then, but little had materialized, and history went slipping by.

In Dallas, however, there was a historical group that was no Johnny-Come-Lately—the Dallas Historical Society. In March, 1920, the effort to found it started with a memorandum and an old yellowed newspaper clipping sent "upstairs" at the *News* for an editorial. Dealey was reviving a favorite subject.

The editorial, written by Alonzo Wasson, was moving and effective:

> . . . **"When and by whom was Dallas named and settled? I ask. And leading citizens are unable to answer me,"** complained a Chicago editor to the **News. "Where is its library of historical data? . . . I lament and marvel!" . . .**[1]

On the heels of the editorial marched a legion of details from Dealey's office. Would Professor R. A. Hearon enlist the aid of the history faculty at Southern Methodist University? . . . Would Mr. W. E. Metzenthin write other historical societies for advice? . . . Why not recruit members from the Country Club roster? . . . Would Mr. Rhodes S. Baker accept the presidency if elected? . . . Nothing hasty and nothing left undone.

On the evening of March 31, 1922, at the Dallas University Club, to the clink of 101 "large glasses of triple-sec sparkling, transparent iced water," in toast to the native citizens of Dallas County present, the Dallas Historical Society was born. Who proposed the iced-water toast? Who else but Dealey?

"The meeting closed," the minutes recorded, "with a rising vote to George B. Dealey for his efforts that successfully materialized the organization of the society."

Dealey had been an unusual witness to the cavalcade of Texas history since 1870 . . . more than 60 years watching the parade of time and events through the eyes of the *News,* the one paper which set its horizons on the far-flung borders of the state. In their day Willard Richardson and Colonel Belo had made the *News* the lamp of Texas history, and Dealey had caught up the spirit. But his interest in history went beyond the faithful chronicle of the day's events. In 1903-04 he compiled "A History of The News," nearly 200 pages of manuscript written by the heads of each department of the paper, intended for publication as a book.[2] He revived the *Texas Almanac and State Industrial Guide* in 1904, inspired greatly by the historical treasure to be found in the *Almanacs* published by the *News* in the 1850's and 1860's. In 1909 he carried out his "divine inspiration" and had the Alamo Replica built on the State Fair grounds, and as predicted, over the years it was visited by hundreds of thousands of Texans . . . "and thus was created a patriotic feeling. . . ."

The year 1935 would mark the fiftieth anniversary year of the Dallas *Morning News,* and years ahead of time Dealey was thinking and planning the Golden Jubilee Edition. It would be the finest of its kind ever published . . . the story of Dallas and the story of the *News* . . . authoritative and comprehensive. Who should be in charge? A tough assignment . . . time-consuming. He hadn't yet decided—it was 1932—when Sam Acheson, a reporter on the *News* staff since 1925, presented him with a copy of his new book, *Joe Bailey—The Last Democrat,* a biography of the late famous senator from Texas. The book was excellent—good biography, good history—and Dealey was immensely pleased that a *News* man had written it . . . notwithstanding the old grudges between the *News* and Joe Bailey. Acheson was the man for the Golden Jubilee Edition! Immediately Acheson was moved from the third floor to the second floor, and put in "the heavy artillery." His assignment: Make the edition a monument to history. Do whatever research necessary. Beware of perpetuating errors. There was no such thing as really correct history. Be sure you're right, then go ahead.

While Acheson was working on the Golden Jubilee Edition, Dealey instructed him to assist in putting new life into the Dallas Historical Society, and to help get it ready for the Texas Centennial year. It needed space for its archives, which, for lack of proper quarters, had been accumulating in a private safe; and it needed to have regular meetings. Above all, the society needed some full-time personnel to speed its progress toward a professional status. Dealey wanted a trained younger person to assume the burden being carried by the society's first and voluntary secretary, C. B. Gillespie. He knew the man he wanted, later a fellow member of the Critic Club, Professor Herbert Gambrell of the history department of Southern Methodist University, and he prevailed on him to work with Acheson in rejuvenating the society. A full-time position of financial secretary and archivist was created and filled by Miss Virginia Leddy, who later became Mrs. Herbert Gambrell.

Where history was concerned, it was Dealey's decade. In 1934 he was made president of the Dallas Historical Society, an office he was to hold for the remainder of his life. In September, 1934, Dallas was designated the Centennial Central Exposition City, and no citizen could claim more credit for the triumph than Dealey. If it was the ready-made, multimillion-dollar State Fair grounds that had cinched it, Dealey figured there. If it was Dallas' 5,500,000-dollar cash pledge for new buildings, he figured there. If it was the Dallas Historical Society, or the "Dallas spirit," or backstage politics, he figured there.

On October 1, 1935, the *News* published its splendid 152-page Golden Jubilee Edition. Printed on special, long-lasting newsprint, beautifully made up, no advertiser allowed more than a single half-page, written with pains-taking thoroughness and scholarly accuracy, it was a paragon of newspaper historical editions. The front page carried a two-column editorial by Dealey, the only editorial he ever wrote completely himself and the only one he ever signed—

> With its predecessor on the Gulf, for more than ninety years, THE DALLAS MORNING NEWS has labored for the material and cultural development of the whole State. Its heart is a Texas heart. . . .

The edition was a "stem-winder," as Dealey had promised a friend. More prestige flowed to Dealey and the *News*. Where matters of history were concerned in connection with Centennial preparations, Dealey was consulted.

"Should the Alamo Replica be eliminated in making way for the new buildings for the Exposition?"

"No, indeed. Rebuild it elsewhere on the grounds."

"What suggestions for the Hall of State building?"

"Design it so that afterwards it might be a permanent museum of Texas history and the headquarters and library of the Dallas Historical Society."

"Any motifs for the building?"

"Somewhere in it there should be a Hall of Six Flags."

Dealey's decade of history materialized almost beyond his expectations. The Centennial Celebration, capturing the fancy of the nation, attracted more than 6,000,000 visitors, and the next year it was continued as the Greater Texas Pan-American Exposition —another success. The Hall of State building was majestic and beautiful, a jewel for the city of Dallas, described by a former Texas governor as "the Westminster Abbey of the Western World." . . . From a towering entrance niche, two vast wings stretching out to embrace all things . . . A Tejas warrior bending a bow, aiming up into the infinite sky . . . Inside, lofty ceilings, gigantic murals, heroic statuary, rich and imaginative paneling.

In 1938 care of the hall was entrusted to the Dallas Historical Society, "whose past performance gave earnest of its capacity to deal expertly with the problems involved."

The impressive ceremony dedicating the Hall of State to its new purpose was arranged to take place on October 12.

"On Columbus Day," many people thought. "How appropriate!"

But it wasn't for Columbus at all. It was a secret salute to Dealey's red-letter day, the date he went to work for the *News*. Dealey's admirers had chosen October 12 because they knew it would please him.

During this period Dr. Herbert Gambrell agreed to serve as curator of the society, and now Dealey had someone to write memoranda to:

Dear Mr. Gambrell:

Fifty years ago there was a cigar store on the South side of Main, between Poydras and Lamar, operated by a Mr. Fendrick.

Outside of his store was an impressive looking wooden Indian. If we could locate that wooden Indian. . . .

—GBD

Dear Mr. Gambrell:

. . . There should be a history of the State Fair. Incidentally, I think one is being prepared by Judge J. J. Eckford. Also, there should be prepared a—
History of Banking in Dallas.
History of the Telephone in Dallas.
History of Real Estate Development.
History of Fraternal Orders.
History of Luncheon Clubs . . . Hotels . . . Oil . . . Transportation . . . Public Education . . . City and County Government . . . Art and Music . . . Amusements . . .

—GBD

The communications from Dealey filled folders, and the folders filled filing cabinets, and still they came.

In the fall of 1938 Sam Acheson completed a book on the history of the *News,* an outgrowth of the Golden Jubilee Edition. Dealey felt he had a stake in the book too, because he had spent a lifetime gathering materials for it, and he had guided its development, read every line, made hundreds of suggestions. What should the book be named? The staff was queried for titles. Ted Dealey supplied the one that clicked—*35,000 Days in Texas.* The fat red-covered book came off the presses, and Dealey was proud of it. He gave away 1000 copies, most of them bearing two autographs—Sam Acheson and G. B. Dealey. The book was the fulfillment of one of his oldest dreams . . . the story of the *News* related for contemporaries and recorded for posterity.

Dated March 23, 1937, a dozen copies of a memorandum, written on pink paper and enclosed in red envelopes, circulated out from Dealey's office to the heads of all departments of the newspaper:

"It is time we give consideration to plans for a new building," the memo began.

A new building? Some of the men had not expected this from

a man who was 78. But why not? Over the years he had planned nine new building and expansion projects for the *News* . . . he was always quick to try new methods and new machines . . . within the past year he had put a substantial investment behind the venture at Lufkin, Texas, to make newsprint from Southern pine. "Plan for the future" was a precept he applied to every endeavor.

Hardly any of the old heads at the *News,* however, could quite grasp the idea of parting company with the comfortable, friendly old quarters they had known practically all their lives. "The Old Lady on Lamar Street," they called her . . . or sometimes "The Old Plantation."

The *News* building was a landmark in Dallas . . . it had been there on Commerce between Lamar and Austin Streets since most people could remember, and the impression was furthered by the inscription carved deep into the broad square face of the huge stone pillar [3] at the corner entrance on Commerce and Lamar:

THIS INSTITUTION

THE NEWS

WAS ESTABLISHED

IN 1842

WHILE TEXAS WAS

A REPUBLIC

Inside, the building was old, but as clean as a whistle, its brass handrails and cuspidors shined to a sparkle, its wooden floors wet-mopped daily, and its lavatories fresh and tidy. Dealey had always demanded cleanliness, and the older he got, the more careful he became with his personal cleanliness and the more severe the standards he set for the building. Even the Negro porters, who continually scrubbed, polished, dusted, and swept, had to wear freshly laundered white jackets each day. To paraphrase the once-popular advertising for *Sapolio,* America's favorite cleanser when Dealey was a young man:

> This was the *News* of fair renown,
> The immaculate paper of Spotless Town.

Nearly every corner, office, and wall of the building reflected tradition and story. In the main lobby on the street floor, Colonel A. H. Belo's portrait and cavalry sword hung to the right of the door. A tipsy reporter one night grabbed up the sword and terrified the crowd in the Employees' Lunchroom until a policeman arrived. Behind the gray marble front counter, a mass of desks, cabinets, etc., spread back over the entire floor, comprising the business and advertising departments. So ingeniously and tightly fitted together was the furniture that nothing but many years of shifting and rearranging could have so completely eliminated the waste of floor space. On cloudy days the pull cords for the lights overhead were a temptation to the workers, but they were restrained by a sense of frugality which permeated the institution, not to mention the likelihood that Dealey would notice the light and come over to turn it off. His thrifty nature was well known, and many *News* men carried their loose change in coin purses because he was continually fostering the idea that a coin purse was the mark of a careful and thrifty man.

Midway in the block-long structure, between the office section and the mechanical section, a marble stairway with deeply worn steps led to the upper floors. An open-type, grilled-cage elevator was handy, but most persons preferred the stairs. The elevator seemed tired, and its slow climb was much like an old-time balloon ascension.

On the second floor the entrance leading east opened into the quarters of the "heavy artillery" . . . first, a many-purpose lobby, around the walls of which were numerous big-framed photographs of 21-year employees, and below the photographs were framed mottoes by the dozen, also two wall-type red fire extinguishers, a small picture of Davy Crockett, and a painting of the Madonna and Child. Among the rooms opening off the lobby was one more fabled than the others—Room 15, known as the Conference Room except between 2:00 and 2:30 in the afternoon, at which time it was the room where Dealey took his afternoon nap on an old-fashioned, hard, leather-covered couch, a daily habit for so long that the memory of the oldest employee ran not to the contrary. If he missed his nap for any reason, he was grouchy the remainder of the day, and consequently unusual quiet prevailed on the second floor from 2:00 to 2:30.

The atmosphere-laden Library was located at the end of the hall that turned left off the lobby. It bulged with 10,000 volumes crowded into tall glassed-in bookcases, it smelled as mellow as old leather bindings and crumbling newsprint, and it had an air as contemplative as the face of Gutenberg, whose bust statue adorned the top of the central bookcase. The Library was Dealey's pride. He had started it in the 1890's, and through the years he had provided for it well. In the United States the newspapers with comparable libraries were rare.

Just off the stairway on the west side of the building was the Employees' Lunchroom. It was always busy and bustling, a place where editors and copy boys, printers and apprentices, perched together on high stools at the counter or sat crowded around small tables. Reproductions of famous Remington paintings of Western scenes graced the walls . . . they were Dealey's selections, that is, on the advice of John Rosenfield, art critic of the *News*.

"In the lunchroom everybody is the same size," Dealey had told T. C. "Doc" Daniell, the lunchroom manager, when he opened it in 1917, and that was the spirit that had been maintained.

"Several years ago," Doc would start his favorite story, "Mr. Dealey put in the rule to close the lunchroom from 2:00 until 2:30. Shortly afterward, he came around a minute or two after 2 o'clock to eat his dinner. He found the main entrance locked, so he started through the kitchen door. A new cook's helper called 'Spark-plug' was sweeping. He was a tall, lanky, redheaded boy who stuttered. Being new and not knowing Mr. Dealey, Spark-plug waved the broom in his face.

" 'Hey, Sh-Sh-Shorty,' he said, 'you're t-t-too late. Come b-b-back at 2:30.'

"If one of the pressmen hadn't been standing across the hall from the lunchroom, no one would ever have known about the incident, because Mr. Dealey went back to his office, returned at 2:30, and never said a word about it."

Dealey was a living legend. Hundreds of stories on him circulated among the employees and his wide circle of outside friends,

and new ones were constantly being added to the collection.
"Did you hear about the mayor asking Mr. Dealey how many
people he has working for him now at the *News?*. . . . 'About
half of them,' he told him."

Whenever a newcomer marveled at the illegibility of Dealey's
handwriting, someone was sure to tell how Dealey signed in at a
Chicago hotel, and the bookkeeper made out his account to "A. E.
Israelsky."

A ride in the car with Dealey and his old Negro chauffeur, Boswell, was always an object lesson in safe driving. They stopped
for all railroad crossings.

"All right to the right, Boswell," Dealey would say, looking
down the track on his side.

"All right to the left, Mistah Dealey," Boswell would say.

"Go ahead, Boswell."

A special office boy served the executive offices, and his desk,
placed just outside the door to Dealey's office, was the same little
slanted top desk young George Dealey had used when he started
to work for the Galveston *News* in 1874. Above the desk on the
wall was a set of typewritten instructions, and among the regular
duties was one that read: "Hand a glass of water to Mr. G. B.
Dealey each hour, no matter what he is doing or who else is in
the office." He had been drinking eight glasses of water a day
since 1899 . . . tap water—iced water being unfavorable to good
digestion.

Lettered in gold on the wall opposite the door to his office was
the motto made famous by the N. W. Ayer advertising agency
before 1900—"Keeping Everlastingly at It Brings Success." The
motto had one drawback, he often said; it made the salesmen who
came to see him too persistent.

Most of the Dealey grandsons were "preordained" for careers
on the *News,* and as each was graduated from college, he would
report to "Grandfather" to learn the newspaper business.

"First, you'll be in circulation," Dealey would explain to them,
with a twinkle in his blue eyes. "After several months, when you
know everything there is to know about circulation, you come tell
me, and then I'll get you transferred to another department."

Calling one of the grandsons to his office one day, he inquired about his training in the advertising department. Was he selling any reader ads?

"They told me they don't sell those around here any more," was the answer.

The entire advertising force sold reader ads for the next several weeks.

After the repeal of Prohibition, the majority of the board of directors of the *News* favored accepting liquor advertising. It was all right, Dealey conceded reluctantly, if "it walked in the door," but no solicitation. Wary of "the Boss" and his convictions on the subject, the advertising managers and other executives secretly planned a meeting to convince him that the paper needed to promote liquor linage. Gathering in his office, the group shifted uneasily in their chairs.

"The competition," one of them said, to open the subject, "is certainly picking up a lot of beer linage lately."

"Fine!" Dealey said, leaning back in his swivel chair, and giving his head a characteristic little jerk that always put an exclamation point to his words, "and the less of it the *News* has, the better I like it!"

The conference turned immediately to the general subject of newspaper promotion, without further mention of wine, beer, or liquor linage.

Dealey believed that all the men connected with the business office or news-editorial work should "dress up," complete with coat, tie, and hat. One Saturday morning, Ted, his son, who was in his 40's and the vice-president of the company, popped in at the office from his ranch wearing a sports shirt and no coat or tie.

"Hadn't you better go home and finish dressing," Dealey asked him, looking over his glasses and not smiling.

Ted went out without a word, and came back later "dressed up."

In each of the men's lavatories in the building, there was a neatly printed little sign fixed to the middle of the inside door, which read: "Gentlemen will please finish dressing before opening the door."

For 50 years Dealey went to the same barber shop, an old-fashioned tonsorial parlor called the Fretz Barber Shop in the early days of Dallas when it was prosperous and had 24 chairs and a Turkish bath in the first basement and a marble bathing pool in the subbasement.

After the shop had changed owners and names several times and had gone down, Dealey was persuaded by his son-in-law, James M. Moroney, an executive in the *News* organization since 1934, to try *his* barber shop at a nearby hotel. It was modern.

After going several times, Dealey told Ted he would have to find another shop.

"Jim's barber shop is a tipping place," he complained. He didn't like "tipping places."

The most common procedure for obtaining a salary raise for an employee at the *News* was for the head of the department in which the employee worked to appeal in person to Dealey. Invariably Dealey asked three questions in the order of their importance, insofar as chances for the raise were concerned:

1. Does he need it? A new baby in the family?

2. What does he do with his money? Does he own his home? Does he gamble?

3. What's he worth to the *News?*

In determining a man's worth, Dealey believed in the importance of effort rather than results—a philosophy he based on more than 60 years' observation of life.

"You are not responsible," he would explain, "I am not responsible, for the results we get. How can it be otherwise? God alone can guarantee results. But we *are* responsible for the effort we make to get our results. So what really counts is the sincerity and quality of our efforts." [4]

He was devoted to the men who had started young and stayed with the *News* all their lives, and he was especially proud of the father-and-son combinations on the paper. One such pair was K. B. Crannell, Sr., and, Jr. In 1939 K. B., Sr., who started as a newsboy in 1910 and later went into the bookkeeping department, suffered a heart attack and went to the hospital. Dealey called in K. B., Jr., who was new on the staff as a bill collector, and instructed him to quit work early each afternoon, go by the hospital to see his father, and then report to him how his father was getting along. At the same time he gave him five 100 dollar bills to give to his father that afternoon.

K. B., Jr., complied with the instructions the first two days, but the third day he thought he was too busy to go by the hospital before quitting time. The following morning a note on his desk asked him to "Please report immediately to Mr. G. B. Dealey."

"I'll give you one more chance," Dealey told him, after a fatherly talk, "but if you miss another single day going by to see your father, I'm going to fire you." Dealey was absolutely serious, and K. B., Jr., did not miss another day until his father had recovered and was out of the hospital.

It was long overdue, but finally—in the late spring of 1939—Dealey was sitting for a portrait.

"Be sure you wear your black alpaca coat," the employees' committee instructed him. The employees had commissioned Douglas Chandor, the famous British-American portraitist, to do the painting for Dealey's sixty-fifth anniversary with the *News*.

The two Englishmen hit it off like old friends—one a tall, lean, pipe-smoking, aristocratic-looking, youthful man . . . the other a medium-built, handsome, wise, and genial old man. Conversation at the sittings ranged widely, but invariably it got around to things about England.

Had Mr. Chandor ever eaten any of the genuine Keiller's Marmalade that was made in England?

Yes, indeed. Wonderful stuff.

Fine! A store in Dallas carried it, and there would be a jar waiting for him tomorrow. Too bad they couldn't get a Hot Cross Bun to go with it. In the old days in Dallas an Englishman named Evans ran a bakery and made lots of the buns at Eastertime . . . always reminded him of his boyhood in the old country . . . "Hot Cross Bun—one a penny, two a penny."

Within a few days the figure on the canvas grew strikingly lifelike, not only in looks but also in spirit.

In order to pose with a half-smoked cigar, Dealey laughingly told the artist, he was being forced to break his doctor's orders. Really?

Yes. The doctor allowed him three cigars a day. But the sittings didn't come at the regular times for these smokes, so he had to light up a fourth. Never mind. He had been smoking 70 years . . . still remembered his first smoke. It was in the then Parliament Fields, near Liverpool. He had made enough money to buy an ounce of tobacco, and with it he got a clay pipe free. Slipping off into the tall grass, he lit up, and the memory of the awful sickness that followed was still as vivid as could be.

The background of the painting took form—one of the bookcases in the *News* Library, the shelves filled with old volumes that looked as if they contained the wisdom of the ages. Chandor deftly touched in a purple haze. He was fond of purple, he said . . . had always loved the purple heather, so familiar to his childhood.

Did Mr. Chandor read the magazine *Punch?* Good, wasn't it? A few years back an English journalist named Gilbert Floyd had kept him supplied with copies. Occasionally he took them home and "the Missus" saw them, but she couldn't find much humor in them. She didn't understand the English brand.

At the final sitting Dealey stayed late, and when Boswell, the Negro chauffeur, came after him, Mrs. Dealey came along to see the painting.

"A wonderful likeness," she declared it.

Dealey was immensely pleased that Ollie liked it. He put great stock in her opinions.

"It sure do look like you," Boswell said on the way home.

Had Boswell noticed, Dealey asked, that the bookshelf directly back of his head was empty? Well, it was. That was the artist's way of saying he was empty-headed, he chuckled.

On the way home, the car approached a railroad crossing, and Dealey looked to the right, while Boswell looked to the left.

"All right to the right, Boswell."

"All right to the left, Mistah Dealey."

"Go ahead, Boswell."

CHAPTER TWENTY-SEVEN

1939=1941

THE 65TH ANNIVERSARY DINNER . . .
"DEAN OF AMERICAN JOURNALISM."
DEALEY DAY AT THE UNIVERSITY OF
TEXAS. FOUNDING THE DALLAS FOUNDA-
TION. THE SUPREME COURT UPHOLDS
DEALEY.

THROUGH THE OPEN WINDOWS, DEALEY COULD HEAR THE WAVES
washing up on the beach, an old familiar sound, even though he
had not lived in Galveston for 50-odd years. Inside the hotel room
it was dark, but outside he could detect the faint gray light of
dawn. A train whistled sharply in the distance. For a moment
time turned back . . . 65 years ago to the day a train whistle had
waked him up . . . on October 12, 1874 . . . the day he went to
work for the *News* . . . an exciting day. But 65 years later he was
even more excited. He spoke to Ollie to see if she was awake. She
was, but she told him to go back to sleep . . . he would need his
strength before the day was over. He tried to catch a few more
winks, but to no avail.

Possibly he was in tune with the exhilaration of other newspapermen all over Texas as they got up early that morning and
prepared to set out for Galveston. Practically all the bigwigs of
the Texas Fourth Estate and others from as far away as New
York were congregating in the Island City to honor "the Dean

of American Journalism" on his sixty-fifth anniversary with the *News*.

During the morning Dealey and Ollie took a ride around the city. There were still a few old landmarks he could point out, among them the Galveston *News* building . . . Colonel Belo had built it in 1883. Along by the wharves they saw a large British freighter, ominous with its two guns fore and aft and its fresh coat of gray paint . . . a pointed reminder of the six-weeks-old war in Europe.

All day the telegrams of congratulations poured in . . . so many that the Western Union office put on an extra helper to handle them.

That night the crowd gathered in the grand banquet hall of the Buccaneer Hotel while a string ensemble played a continuous medley of Dealey favorites . . . "Blue Danube Waltz" . . . "Light Cavalry" . . . "Drink to Me Only with Thine Eyes" . . . "The Student Prince" . . . "Believe Me If All Those Endearing Young Charms." Sitting at the head table waving at the guests as they came in was Dealey, enjoying the occasion to the fullest. He caught the eye of Dr. J. Shirley Sweeney, his personal physician, and beckoned to him.

"How am I doing, Dr. Sweeney? Feel my pulse," he said, with a twinkle in his eye, reaching his arm across the table.

Dr. Sweeney felt his pulse. "Great!" he said. It was fast, but whose pulse wouldn't have been under the circumstances?

Acting for the Texas Newspaper Publishers Association, host of the occasion, Toastmaster Amon G. Carter, publisher of the Fort Worth *Star-Telegram,* kept a light-humored air to the proceedings.

Four speakers told the saga of George Bannerman Dealey, and former Governor of Texas W. P. Hobby, publisher of the Houston *Post,* transcended himself in a burst of oratory that captured the meaning of the occasion:

> Whether we draw in the pure ozone from the Davis Mountains or breathe the more luxuriant air of the Hill Country or wash in the waves of the Gulf; whether we are fanned by the scarlet winds

of the Panhandle or lulled by the gentle zephyrs of the piney woods
. . . it is all Texas, Texas just the same and everywhere; it is
Texas whose land has been diversified and enriched through the
lessons in agriculture taught by Col. G. B. Dealey; whose art has
been ornamented and chastened by his conceptions; . . . literature
embellished by his pen . . . politics made cleaner by his precepts
. . . history made authentic by his research . . . culture broadened
by his publications. . . .

Standing to respond, Dealey appeared small behind the elon-
gated head table, but as he spoke, the calm assurance, the humble
spirit, the infectious humor, the lovable nature, and deep, deep
human understanding reached out to the audience, and they saw
a man with a heart as big as Texas . . . the man of greatest stature
in the history of Texas journalism.

He made the usual disclaimer, saying he was "a person of only
mediocre ability. It is clear to me that this demonstration is
symbolic. I am being honored as the present head of a great newspaper."

He talked of his boyhood in Galveston, his early days on the
Galveston *News,* his association with "the Big Six"—the men
who made the *News* a great institution—and he told the "mince
pie story":

"Naw, suh, that ain't mince pie . . . that's lemon custard . . .
shoo, flies, shoo!"

About the celebration, Peter Molyneaux, an old and revered
journalist of the state, wrote in his publication, *The Texas
Weekly:*

> **Mr. Dealey was rightfully saluted as
> "dean of American journalism." For
> when young Dealey started his career,
> Charles A. Dana still had twenty years
> ahead of him as editor of *The New
> York Sun;* James Gordon Bennett's
> *New York Herald* was at the height of
> its prestige . . . Joseph Pulitzer's pur-
> chase of *The New York World* was
> still more than eight years in the
> future, and the founding of the *Kansas
> City Star* by William R. Nelson was**

six years away . . . and it would be
twenty-one years before Adolph Ochs
would begin remolding *The New York
Times.* All of these men . . . were
Dealey's contemporaries, and all have
passed on except Hearst, who was still
a student at Harvard when Dealey was
moving from Galveston to Dallas to
help establish *The Dallas Morning
News.* He was rightfully saluted, therefore, as "the Dean of American Journalism."

In January, 1940, Dealey assumed the position of chairman of
the board and shifted the presidency of the *News* to Ted, his son,
and made his son-in-law, James M. Moroney, vice-president. It
was his intention to turn over complete charge of the paper to Ted
and Jim and the younger men in the organization . . . except, as
he was accustomed to say to new editors-in-chief: "there will be
no departure from the well-known traditions and policies of the
News without approval from me." The vigilance over policy and
tradition would never be relaxed as long as he lived. The daily
conferences with the managing editor at 10:00 A.M. and 4:00 P.M.,
and the submission of all editorials to him before they were published—these things continued the same as ever. It might be only
twice or three times a year that he suggested a change in an editorial, but that wasn't important. The important thing was that
the editorial writers should know that he would read the editorials
before they were published. It served his ends toward guarding
policy and tradition.

He had a world of pet projects he wanted to give more time to
. . . the Family Service (formerly the United Charities), the Freeman Memorial Clinic, a new slum clearance drive, the Dallas
Foundation, to mention a few. It was fortunate to have a son
who was a vigorous and competent executive to put in charge of
the paper. Ted had a tremendous job on his hands, but he had been
training for it practically all his life, nearly 20 years as a reporter
and editor and the last six years at a desk a few steps from his
father's. Ted was 48. When Dealey was 48, back in 1907, the job

of managing the newspaper was not as complex as it was now in 1940. Back then the Dallas paper had 37,000 daily circulation; now it had 102,000. Back then the volume of advertising required an average daily issue of 14 pages; now more than twice as many. Back then the employees numbered about 200; now more than 650.

The properties were in excellent financial condition. The indebtedness assumed at the time of purchase of A. H. Belo & Co. was entirely paid off. The Dallas *Morning News* and WFAA were making good profits, and the *Texas Almanac and State Industrial Guide* was paying its way. *The Semi-Weekly Farm News* was losing a little money, but the old perennial money-loser, the Dallas *Journal,* had been sold.

In retrospect Dealey occasionally wondered if the sale of the *Journal* in June, 1938, had been the right thing to do. When an acceptable purchaser had offered to buy it, they had accepted. In the inner council the argument that had prevailed was to grasp the opportunity to get rid of "the weak sister." In 24 years it had never made a profit. Two years after the sale, however, when the *Dispatch-Journal* (the two papers having been merged) was obviously on its way out, leaving the afternoon field in Dallas exclusively to the Dallas *Times-Herald,* it was apparent that the *Times-Herald* would be a more formidable competitor for circulation than it ever had been while the afternoon field was divided.

But all things considered, Dealey was convinced the sale of the *Journal* was the right thing. Before the sale, their efforts and talent had been divided between two newspapers. Now their best efforts and best brains were being concentrated on the Dallas *Morning News,* and they were not plagued with the eternal rush that prevailed on afternoon papers, leaving them half edited at press time. Over the long haul, the *News* would rise to greater heights.

"Dealey Day" was declared on the University of Texas campus November 4, 1940, and Dealey was honored with a banquet by the School of Journalism.

"The big point for every one of you journalists to remember," he told the students, in a patient, fatherly voice, "when you start out in life is to develop some good purpose and stick to it . . . Keeping everlastingly at it brings success."

It was the same simple truth he always preached . . . simple but irresistible and irrefutable when one starts "at it" at 15 and keeps "at it" past 80.

He was still keeping at it. The month before he had dedicated the new building for the Texas Children's Hospital, after 12 years of keeping at it. He was raising money for more live oak trees on the Southern Methodist University campus—30 years of keeping at the interests of the university. He was heading the drive to liquidate the debt on the Westminster Presbyterian Church— more than 40 years of keeping at church business . . . chairman of the Board of Trustees since 1909. It was the same with other projects.

His newest undertaking—newest but 11 years old at that—was the Dallas Foundation, and he was keeping at it, hoping to see it firmly established before he "passed out of the picture" (a phrase he used increasingly of late). About every three months he sent a memorandum to the editor-in-chief or the managing editor of the *News,* asking, "Isn't it about time for something on the Dallas Foundation?"

In 1929 he had combined with Eugene P. Locke and George Waverley Briggs to write the charter for the Dallas Foundation, then called the Dallas Community Trust. Its purpose was to create a self-perpetuating body to receive and administer philanthropic endowments given in the interests of Dallas . . . and to adapt their use to the inevitable changes of time. It would avoid the fate, for example, of Benjamin Franklin's fund in perpetuity for the relief of itinerant printers. Also, it provided the first practical method for men of small or moderate financial means but philanthropic inclinations to mingle their gifts with other funds in one united trust for the public good.

Dealey visualized a great fund, in some distant day amounting to many millions of dollars, which would build hospitals, create parks, endow university branches, and provide many other of the finer things in life for Dallas people.

"A community trust is necessarily of slow growth," Dealey repeatedly said, when doubt was expressed over its progress. "It is for all time, and since it has no pressing demands, it can afford to wait for bequests and donations until philanthropic-spirited people—moved by increasing knowledge of its usefulness—desire to provide them." [1]

He intended to keep at it until the idea caught on.

Beginning in midsummer, 1940, Dealey faced a new experience. He was a defendant before the law. On the docket it was the case of Philip B. Fleming, administrator of the Wage and Hour Division, United States Department of Labor, versus A. H. Belo Corporation. But to Dealey it was personal . . . the government vs. G. B. Dealey. The *News* was accused of violating the Fair Labor Standards Act, better known as the Wage and Hour Law.

Here was irony. For more than 40 years he had worked to raise the working conditions of employees and to maintain above-average wages. But in 1940 the record of the past meant nothing to the Labor Department. It refused to consider that there might be a better plan than a 40-cent minimum wage, a 40-hour week, and time-and-a-half for overtime. The *News* must comply or else.

The crux of the controversy was whether the *News* would be able to continue to deal with its employees individually on a man-to-man basis or on a mass contractual basis. Dealey balked at the coercion. It was all wrong for a newspaper.

The *News* drew up two plans. One offered the employees the Labor Department's formula. The other offered the employees the same plan they had always worked under. It was called simply the "Belo Plan." It provided the same monthly salary which each employee had previously been getting, which in every case, except for office boys, was more than the minimum wage prescribed by the Wage and Hour Law. The Belo Plan neither imposed undue hardships on the company because of the nature of newspaper work, with its occasional long hours, nor took away the liberal practices of the company toward employees, including full pay while sick no matter how long, no punching of time clocks, a two-week annual paid vacation, a 2500-dollar paid-up life insurance policy, no limitation on rest periods for drinks and snacks, liberal pensions for retired employees, and other considerations.

Every employee voluntarily chose the Belo Plan.

The test came in Federal Judge William H. Atwell's court on February 3, 1941. Testimony proceeded all day:

Q. Will you state how many employees there are of that character, superannuated at the present time?

A. Yes, sir, twenty-eight [M. M. Donosky, treasurer of A. H. Belo Corporation, testifying].

Q. Will you state what pay was paid to those employees during the last year?

A. $64,636.

Q. Now do you have a memorandum there of the length of service of the various groups of employees of the newspaper and WFAA?

A. . . . [For employees having] from ten to fifteen years of service, it is eighty-five in number. From fifteen to twenty years, it is seventy, and over twenty years, one hundred even. . . .

Q. Your name is Ruth Buckner?

A. That is right. . . . [Ruth Buckner, secretary to the *News'* circulation manager, testifying].

Q. Has your contract been fulfilled one hundred per cent in all payment of wages to you?

A. I would say in my case it has been fulfilled about two hundred and fifty per cent, because I was ill a great deal last year, and I never missed getting my pay check a single week.[2]

All day long the plaintiff got the worst of it. Not a single witness made a damaging statement against A. H. Belo Corporation. No employee was dissatisfied. None unhappy. Instead, all professed or implied loyalty to the company and esteem for their employer.

In his oral opinion the following day, Judge Atwell said:

The two suits spark from a clash in systems. . . . One deals only in dollars and cents. The other with happiness of employer and employee, vacations, pay when sick, or, absent, as well as with dollars and cents. Neither system is fixed by statute. Since the citizen is free to keep the law by going in any direction he chooses, he may not be compelled to forego that right. . . .

I find the following facts:

No. 1. That there has been no violation of the wage and hour statute by the A. H. Belo Corporation. . . .[3]

It was a day of triumph for Dealey.

On the evening of the day Judge Atwell rendered his opinion, the Dallas Historical Society was holding a function at the Hall of State, at which both Dealey and the judge were present.

"Would it be appropriate to express my pleasure and appreciation to Judge Atwell?" Dealey asked a friend.

Perhaps the judge was expecting it, the friend suggested.

"I was wondering if you enjoyed the trial," the judge laughed, when Dealey came over.

The United States Circuit Court of Appeals promptly upheld Judge Atwell's decision, and on June 13, 1942, it was sustained by the United States Supreme Court. The Belo Plan caught on and was soon copied in many parts of the country. It was one of Dealey's finest contributions to labor and to the law.

CHAPTER TWENTY-EIGHT

1941-1946

**THE TRIBE GATHERS FOR THANKSGIV-
ING. *NEWS* MEN GO TO WAR. KEEPING
TRACK OF THE GRANDSONS IN SERVICE.
PLANNING THE NEW BUILDING. THE LAST
EVENING WITH THE CRITIC CLUB.**

TALK TURNED TO THE EVER-WIDENING WAR . . . THE NAZI PUSH
on Moscow . . . the recent British success in Libya. Hadn't somebody better stop the Japs? Was Roosevelt's lend-lease getting us
too close to the brink?

It was the evening before Thanksgiving Day, 1941, and a little
group was chatting in Dealey's office. No conclusions were
reached, but someone remarked tellingly that America might well
count its blessings the next day.

In the shadow of the war Thanksgiving Day took on a deeper
meaning . . . an added closeness of feeling where family groups
gathered . . . a vague dread of the future by those who gave it
any thought. But very few had any real awareness of how late
the hour was.

At the James M. Moroney home (Maidie's house), the Dealey
family had a partial gathering on Thanksgiving Day. The two
Moroney daughters, Betty and Jean, were home, also James, Jr.,
and Jean's husband and daughter. Dealey and Ollie arrived early,
in time for a mid-morning coffee, and Maidie slipped a little
cognac into "Papa's" cup.

"The coffee at 'Pud's' always tastes different," Dealey remarked, "but it's very good."

Dr. and Mrs. Rice R. Jackson (Annie) got there before lunch, but their four sons—Henry Allen, Rice, Jr., Gordon, and Gilbert —were out of the city. The last arrivals were Dr. and Mrs. Henry B. Decherd (Fannie) and their son, Ben, with his wife.

As a prerogative of the "Grandfather," Dealey demanded a kiss of all granddaughters and granddaughters-in-law. In paying the tribute, one of them planted a big "lipsticky" kiss on his forehead, and unknowingly he sported the mark for half an hour, to the amusement of the crowd, until Ollie discovered what the fun was about and came to his rescue.

There was much laughter and banter at the dinner table, and Dealey had a new story to tell on himself. He and Ollie had recently been to see the motion picture, *Lloyds of London,* and he had recommended it to one of the employees at the *News,* adding that he had just taken out a fairly large life insurance policy with Lloyds.

"You did?" the man responded. "Well, I've heard they'll insure anything."

Before the day was over, Ollie had been persuaded to demonstrate her fluency in Spanish and tell how "Papa" ordered soap in Mexico City and got a bowl of soup. The newest granddaughter-in-law was shown that "Grandfather" really carried several straight pins sticking on the underside of his coat lapel. Why? Because pins were handy to have around.

It seemed that Thanksgiving Day had hardly been over any time when the Japanese attack on Pearl Harbor came on December 7, and the United States was precipitated into the war.

Dealey faced the war problems of publishing a newspaper with the composure that came of his 82 years and his experience with two previous wars. Although well advanced in age, he was in excellent health, and there were no signs of any decline in his mental acumen and vitality. Of course age had brought a few more wrinkles in face and neck, whiter hair and mustache if possible, and a quieter walking pace, although he still did his early-morning walk at a good clip.

The wartime personnel problems of the *News* naturally gravitated to him. When an employee got his draft notice or decided to volunteer, it helped to have somebody around who understood a man's innermost feelings, and who would talk with him until he was talked out . . . two or three hours if necessary. Dealey's job. He enjoyed helping the men get their personal affairs in order, lending them money, looking after their families, and assuring them their jobs would be waiting when they got back.

One of the first *News* men to go into service was Associate Editor-in-Chief William B. Ruggles, a reserve officer in the infantry. On the morning he came by Dealey's office to say good-by, Dealey told him the company would make up the difference between his major's pay and his salary on the *News*.

"But I didn't ask for that," Ruggles said.

"Well, it came up at the board of directors' meeting," Dealey said.

Ruggles didn't take the offer, but he never forgot the consideration.

Dealey's volume of correspondence, always a marvel to his associates, increased with the tempo of the war, and an amazing number of the letters carried gifts and donations.

"Wish I could send more than $100," he explained to a friend soliciting for the United China Relief, "but money these days passes through my hands like lightning through a crab apple tree."

Never had so many good causes needed money, it seemed. He tried to support them all with at least a modest contribution, and many relatives and friends who were hard pressed by the war received unsolicited gifts with unfailing regularity. In each letter to "Dear Cousin Lillie," "Dear Cousin Annie," "Dear Cousin Florence," and other relatives in England and elsewhere, there was either a draft for five pounds or a notice of a food parcel on the way.

He prized his correspondence with Commander Samuel D. Dealey, his nephew. The gallant submarine commander, who had sunk nine enemy ships in his first two patrols in the Pacific, was his idea of a real war hero. Commander Dealey's last letter to him was written October 22, 1943:

Dear Uncle George:

Once again we are practically worn out from relaxing and are ready to go on another hunting trip for a rest. . . .

I notice, in letters from the folks, that you were worried for fear that our successes on previous trips might lead to over-confidence. No, there isn't much danger of that. Those fellows on the other team are "playing for keeps" too.

. . . Please give my love to Aunt Nellie.

Best regards,

Sam

He kept the battle flag Sam had sent him on his desk for good luck. The USS *Harder* on its fifth patrol sank five Japanese destroyers, another astounding victory. But from its sixth patrol the *Harder* never returned; apparently the enemy had scored a hit "for keeps." Posthumously, Commander Dealey was awarded the Congressional Medal of Honor.

By the end of 1943 most of Dealey's grandsons were in service, and no one kept up with their whereabouts better than he did. In a letter dated November 22, 1943, to "Dear Beth,"[1] he wrote a typical news roundup on "the boys":

Capt. Ben Decherd (Fannie's son) is still aide to General Walter Krueger and is located somewhere in the South Pacific.

Annie is doing as well as could be expected of a mother with three sons in the service. Her son, Rice Jackson, Jr., Lieutenant in the Navy, whom I saw yesterday, is shortly leaving for Hawaii, and from there, I suppose, for duty in the South Pacific. Another son, Gilbert, a Lieutenant in the Army, also was at our house yesterday. He received his commission a short time ago in Florida, was sent to California, and now has some other assignment, which I can't remember. Gilbert's twin, Gordon, also a Lieutenant in the Army, is somewhere in the Northwest—Alaska or the Aleutians.

Al Dealey, Walter's boy, is in the Marine Corps, having joined a week before Pearl Harbor. He is a Lieutenant, and is still in the States.

Joe Dealey, Ted's son, is at Bradley Field, Windsor Locks, Conn. He expects to go to officers school very soon.

Maidie Moroney's boy, Jimmy, is now in Boston, Mass., having received his commission as Ensign in the Navy last month. Her daughter, Betty, has a husband, Lt. Bobby Gardner, USNR, who has been located at Daytona Beach, Fla., is now on his way to San Francisco, and overseas from there, I suppose. James J. Laney, who is the husband of Maidie's other daughter, Jean, is a Lieutenant in the Navy and was in on the Guadalcanal fighting.

During 1944 Dealey was a good soldier on the home front. He kept strictly to the limits of his ration cards, gave rides to employees in his car to and from work, and made it his particular concern to "hold down the fort" for the institutions which he had spent a lifetime building up. First of course there was the *News*. The young employees had been drained off for the armed services, but somebody had to run the newspaper, and when older employees spoke of volunteering, he spent hours reasoning with them, insisting they could do more for the war effort on the *News* than half a dozen average soldiers could do anywhere else. Some he persuaded, and some he didn't.

There was no medal of honor or service ribbon for "holding down forts" on the home front, but he got his rewards in letters of appreciation such as the one from Mrs. Dora B. Foster, the executive director of the Freeman Memorial Clinic, who wrote: "You never let your interest in our work lag a bit no matter what the ache in your heart might be. Your ability to carry on has given me the lift I needed."

He was in the vanguard of those who first urged postwar planning. In June, 1944, he attended the Citizens' Conference on Postwar Planning held in St. Louis, and, hewing to an old theme, he pleaded for civic attractiveness, the clearance of city slums, and city planning . . . "Let us prepare for the day of victory and for the return of our boys by making their home towns look as presentable and as attractive as possible," he urged.

The trip to St. Louis proved more strenuous physically than he had expected, but after a month's rest at Boulder, Colorado, where he and Ollie had been spending a part of August and September the last few years, he felt strong again. He liked the rest sanitarium where they stayed in all respects except one. Smoking was prohibited on the premises, and he still loved his cigars. Two cigars a day were all his doctor allowed him of late. But two cigars could be the spice of life, and twice a day he would walk over to the nearby cottage of his longtime Dallas friends, Colonel and Mrs. John E. Owens,[2] and have his smoke.

For a man of 85, his health was excellent, but it had to be guarded. About this time certain British friends and admirers proposed the bestowal upon him by King George VI of the Order of the British Empire (O.B.E.), but several members of the family felt that the excitement of the ceremony and the strain of the trip involved would overtax his strength. The plans were never carried out, and he never knew of the proposal. His last notable honor had been at the University of Texas in 1943 when he was made an honorary member of Phi Beta Kappa. A year previous to that he was the Honorary National President of Sigma Delta Chi, professional journalism fraternity.

After Victory Day in Europe, May 8, 1945, the numbers of troops returning to the United States from Europe began to swell rapidly week by week. The war with Japan in the Pacific was still raging, but most people in America could not help feeling—come what might—that the worst was over. Right or wrong, it was a feeling of excitement and joy and expectation . . . both for those waiting and for those returning.

Dealey experienced the same excited feeling, tempered with age, of course. He felt an urgency to see his grandsons safely back and with their families. One grandson-in-law had been lost—Lieutenant Bobby Gardner, Betty Moroney's husband—but none of the grandsons had been killed. He was anxious to see the many *News* men return to the fold, too, and to see close friends who had been away a long time. He wanted to see them before something unexpected happened. Only a man of 85 would understand exactly how he felt. For the first time in his life something inside told him—in a way he recognized—that the thread of life was spinning out.

The afternoon of July 4, 1945, was a cloudy day with a few light showers of rain, which made a steamy mist on the sidewalks and pavement and produced the peculiar smell that raindrops make on hot asphalt, a pleasant smell which drifted in the open windows of the *News* building. Dealey sat alone at his desk for more than an hour and worked at a letter he was writing in longhand. Finally he folded the four pages, sealed them in a regular letterhead envelope, and scrawled obliquely across the face of it: "To Mr. Edward M. (Ted) Dealey—To be opened on my death. (It contains suggestions as to my funeral.)—G. B. Dealey."

He stepped over to Ted's desk and handed the letter to him.

"You'll be a hundred years old when I open it," Ted said, as he got up and put the letter in the safe. Neither of them said anything further, and each went back to his desk and continued working the remainder of the afternoon.

He kept busy as ever during July and August, nine hours a day and six days a week. During the latter part of August, he and Ollie delayed their annual visit to Boulder, Colorado, while Ted made a flying trip to Japan to attend the surrender of the Japanese and to report the story for the *News*. When Ollie packed their bags for Colorado, she made sure to put in a pair of salt and pepper shakers, because the food at the rest sanitarium wasn't seasoned enough to suit them.

At the end of September both were glad to get back home. Colorado had some grand and inspiring scenery, but they found nothing they liked as well as the wooded ravine across the street from 3704 Alice Circle, a little spot filled with familiar trees, undergrowth, and wild flowers, and in the spring burgeoning with redbud and dogwood.

Dealey was happy to be on deck at the office again, too. Numerous matters needed attention. The Alamo Replica on the State Fair grounds needed repairs, and he got behind the proper authorities promptly. It was time to revive the "G. B. Dealey Award for Music," a small prize given each year to some young talented musician. The award had been discontinued during the war, but he asked John Rosenfield, the drama, art, and amusements editor of the *News,* to help promote it again. A new wing was needed for the overcrowded Freeman Memorial Clinic, and he volunteered for the fund-raising committee. Austin College at Sherman, Texas, asked his aid in raising 100,000 dollars. "I think I am one who knows what money is for," he replied, "and it has been my practice for years to get rid of it pretty promptly as it comes to me. Consequently I do not have much left . . . but I will promise to give you some modest sum between now and the end of the year." Later he sent 500 dollars.

Planning the new building for the *News* occupied much of his time. Originally the plans had called for an expansion on the block where they were already located, but they were unable to buy the entire block, and the situation was not ideal. Late one Saturday afternoon in 1940, Leven T. Deputy, the mechanical superintendent, dropped by Dealey's office to go over some details on the building plans.

"You don't want to build here, do you?" Dealey asked, sensing a resigned attitude in Deputy. He had great faith in the mechanical superintendent's judgment.

"No, sir, I don't," Deputy answered frankly.

A few days later the old plans were scrapped—three years' planning thrown out the window—and they began looking for a new site. For guidance Dealey referred to George E. Kessler's original City Plan for Dallas, in which Kessler had said that Dallas should have a Union Station with a park in front, and that on the three other blocks around the park there should be three monumental buildings. When people would step out of the railroad station, they would say, "This is a beautiful city."

Thirty-five years after Kessler conceived the plan, Dallas had the monumental Union Station, the attractive plaza in front, and the 14-story Jefferson Hotel * on the north block. Now the *News* would build on the south side, and it would take only one more building on the east side to complete the picture Kessler had in mind.

---
* Later named the Hotel Dallas.

Often at the conferences with the building committee and the architect, Dealey would remind them that they were building for 50 or 100 years in the future.

"Nothing was ever built large enough in Dallas," he would say.

The new building for the *News* would be, though. Every part of it would be large enough to accommodate an 80-page daily paper of 500,000 circulation, a newspaper large enough to serve a city of 2,000,000 people.

Near the end of 1945 Deputy asked how far back from the curb to set the building.

"Put it back far enough so we can have a front yard and landscape it with grass, shrubbery, and trees, and put up two flagpoles," Dealey instructed. "Let's add to the beauty of the plaza in front of us, and in no way detract from it."

After his nap and cigar on February 25, Dealey spent a short time in the *News* Library looking up some information. Before leaving the room, he complimented the two librarians on the attractiveness of a bright potted plant on the desk.

"When he gave me a ride the other night," the assistant librarian said, as Dealey went down the hall, "it was drizzling, and he insisted on getting out and holding his umbrella over me all the way to my front door. I asked him to come in for a cup of hot tea, and that twinkle came in his eyes, and he said, 'What, and get called on the carpet when I get home late!' "

That evening 14 members of the Critic Club met together at the Dallas Woman's Club to have dinner and hear a paper. While eating, Dealey talked with Dr. Herbert Gambrell . . . telling him that the mayor and a committee of councilmen were planning to visit the Hall of State at his invitation to learn more about the fine work of the Historical Society. He chatted with George Waverley Briggs about Dallas Foundation matters . . . suggesting two persons who might make bequests.

Before the discussion of the host's paper, he asked to be excused. He didn't feel well, he said, and also Mrs. Dealey was ill and he wanted to get on home early. Getting his hat and coat in the corner of the large dining hall, he gave a debonair little wave of the hand to the men around the table, then turned and walked with his quiet, courtly manner along the raised gallery toward the door, disappearing from sight and reappearing as he passed each column.

He found Ollie feeling better, but told her he had indigestion, and took some bicarbonate of soda for it. He didn't rest well that night.

The next morning he telephoned Ted he didn't believe he would come down if things were going all right at the office. Stopping by Ollie's bed to give her a glass of water, he asked her to call Dr. Sweeney and ask him to drop by. But he was taking a nap by the time the doctor was reached, and it was agreed he would come by after hospital calls.

About noon when Dealey waked from his nap, he told Ollie he was feeling better. Hearing the doorbell, he got up from his bed and, when the doctor came into the room, was pulling a heavy chair to the side of the bed. His breathing was so labored that Dr. Sweeney was alarmed.

"You shouldn't have moved that heavy chair, Mr. Dealey," Dr. Sweeney remonstrated, as Dealey lay back on the bed.

"I wanted you to have a comfortable place to sit down," he said, managing a smile, and the old twinkle came in his eyes.

His breathing became more labored. Dr. Sweeney reached an arm under him and raised him up.

"Thank you, Dr. Sweeney," he gasped.

The doctor called Mrs. Moroney (Maidie), who was in the next room.

"Don't worry ... everything's ... going to be all right," Dealey gasped, as Maidie came in. A moment later he lost consciousness.

Maidie quickly telephoned to Ted, Annie, and Fannie, but before any of them could reach the house, he was dead, of a massive coronary occlusion.

Ted sent for the letter his father had written to be opened upon his death.

"My dear Ted," it began. "In the course of time my earthly end will arrive. In view of this I deem it prudent to set down for serious consideration, when that time arrives, my thoughts and desires concerning my funeral."

The first suggestion was that the funeral be held at the First Presbyterian Church, despite the fact that he was chairman of the Board of Trustees of the Westminster Presbyterian Church. The reason, the letter explained, was that probably a large number of the *News* employees would want to attend the funeral, and most of them lived nearer the First Presbyterian Church and it would be more convenient for them.

The letter continued:

> I especially request a minimum of publicity in the *News* . . . All the eulogy about me appropriate has been printed in our paper many times and need not be repeated.

> When I go it will be firmly believing in our Heavenly Father, the Holy Ghost, and earnestly trusting to forgiveness for my sins through Jesus Christ our Savior.

> To you, my beloved son, I drop the mantle of my life's work, with the firm belief that your record will be far better than mine.

> The following was . . . used by His Majesty, King George VI, in a worldwide broadcast from Sandringham, England, on Christmas Day, 1939:

> "I said to a man who stood at the gate of the year. Give me a light that I may tread safely into the unknown and he replied, 'Go out into the darkness and put your hand into the hand of God. That shall be to you better than a light and safer than a known way!'"

> I like the foregoing. My final advice is that you keep in touch with God, day by day in every way. Let Him guide you, and you will win out. You are a fine man, Ted, and have from first to last been a great help and blessing to me.

> Lovingly your father,
>
> G. B. Dealey

At the *News* the word passed swiftly through the building. On the second floor Stuart McGregor went quickly from office to office, opening each door and giving the message. One of the librarians followed unwittingly along behind him.

"I don't believe it! I don't believe it!" John Knott, the veteran cartoonist said, and then turned and started sketching rapidly on his drawing board, making odd meaningless shapes.

The editorial council assembled in Room 15 for a brief conference. Bill Ruggles, the editor-in-chief, suggested that each of them write an editorial and let Ted Dealey select the one he liked.

That afternoon the work went on. A few noticed that the building had never seemed so quiet. Everyone bent over his desk and worked more steadily than he had ever worked before.

Copy started coming up to the composing room.

"The arts, too, have lost their oldest and best friend," began John Rosenfield's column, "The Passing Show." ". . . I speak of his day-in-day-out apportionment of newspaper space . . . his adequate staffing of an amusements department. . . . Mr. Dealey did not make the arts his hobby; they were part of his business."

City Editor Ted Barrett carefully edited the lead story . . . marked it for 10 lines dc—12/14 . . . "George Bannerman Dealey, revered 86-year-old dean of American journalism and publisher of The Dallas Morning News, is dead. Journalist, builder of city and state, civic captain and philanthropist. . . ."

The first rush of telegrams filled eight columns of type. From the Speaker of the House in Washington: "Truly one of the builders of Texas. . . ." From the general manager of the Associated Press: "An exemplar of all that is best in American journalism. . . . He made one of the world's great newspapers. . . ." From the president of the University of Texas: "A true champion of education . . . a steadfast friend of the University. . . ." From the governor of Texas: "Men a hundred years from now will look upon his constructive works with gratitude. . . ."

Lynn Landrum's editorial was chosen from the six written by the editorial staff of the *News:*

> The head of The Dallas News was more than its head. He was its heart. There was no worker on The News who has not known the greatness and kindness of that heart. . . . He gathered years, but was never truly old. He grew

rich in experience, but never poor in
faith. He was loaded with honors without ever stopping to think more highly
of himself than he ought to think. . . .
and the corridors of memory will echo
the quiet chuckle and gentle wisdom
which were his. The marks of the man
are all over the institution into which
he poured all that he was and all that
he dreamed. As long as it lives, he will
live also. . . .

They missed him greatly at the *News*. But like Richardson and
Belo before him, Dealey had built an institution . . . with "every
possible safeguard around it" . . . that would continue to grow
after he passed on.

It was a period for new growth in America. The nation was on
the move and teeming with the boundless energy of postwar read-
justment, reconversion, and expansion. New horizons spread before every city and state, and the *News* had its mission . . . greater
than ever . . . "to assist in every possible manner in the material,
mental, and spiritual development of the State and its people."

Notes

CHAPTER TWO

1. His first home was in Manchester, England, where he was born September 18, 1859, and lived until he was six or seven years old. It is known definitely that the family was living in Liverpool in 1866 and remained there until their financial misfortune in 1870. Losing everything, George Dealey, Sr., decided to take the family to America. Money was borrowed to meet the expenses of the trip, and the circumstance determining their destination was that a relative lived in Galveston, Texas.

2. George Dunlop, in *The Texas Coaster*, Richmond, Texas, October 18, 1895.

CHAPTER TEN

1. The quoted excerpts from the final conversation between Dealey and Colonel Belo were developed from an intensive study of (1) the letters exchanged between Dealey and Alfred Belo, Jr., immediately after the death of Colonel Belo, which mentioned certain remarks made at that time, and (2) other materials such as the issues of the Dallas *Morning News* immediately preceding and following his death.

2. The Dallas *Morning News*, April 21, 1901, p. 2.

CHAPTER ELEVEN

1. From a memorandum by D. P. Toomey to Dealey, dated July 31, 1902.

2. From letters written by R. G. Lowe to Alfred Belo, Jr., dated January 6 and 10, 1905.

CHAPTER FOURTEEN

1. On the night of May 3, 1892, Governor James Stephen Hogg debated George Clark, "the Little Giant" of the Texas bar, before a crowd of 10,000 people in an open field. The *News* had a corps of

shorthand reporters, staff correspondents, and telegraphers on hand
and carried a verbatim report of the debate in the next morning's
issue.

2. In October, 1914, the estate was purchased. At Dealey's suggestion, it was named Reverchon Park, after Julius Reverchon. Dealey
wrote of Reverchon in July, 1945, "He was one of the members of
the French Colony located west of Dallas and was a remarkable
botanist. In the course of his lifetime he gathered a great collection of
plants, shrubs and flowers which became very valuable. He wanted to
keep the collection in Dallas, but no one seemed interested, and it was
afterwards sold to the Botanical Gardens in St. Louis."

CHAPTER FIFTEEN

1. Quoted by Dealey in a paper delivered to the Critic Club,
January 2, 1934. The quotation is taken from "This Mad-House
World" by Charles E. Russell, *Scribner's Magazine,* October, 1933.

2. *Op. cit.,* pp. 224-225.

CHAPTER SEVENTEEN

1. Carried in the *News,* February 12, 1911.

CHAPTER NINETEEN

1. The 33rd Degree was conferred on Dealey in Galveston, December 11, 1909.

CHAPTER TWENTY

1. The quotation is from a "Special Message to the Stockholders of
A. H. Belo & Co.," dated November 7, 1923. In the same message
Dealey said: "Possibly none of these men [the men who had built the
News] ever conceived the day when it would become necessary for
the daughter at Dallas to part company with the mother at Galveston.
Yet it was inevitable. The passing of time brings changing scenes.
Centers of population shift. New communities spring up. Others die.
New generations appear. Time was when *The Galveston News*
proudly carried under its head the words 'Circulation larger than that
of all other daily papers in Texas combined.' A few years pass and we
see Galveston cut off from the mainland by the city of Houston, a
thriving, growing community. The fight is hard, but the die is cast.
For several years past we have known that it was impossible, eco-
nomically, to publish a paper of the calibre that we wished, in so
small, though so staunch, a city as Galveston when fifty miles inland
there lay a city well able to support newspapers of the first class and

better able to circulate them because of geographical and other advantages."

CHAPTER TWENTY-TWO

1. In Dealey's copy of *Great Expectations,* still in the Library of the *News,* the passage is found on p. 263. (The edition is printed by Chapman and Hall, Ltd., London, undated.) Briggs relates that he looked up the passage that evening after the conversation and found that Dealey had quoted it almost verbatim.

2. John F. Lubben, the Secretary-Treasurer of A. H. Belo & Co. since 1906, had moved from Galveston to Dallas at the time of the sale of the Galveston *News.* His connection with the firm went back to 1881. He and Dealey had been close friends since boyhood. — Tom Finty, Jr., joined the *News* in 1897 and served brilliantly in various editorial capacities. Since 1914 he had been editor-in-chief of the *Journal.* —E. B. Doran began as a reporter in 1895 and later was made city editor of the *News.* In 1914 he became managing editor of the *Journal,* and in 1918 he was made a director of news and telegraph of both papers in Dallas.

CHAPTER TWENTY-FOUR

1. The plan was named for Charles E. Ulrickson, who headed the citizens' committee named by Mayor Louis Blaylock in 1925 to draw up a long-range public improvement program under the Kessler Plan. Mr. Ulrickson had come to Dallas in 1916 as vice-president and general manager of the Trinity Portland Cement Company. His civic leadership encompassed many other interests and activities in addition to the work of the committee which bore his name.

2. The city bond issue was for $23,900,000. There were still two more bond issues to be voted on the following spring—one for $3,-339,000 by the county and the other for $6,500,000 by the property owners within the Reclamation District, who literally were paying for the cost of the levee themselves—but the success of the city vote made the passage of the next two issues a practical certainty.

3. At its annual winter meeting of 1928, held in Dallas in February, the Texas Newspaper Publishers Association passed a resolution naming Dealey the "Dean of the Texas Press. —The article, "42 Pictures of Davy Crockett Help Run The Dallas News," written by George W. Gray, appeared in the February issue, 1927, of the *American Magazine.* —The Dallas Chamber of Commerce banquet given in honor of Dealey took place November 26, 1929. —The biographical sketch of Dealey carried by *Editor & Publisher* in its "Romances of American Journalism" appeared July 28, 1928.

4. Mr. Freeman endowed the clinic in memory of his son, Richmond.

CHAPTER TWENTY-FIVE

1. May 15, 1933.

CHAPTER TWENTY-SIX

1. March 21, 1920.

2. The manuscript was never published, but was kept in Dealey's personal filing cabinet until after his death.

3. The stone bearing the inscription was later removed and incorporated into the new building of the *News,* which was completed in 1949.

4. From George W. Gray's article, previously cited, in the *American Magazine,* February, 1927, p. 10.

CHAPTER TWENTY-SEVEN

1. From "After Thirty Years," a paper delivered to the Critic Club by George Waverley Briggs, October 27, 1952, p. 8.

2. Excerpts taken from pp. 80, 95, 183-184, respectively, in the *Transcript of Record in the United States Circuit Court of Appeals, Fifth Circuit, No. 9867, Philip B. Fleming, Administrator of the Wage and Hour Division, United States Department of Labor, Appellant, versus A. H. Belo Corporation, Appellee.* Filed April 29, 1941.

3. *Ibid.,* pp. 188-189.

CHAPTER TWENTY-EIGHT

1. Mrs. Gurney Edwards of Providence, R. I.

2. Colonel Owens was a vice-president of the Republic National Bank of Dallas. For many years he was a member of the Critic Club.

Appendices

A. A STUDY OF THE ANCESTRY OF GEORGE BANNERMAN DEALEY

PARENTS AND FAMILY

Father of George B. Dealey was George Dealey, *born* January 20, 1829, Brunswick Road, West Derby, Liverpool, England; *died* March 31, 1894, Holmes Street, Dallas, Texas.

Mother of George B. Dealey was Mary Ann Nellins, *born* August 26, 1829, Granshaw, County Monaghan, Ireland; *died* June 9, 1913, Colonial & Lenway Streets, Dallas, Texas.

Children of George and Mary Ann Dealey:

George William,	*born* December 23, 1851, Duke St., Everton, Liverpool, England; *died* September 27, 1852, same address.
Elizabeth Ann,	*born* March 30, 1853, Duke St., Everton, Liverpool, England; *died* July 21, 1918, E. Platte St., Colorado Springs, Colorado.
Thomas William,	*born* January 6, 1855, High St., Everton, Liverpool, England; *died* February 15, 1906, Mineral Wells, Texas.
Leonora Jane,	*born* January 23, 1858, Victoria Road, Rusholme, Manchester, England; still living in 1954.

GEORGE BANNERMAN,

	born September 18, 1859, Queen St., Rusholme, Manchester, England; *died* February 26, 1946, 3704 Alice Circle, Dallas, Texas.
James Quayle,	*born* August 13, 1861, Walmer St., Rusholme, Manchester, England; *died* January 22, 1937, Dallas, Texas.

Charles Louis,   *born* July 6, 1863, Coke St., Cheetham Hill,
                    Manchester, England; *died* (date unknown).
Caroline Eleanor,   *born* November 30, 1864, Freehold St., North-
                    ampton, England; *died* April 2, 1914, Colonial
                    & Lenway Sts., Dallas, Texas.
Frances Mary,   *born* October 25, 1866, Eden St., Windsor,
                    Liverpool, England; *died* April 11, 1871,
                    Mechanic St., Galveston, Texas.
Samuel David,   *born* August 20, 1869, Alt St., Windsor, Liver-
                    pool, England; *died* February 9, 1912, at
                    Mineral Wells, Texas.

PATERNAL GRANDPARENTS AND FAMILY

Paternal Grandfather of George B. Dealey was Thomas Dealey, *born*
September 16, 1793, Liverpool, England; *died* 1870.

Paternal Grandmother of George B. Dealey was Leonora Quayle,
born August 28, 1793, Isle of Man (?); *died* 1875.

Children of Thomas William and Leonora Dealey:

Leonora Emma, *born* November 6, 1812, *died* 1891.
Elizabeth, *born* August 13, 1814, *died* 1875.
James Quayle, *born* December 21, 1815, *died* May 16, 1817.
William Henry, *born* February 26, 1817, *died* November 26, 1820.
Henrietta, *born* August 22, 1818, *died* November 28, 1820.
Thomas Bannerman, *born* March 11, 1820, *died* January, 1883.
Frances Amelia, *born* October 11, 1821, *died* March 2, 1881.
Margaret *born* August 2, 1824, *died* October 20, 1846.
Robert, *born* September 27, 1826, *died* (date unknown).
GEORGE, *born* January 20, 1829, *died* March 31, 1894.
Samuel, *born* May 19, 1831, *died* (date unknown).
Eleanor, *born* February 7, 1834, *died* 1906.

MATERNAL GRANDPARENTS AND FAMILY

Maternal Grandfather of George B. Dealey was William Nellins, *born*
1757 in Dublin, Ireland; *died* 1846 at age of 89. (One source says
William Nellins died at age of 82 . . . if this is the case, then his
date of birth would be 1764.)

Maternal Grandmother of George B. Dealey was Jane Johnstone,
born (date unknown) in Granshaw, Ireland, *died* at age of 62.

Children of William and Jane Nellins:
    Margaret
    MARY ANN, *born* August 26, 1829; *died* June 9, 1913.
    Jane
    Catherine
    Lizzie   (No data as to dates of birth or death available for
    Caroline   any of the children of William and Jane Nellins,
    Harriet   except for Mary Ann.)
    James
    Hugh
    William
    Two other sons, names unknown.

B. RULES PROMULGATED BY THE *NEWS'* MANAGEMENT
March 15, 1899

(This document is published here not only as material significant to the story developed in Chapter 8, but also as a
crystallization of the policies and organization which helped
make the *News* a superior newspaper.)

The Editorial Council consists of the Managing Editor, Mr. W. J.
Walter, and the two editorial writers, Mr. Doremus and Mr. Clark
(or their successors), with Mr. Jenkins as advisor. Its duties are to
exercise full control over the editorial and news columns of both the
papers. In the matter of affairs specially pertinent to the Galveston
territory, the management there will control without reference to the
council, but on lines clearly defined as the policy of the paper. The
hours of duty are so arranged as to have at least one member of the
council on duty from 9 A.M. to the time of paper going to press. The
Council meets daily in conference to discuss and determine all questions in its jurisdiction.

(2) In an advisory capacity the council shall have general supervision over the two managing editors.

(3) The Managing Editors shall be expected to perform all such
duties appertaining to that position in providing for news gathering
in and outside of the cities of publication, and they will be held responsible for covering news features of every kind in their respective
territories.

(4) In the adoption of an editorial and news policy it shall be the

desire and intention to follow the well beaten track laid down by The News management during the past thirty years. Fractiousness of all kinds is to be avoided. Fairness and justice to be accorded all men and measures. Personal journalism of every description must be avoided. If the Managing Editor violates a well established rule, he must personally assume the responsibility therefor.

(5) If the Managing Editor is instructed by any one in authority over him to perform a service inconsistent with established rules he must require such instructions in writing for his own protection, and such instructions must be submitted to the council, who will refer the matter to the management.

(6) The Managing Editor in handling matter tendered for publication which contains advertising features, shall submit the same to the Business Manager, who is authorized to pass upon said features—the Business Manager being held responsible to the management for the judicious use of this authority.

(7) The Business Manager shall be consulted on matters pertaining to expenditures and his opinion obtained prior to taking action, whenever it is practicable to do so without impairing the efficiency of the editorial department.

(8) The Business Manager will also be expected from time to time to make suggestions to the council regarding matters which from his contact with the public he may think it advisable to take action upon, and to suggest news features, topics of interest to be treated, etc.

(9) The heads of mechanical departments will make their reports, requisitions for supplies, material, etc., to the Business Manager, and any matter whether of a business or private character (in so far as the latter may affect the business of the office, such as absence from duty caused by sickness or otherwise, etc.) shall be stated to the Business Manager, who will take action himself or refer the matter to the proper authority. He is looked to by the management for regularity, discipline and results in said departments as well as his own immediate department.

> D. C. JENKINS, Director   A. H. BELO, President
> T. W. DEALEY, Secretary   R. G. LOWE, V-President
> Dallas, March 15th, '99.

C. AN INTERESTING STUDY OF NEWS-PAPERS CARRYING FRONT-PAGE AD-VERTISING IN 1902

From a memorandum by Dealey, dated October 18, 1902

THE FOLLOWING METROPOLITAN NEWSPAPERS, OR PAPERS WHICH CAN BE COMPARED WITH THE NEWS, *DO* RUN ADVS. ON FIRST PAGE:

Daily Journal, Providence, R.I.
Herald, New York, N.Y.
Sun, Baltimore, Md.
Herald, Boston, Mass.
Times, Buffalo, N.Y.
Morning News, Memphis, Tenn.
Post-Intelligencer, Seattle, Wash.

TOTAL OF SEVEN

THE FOLLOWING METROPOLITAN NEWSPAPERS, OR PAPERS WHICH CAN BE COMPARED WITH THE NEWS, *DO NOT* RUN ANY ADVS. ON FIRST PAGE:

Call, San Francisco, Calif.
Journal, New York, N.Y.
Dispatch, Richmond, Va.
Register and Leader, Des Moines, Iowa.
Courier Journal, Louisville, Ky.
Times, Shreveport, La.
Hartford Courant, Hartford, Conn.
News, Nashville, Tenn.
Daily States, New Orleans, La.
Argus, Albany, N.Y.
Sentinel, Indianapolis, Ind.
Drovers Journal, Chicago, Ill.
Inter-Ocean, Chicago, Ill.
Scimitar, Memphis, Tenn.
Picayune, New Orleans, La.
Free Press, Detroit, Mich.
Times Democrat, New Orleans, La.
World, New York, N.Y.
News and Courier, Charleston, S.C.
Tribune, Salt Lake, Utah.

State, Columbia, S.C.
Post, Denver, Colo.
Mail and Express, New York, N.Y.
Commercial, New York, N.Y.
News, Chicago, Ill.
Press, Philadelphia, Pa.
Evening Telegraph, Colorado Springs, Colo.
Drover's Telegraph, Kansas City, Mo.
Age-Herald, Birmingham, Ala.
Commercial Appeal, Memphis, Tenn.
Chronicle, Chicago, Ill.
Post, New York, N.Y.
Times Union and Citizen, Jacksonville, Fla.
Union, San Diego, Calif.
Constitution, Atlanta, Ga.
Banner, Nashville, Tenn.
Times, Denver, Colo.
Record Herald, Chicago, Ill.
News, Indianapolis, Ind.
Commercial Advertiser, New York, N.Y.
American, Nashville, Tenn.
Dispatch, Pittsburgh, Pa.
Tribune Commercial, Cincinnati, Ohio
North American, Philadelphia, Pa.
Star, Kansas City, Mo.
Journal, Kansas City, Mo.
Republic, St. Louis, Mo.
Globe-Democrat, St. Louis, Mo.
Post-Dispatch, St. Louis, Mo.
Post, Washington, D.C.
Leader, Cleveland, Ohio
Gazette, Colorado Springs, Colo.

TOTAL OF FIFTY-TWO

A few weeks after his 15th birthday G. B. Dealey went to work as an office boy for the Galveston *News*.

At the age of 19 Mr. Dealey was a clerk in the mailing room of the Galveston *News*.

At the age of 50 Mr. Dealey had become Vice-President and General Manager of the Dallas-Galveston papers.

In 1896, when he was 37, Mr. Dealey was made manager of the Dallas organization.

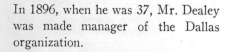